ITINERARIES IN CONFLICT

ITINERARIES IN CONFLICT

Israelis,

Palestinians,

and the

Political Lives

of Tourism

Rebecca L. Stein

DUKE UNIVERSITY PRESS   DURHAM AND LONDON   2008

© 2008 Duke University Press

All rights reserved

Printed in the United States of America on acid-free paper ∞

Designed by Heather Hensley

Typeset in Monotype Dante by Tseng Information Systems, Inc.

Library of Congress Cataloging-in-Publication Data appear

on the last printed page of this book.

Contents

Acknowledgments

This book emerged through years of dialogue with colleagues, friends, and family members who helped imagine its contours and sustained me during the writing project. It is also the product of a political itinerary, of my personal involvement in the struggle for peace and social justice in Israel and Palestine. As such, its roots can be traced to my first few years in Jerusalem (1991–93), working with the Israeli peace movement, documenting and protesting Israeli human rights abuses in the occupied Palestinian territories—years that left me wondering how such abuses, and the discourses that sustained them, articulated with everyday Israeli cultural practices within the Green Line. This project propelled me to graduate school and became, in part, the book before you.

During my graduate work at Stanford University, Paulla Ebron, Suvir Kaul, Smadar Lavie, David Palumbo-Liu, Mary Pratt, and Ramon Saldivar provided cogent scholarly models. Particular thanks are due to Akhil Gupta and Sylvia Yanagisako for generous mentoring; to Joel Beinin for guiding me in the complexities of Israeli and Palestinian history; and to Caren Kaplan at the University of California, Berkeley, for extending both her intellectual and personal support. Friends in the Bay Area—Robin

Balliger, Bruce Braun, Charles Hirshkind, Jake Kosek, Saba Mahmood, Anand Pandian, and Miriam Ticktin—provided sharp interlocution and spirited dinner party fare. Donald Moore offered tireless intellectual engagement. Sarah Steinberg nurtured with wisdom and humor.

In subsequent years, colleagues at the University of California, Berkeley, Amherst College, and the University of Minnesota gave considerable encouragement and critical engagement: Amrita Basu, Daphne Berdahl, Lawrence Cohen, Tom Dumm, Judith Frank, Karen Ho, John Ingham, Jean Langford, Pavel Machela, and Austin Sarat. Particular thanks to Andrew Parker at Amherst College for incomparable mentorship and friendship.

At Duke University, I owe a tremendous debt to my colleagues in the Department of Cultural Anthropology for building such a dynamic intellectual community: Anne Alison, Lee Baker, Kathy Ewing, Ralph Litzinger, Diane Nelson, Mark O'Barr, Charlie Piot, Irene Silverblatt, and Orin Starn. Many colleagues in other departments have been equally engaged critics and supportive friends, particularly Banu Gokariksel, Erdag Goknar, Negar Mottahedeh, Robyn Wiegman, Ara Wilson, and coparticipants in the "Feminism, Transnational, International" reading group.

Numerous individuals in other academic locations have also shaped this book: Ann Anagnost, Yael Ben Zvi, Edward Brunner, Matti Bunzl, Elliott Colla, Virginia Dominguez, Gil Eyal, Kaylin Goldstein, Rhoda Kanaaneh, Elizabeth Povinelli, Ella Shohat, Matthew Sparke, Ted Swedenburg, Salim Tamari, Eric Zakim, and my colleagues on the editorial board of *Middle East Report*. Robert Blecher and Shira Robinson have been invaluable readers and political interlocutors throughout. Neta Bar, Alvarro Jarrin, Itamar Radai, Galit Shapira, and Lior Flum provided crucial research assistance. At Duke University Press, Ken Wissoker enthusiastically supported this project from its early days; Ken's pioneering vision of interdisciplinary scholarship has been crucial to the book's realization. Thanks as well to the press's anonymous readers for their insightful suggestions and to Mandy Early and Mark Mastromarino for skillfully guiding this book through production.

A number of institutions have supported the research associated with this project, including the Social Science Research Council, the Stanford Program in Jewish Studies, the Stanford Institute for International Studies, as well as Amherst College, the University of Minnesota, and Duke University, which provided research grants. Work at numerous libraries and archives has also been crucial, as has the support of dedicated research librarians: Heidi Lerner at Stanford University; Irene Munster, Rachel Ariel, Christof Galli, and Dannette Patchner at Duke University; and Jeffrey Spurr and the staff of the Harvard Judaica Collection at Harvard University. Thanks, as well, to the National Archives in Jerusalem and Israeli Ministry of Tourism for access to Ministry archives and meetings.

I owe a tremendous debt of gratitude to the many communities, families, and individuals in Israel who participated in this study (many of whom chose to remain anonymous), supported me during the research project, and gave this book vitality. During the initial fieldwork on which this book was based (1995–96), Yaron Ezrahi, Ilan Pappe, and Tanya Reinhart provided intellectual guidance. In this and subsequent research periods (1998; 2002), Julie Nevo, Sara and Svi Navoponsky, and Jeff and Judith Green were my families away from home. Geoff Hartman, Shira Katz, Nathan Krystall, Jessi Roemer, Yifat Susskind, and Jeff Yas taught me about the powerful ways that political critique and community could nurture each other. Thanks, as well, to Meron Benvenisti, Shlomo Serry, and Vivienne Silver-Brody for permission to use the historical images that appear here.

Other debts are harder to enumerate and repay. My family has been a source of constant encouragement and love. I thank my parents, Carole and Richard Stein, for scrupulous editing and unconditional support for the political vision from which this project emerges; my sister, Sarah Abrevaya Stein, for helping me live by her profound example as a deeply committed scholar, parent, and friend; and my grandfather Jay Stein, for his humbling ability to learn at any age. I owe my greatest thanks to my partner, Andrew Janiak, whose intelligence, compassion, and joy has both sustained and changed me, providing a powerful model for how to live and think differently. I dedicate this book to him and to Isaac, the wondrous person we are creating together.

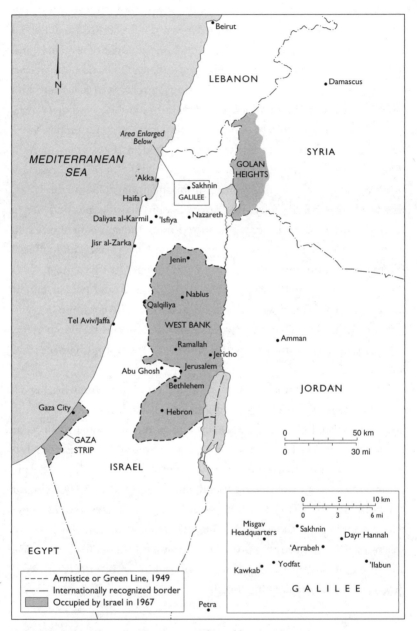

Map I. Israel, the Palestinian Territories, and Neighboring States.
CARTOGRAPHY BY BILL NELSON.

Introduction

At the end of an unpaved road in the Palestinian village of 'Arrabeh, Omar Hassan caters to Jewish Israeli tourists. The establishment he runs, part restaurant and part cultural curiosity, is difficult to find, as the access road lacks streetlights and proper signage. But determined visitors watch for the Hebrew placards directing them "To the Peace Tent" that Hassan has affixed to telephone poles. The tent was originally erected for a family party. But Hassan has refashioned it for commercial usage, lining the interior with carpets and adorning the entrance with Arab coffeepots and photographs of traditional Bedouin costumes. This décor is unremarkable. Hassan, himself a Palestinian citizen of Israel, has reiterated the terms of an Orientalist archive recognizable to his Jewish clients in order to secure profitability.[1]

It is the winter of 1996. The so-called Middle East Peace Process is underway, and Israeli itineraries are changing. Israeli diplomacy with neighboring Arab countries has altered the terms of Israeli tourism. Arab places within the borders of Israel, places feared and avoided by most Jewish Israelis in prior decades, are becoming tourist destinations. Hassan's tent is a coordinate within this emerging tourist landscape. It is a fragile landscape, haunted by histories of political enmity that threaten the market's viability. To moderate these histories, Hassan has interspersed the Orientalist décor with the markers of Israeli nationalism. A photograph of the recently assassinated Israeli prime minister, seated next to the Israeli flag, is displayed in this spirit. The image is a familiar one among the customers Hassan serves, drawn from the prevailing memorial record, and it shares the wall with an Arabic coffeepot and a snapshot of Hassan standing with the Israeli minister of tourism. Such composite displays are crucial for most Jewish Israeli tourists, promising authentic Arab culture without political threat. Their patronage depends on this dual guarantee.

These visitors, most of European descent, have toured Arab places before. Many were avid travelers in the West Bank in the decades following Israel's occupation of the Palestinian territories in 1967, enjoying the open markets of Jerusalem's Old City, restaurants in Bethlehem and Jericho, and souvenir shopping in Hebron. They traveled to Egypt and Jordan after the peace treaties with Israel in 1978 and 1994, respectively. Yet their visit to Hassan's tent is different. For many Jewish tourists, this is their first leisure visit to a Palestinian village inside Israel's borders. Peace, many say, is making it possible.

The popularity of the Peace Tent among Israeli Jews during the 1990s signaled an important shift in dominant Israeli imaginations. In the era of the Middle East Peace Process, also known as the Oslo process, Arab culture was being perceived and acknowledged differently by many Israeli Jews. In the process, the Israeli nation-state was being redefined, its landscapes redrawn, its histories reconsidered. The presence of Jewish Israeli tourists in the Palestinian Galilee marked the emergence of a new form of Israeliness, a new modality of national identity that would not have been possible before the political developments of this decade, before the diplomatic and economic agreements that the Oslo process spawned. The tourist market was not merely a byproduct of such shifts in national sensibilities, but was itself an important site of national reformation. In the 1990s, through the tools and spaces of tourism, Israel was being reimagined.

This is a book about the ways that Israeli tourist practices have participated in reformulating the Israeli nation-state amidst transnational political processes in the Middle East. My investigation of this reformulation focuses on what I will call *national intelligibility*—a concept that designates that which is recognizable according to the dominant national script.[2] It identifies what we might call a national protocol of recognition, one that effectively regulates modes of perception, that which can be perceived, and how perceived things are to be understood or categorized within its terms. This discourse is also an engine of subject formation, one that sorts intelligible subjects from unintelligible ones within the broader field of the perceptible. At issue, then, is a complex interrelation of perception, recognition, and subjectivity, an interrelation that itself is subject to constant, if irregular, change. National intelligibility is a historically contingent discourse that can shift dramatically during periods of profound transition or upheaval within the nation-state, on its borders, and within adjacent territories. I contend that it is also a performative discourse that is sustained through iterative practices and can thus be contested and altered through such practices.[3] That is to say, its norms of recognition are never secure. The lexicon of intelligibility is always being produced and, as such, can be revised.

In this book I am interested in a period of profound political transition when the terms of Israeli intelligibility were quite dramatically in flux. I focus on Israeli tourist culture during the era of the Oslo process, beginning in earnest with the Oslo Accords of 1993—an internationally recognized rapprochement between Israel and the Palestinians which set the terms for a negotiated settlement of the conflict—and concluding with the outbreak of the second Palestinian uprising in 2000.[4] I argue that this regional political process had numerous effects on the ways that Israelis imagined their nation-state, altering normative Israeli practices of seeing and logics of recognition. Israeli diplomacy with neighboring Arab states, and the transnational process it spawned, coupled with concurrent changes in domestic policy, produced a substantive shift in the ways that national identity, space, and history could be conceived and represented. These shifts, I contend, were dramatically manifest within tourist culture. As a body of both spatial and representational practices, tourism provided a convenient toolbox with which to forge new notions of national identity befitting the altered regional landscape.

Consider, again, the Peace Tent. During the period of political flux that Oslo catalyzed, a Palestinian village once feared by Israeli Jews became newly visible as part of the Israeli landscape. This is not to suggest a prior unintelligibility or invisibility that was somehow corrected. The village had always been perceptible to Israeli Jews, but primarily as a site of threat. What had changed was its symbolic charge, its significance in the prevailing Israeli imagination. I am thus speaking less about the Peace Tent than the fantasy it conjured, its changing figuration, its new status as a spatial coordinate of Israeli tourist desire. Yet the terms of this figuration were never under tourist control, not in any strict sense. That is, even the most reassuring itineraries, even those Arab places offering the conjoined décor of Orientalism and Israeli nationalism, could generate profoundly unsettling encounters between guests and hosts, bringing Jewish travelers into contact with a set of Palestinian histories that the state had long endeavored to suppress. In some cases, these encounters produced substantial cracks in normative Israeli logics. Some such encounters challenged the very legitimacy of the nation-state, revising its intelligibility in powerful ways.

Most of this inquiry focuses on the years when the Oslo process was at its height—namely, during the Labor administrations of Prime Ministers Yitzhak Rabin and Shimon Peres (1992–96).[5] The Accords, coupled with the subsequent end of the forty-year Arab boycott of Israeli goods and commercial partnerships, substantially altered Israel's relationship to the Arab Middle East.[6] In its wake, the Israeli state began to pursue new diplomatic and economic relations with neighboring Arab states following a template of peacemaking through economic liberalization, beginning with a peace accord with Jordan in 1994, which ended their official state of war. Without the Arab boycott as an obstacle, Israel also increased its trade with North African countries, particularly Morocco and Tunisia; opened trade offices in Qatar and Oman; escalated diplomatic negotiations with Syria; and pursued joint ventures with Jordan, Egypt, and the Palestinians in such matters as tourism, transportation, water, and the environment.[7] Israeli Foreign Minister Shimon Peres spoke of the "New Middle East" that economic liberalization would deliver, including a regional common market with Tel Aviv at its center.[8] Israel's relationship to and within the Arab Middle East was being radically reconfigured.

Inside Israel's borders, political change was no less substantial. The national economy was liberalizing and expanding.[9] The ethnic makeup of the Israeli Parliament was changing.[10] Israeli demographics were shifting due to massive immigration from Russia and a growing population of foreign laborers, and many minority populations were being acknowledged by the state in new ways, particularly during the Rabin-Peres administration.[11] The Oslo process also altered the ways that Israeli history could be told. In the Israeli academy, scholars were rethinking the foundational Zionist myths and accounts of state formation, and these new scholarly accounts began to circulate in the popular national media.[12] Whereas regional conflict had necessitated historical defenses of the nation-state, there was a sense that political reconciliation had enabled their critical reevaluation.

This book is particularly attentive to the changing status of Israel's Palestinian citizenry within this altered political landscape, a population that includes those communities that remained within Israel's borders after state formation in 1948.[13] In the 1990s, they composed nearly a quarter of the Israeli population. Collectively, they have been subject to decades of state repression, underdevelopment, and political disenfranchisement aimed at preventing any real or perceived threat to the Jewish state. Yet during the Labor administration, state policy toward the Arab minority was modified. After decades of sanctioned underdevelopment, government budgets for the so-called Arab sector grew considerably.[14] Official discourse was also changing, as the state encouraged Jewish Israelis to "coexist" with their Arab conationals. The rhetoric of coexistence (*dukiyum*) was first applied to Israel's new relationship with neighboring Arab states in the context of the Oslo process and only later, after it had gained a conceptual hold, was extended to include Israel's Arab population. Although this discursive shift had limited political effects, as subsequent chapters will suggest, it was nonetheless significant. Arab citizens of Israel, long perceived as Israel's enemy within, were being symbolically included in the nation's multicultural tableau.[15] Israel's Arab population, in other words, was becoming intelligible in new ways within dominant imaginations. It should be stressed that Israel's internal Arab population had always been perceptible to the Israeli state. Indeed, the state lauded its history of comprehension in this area. But these Arabs had been primarily comprehensible as political threats. Oslo helped to alter their perceived political valence.

How did tourism articulate with these political changes? This shifting political landscape, the combination of changing regional diplomacy and domestic policy, catalyzed tourist appetites. More pointedly, I argue that among elite Jewish Israelis of European descent (Ashkenazi Jews), these political changes invigorated a desire for Arabness—that is, for Arab places, culinary traditions, cultural practices, and histories. These desires were by no means novel. In their broadest construal, they can be traced to the early decades of state building by Zionist settlers in Palestine, when the idealization of Arab culture was harnessed to the Jewish nation-making project.[16] In the decades after state formation in 1948, idealization would be replaced by a regulatory discourse about the Arab political threat, one manifest in the work of anthropologists, journalists, state officials, and intelligence officers alike.[17] In the 1990s, under pressure from the changing political landscape, the symbolic valence of Arabness shifted. Arab persons, cultures, and places were no longer perceived as threats in the dominant Israeli imagination—or, more precisely, not merely so. Their significance was being revised. Now they could also be desired, enjoyed, and consumed.

These new valences of Arab intelligibility were powerfully manifest within Israeli tourist cultures chiefly with the emergence of a new set of regional itineraries. Israeli diplomacy with neighboring Arab countries was making the region newly available as an object of Israeli tourist desire. Jordan was the first new regional destination of this era. In the immediate aftermath of its peace treaty with Israel in 1994, hundreds of thousands of Israelis traveled to Petra and Amman for a brief holiday. Israeli tourism to Morocco also increased during this period, following low-level diplomatic relations with Israel in the same year, as did Israeli leisure travel to Egypt and the Sinai Peninsula. Jewish Israeli tourist fantasies were also in flux. As Israel pursued diplomatic talks with Syria in the winter of 1995, articles in Israeli newspapers prepared readers for a visit to Damascus, while others lauded the pleasures of Beirut and Tunis, detailing their historic sites and culinary specialties. These itineraries were still impossibilities, as much of the Middle East and North Africa remained off-limits to Israeli passport holders. Nonetheless, these imaginary routes were important barometers of ideological change. Regional routes that had been officially unavailable to Israeli passport holders since 1948 were becoming thinkable in new ways thanks to shifts in the terms of regional diplomacy. While tourism was a byproduct of such processes, it was also the theater in which Israelis actively negotiated these political changes. Tourist practices and discourses translated the vagaries of diplomatic processes and domestic policy into an everyday language of routes and consumer pleasures. The very intelligibility of the Arab Middle East was changing, and tourism was an important means of both enunciating and negotiating such changes.

The political processes of this period, and the newly modified intelligibility of Arabness, also produced new Israeli itineraries within the nation-state. Beginning in the mid-1990s, Palestinian villages in Israel's Galilee region were collaboratively refashioned as tourist sites by local Palestinian entrepreneurs and Israeli state officials, sites designed explicitly for Jewish Israeli visitors. The state discourse of coexistence played a crucial role in the market's emergence. At work was a phenomenon that we might call *consumer coexistence*. Following the state's injunction to coexist, many Jewish tourists engaged in an incitement to cultural difference: they invited Palestinian citizens of Israel to perform their ethnic identity in the tourist marketplace, to remake their cultural difference into a tourist commodity. Such demands, however implicit in form, represented a substantial shift in normative Israeli epistemologies. The state had long demanded spectacles of loyalty and performances of Israeli identity from the internal Arab population. While these demands did not dissipate in the 1990s, they were tempered by others. In the tourist arena, the same population was being asked by state officials and Jewish Israeli tourists alike to perform as Arabs — that is, to recover some of the ethnic markings that they had long been asked to disavow.

The ethnic tourist market that emerged took a relatively predictable form, reliant on a conventional set of cultural rituals and discourses.[18] Indeed, it is precisely the market's conventional form that interests me, as it signaled a radical shift in prevailing Israeli imaginations. Arab communities and places within Israel's borders were now becoming intelligible as banal objects of enjoyment. Arab villages, persons, and histories could now be slotted into a culturally interchangeable ethnic tourist economy, with relatively consistent taxonomies and measures of value. Yet, as I will suggest, these taxonomies generated highly localized effects. Through predictable tourist structures, new perceptions of the Palestinian minority were being forged.

While these tourist cultures were predicated on a revision in the terms of national intelligibility, they were also dynamic arenas of revision in their own right by which Israelis were actively negotiating and adjusting the contours of the dominant national optic. Space was an essential element in this process. Prior to the Oslo process, Israel's very proximity to its Arab neighbors had been largely obscured within prevailing political discourses, overwritten by the terms of political enmity, both real and imagined. The Oslo process changed this "imaginary geography," making these proximities thinkable in new ways.[19] But tourism made these geographies more thinkable still, making them perceptible in a way that the language of diplomacy could not. Israeli tourism to Jordan is a case in point. The voyage between Tel Aviv and Amman, now possible in just over an hour by car, changed the ways that regional geography could be described. The same could be said about Israeli tourist fantasies about Damascus, Beirut, and Tunis—fantasies anchored in a celebration of surprising nearness. Jewish Israeli tourism within the Palestinian Galilee had similar spatial effects. For many tourists, the proximity between Jewish and Palestinian places inside Israel had also been unthinkable, subsumed by the terms of interethnic enmity. Jews who traveled to Palestinian villages effectively recast the terms of national geography by re-marking Arab spaces as proximate, as newly visible coordinates on a state-sanctioned cartography of Israeli leisure. During the Oslo period, geography could be enunciated in new ways, and tourism provided the tools.

Yet the tourist cultures that Oslo spawned were fragile forms. Consumer coexistence, like its analogue in the political arena, was predicated on a highly contingent form of political tolerance.[20] Most tourists sought Arab culture in denationalized form, stripped of explicit Palestinian histories. At the same time, most had little patience for the histories of discrimination and dispossession to which Palestinian citizens had been subject. The explicit presence of these histories or nationalist markers threatened market viability, discouraging tourists from returning. Nor were most Jewish Israeli tourists willing to use the term "Palestinian" to designate their Arab conationals, preferring the state-sponsored vocabulary organized through ethnoreligious categories. Within its terms, Christian and Muslim Arabs were marked as "Arab-Israelis" while Bedouin, Druze, and Circassian populations were categorized as Israel's "non-Jewish minorities." Of course, these categories were highly political: "Arab" signified an enemy population, while "non-Jewish minorities" were understood as Israel's potential allies.[21] Some Palestinian hosts shaped their tourist offerings according to the political logics employed by tourists in an effort to maximize their profits. Others refused such logics, using tourism as a stage to enunciate the very histories that Jewish Israeli tourists refused. In such moments, the tourist market was transformed into an arena of active struggle over the material and symbolic conditions of Israeli belonging, highlighting the discrepant positions that Arab and Jewish citizens occupy within the Jewish state.[22]

The scope of political revision during this period should not be overstated. Neither the Oslo process nor the domestic policies of the Labor administration were universally embraced by Israelis. It follows that not all Israelis, particularly those on the political right, endorsed a shift in national ways of knowing. And the terms of Arab revaluation that Oslo spawned were highly delimited. Many Arab persons, things, and histories retained their perceived threat and, as such, could not be transformed into tourist commodities. Even as Palestinian villages in the Galilee were remade as tourist sites, Arab Jewish (e.g., Mizrahi) places within Israel's borders did not acquire analogous tourist appeal.[23] The same could be said about the occupied Palestinian territories. Even as Jewish Israeli tourists were imagining their future routes to Damascus and Beirut, few returned to the West Bank as tourists or hikers during this period to revisit places they had enjoyed before the Palestinian uprising. In large measure, the contingent nature of Arab revaluation had its roots in the political terms of the Oslo process. Although the state promised free movement for all regional actors throughout a Middle East without borders, Oslo's neoliberal economic order depended on concurrent restrictions on Palestinian movement, implemented through closures and curfews, militarized checkpoints, Israeli control of borders and ports, visa restrictions, and the eventual separation barrier.[24] While Israeli capital crossed Israel's borders with increasing ease during this period, those borders were newly fortified to prevent the entry of unwanted Arabs into Israeli territory. And even as the Israeli media was reconsidering the proximity between Tel Aviv and Amman, the Israeli state was carefully regulating the distances and divides between Jewish Israeli cities and Palestinian ones in the Occupied Territories. The selective terms of Israeli tourism were a measure of this uneven political landscape.

Routes: Travel and Scholarship

The itineraries examined in this study are situated within a long history of tourism and travel through the Middle East. The tradition of Christian, Muslim, and Jewish pilgrimage to the Holy Land was already well established in the late 1880s, when the Zionist movement began to settle in Palestine.[25] While pilgrims and other travelers had traversed the region for centuries, most scholars trace the arrival of so-called tourists to the mid-nineteenth century, when the development of steam navigation, the growth of railway lines, and the construction of the Suez Canal (1869) made travel to and around the Middle East speedier and more affordable, thereby extending its pleasures to a broader class spectrum of consumers.[26] International tourist companies began operating in the region in the 1860s, offering excursions into the "enchanted Orient."[27]

In some regards, the itineraries introduced in this book are anything but novel. Many of the routes enjoyed and imagined by Israelis during the Oslo period have their precedent in prestate history. In the first decades of the twentieth century, middle-class Jewish settlers in Palestine enjoyed a set of transregional itineraries. They took the daily shuttle service between Haifa and Beirut, the Hejaz railway from Haifa to Beirut, or passenger trucks from Tel Aviv to Damascus and Baghdad.[28] At the same time, these Jewish residents of Palestine were avidly touring the Land of Israel (*Eretz Yisrael*) in the context of a national pedagogical project committed to intimate knowledge of the ancient homeland. The hike (*ha-tiyul*) was a crucial element of this nationalist pedagogy, a practice imagined as a means of territorial conquest and of nationalizing the Jewish traveler through embodied experience of the land.[29] As Western tourism to Palestine increased, Zionist institutions began working with tourist agencies to introduce Western Jews to the burgeoning infrastructures of Zionist settlement, attracting them with specially designed guidebooks, posters, and promotional films (see figure 3).[30] Throughout the Mandate period, British authorities placed strict regulations on the movement of these visitors into Palestine to ensure that "no Jews would enter the country in the guise of tourists."[31]

Figure I. The pedagogical power of the hike [*ha-tiyul*]. Jewish travelers from Palestine with their guide, David Benvenisti, 1941. PHOTO: DAVID SERRY.

Regional routes were closed to Israeli tourists after the establishment of the state in 1948. But their itineraries would shift considerably following Israel's occupation of the West Bank, the Gaza Strip, Golan Heights, and the Sinai Peninsula in 1967 as sites in these territories became newly available as Jewish Israeli destinations. Jews flocked to East Jerusalem's Old City for its culinary offerings, to the Sinai coast for natural beauty and Bedouin culture, and to the markets and restaurants of Bethlehem and Ramallah for inexpensive shopping on Friday afternoons. Palestinian residents of the newly occupied territories also crossed into Israel in large numbers after the cessation of the 1967 War, returning to homes, landscapes, and families from which they had been separated in 1948. Jewish Israeli travel through the Palestinian territories would continue in varying degrees until the outbreak of the first Palestinian uprising (1987–93), when most of these itineraries came to a decisive end. Jewish settlers and territorial nationalists were an exception in this regard, continuing their travel in the Occupied Territories as a means of advancing the Zionist project. By the end of the 1990s, small numbers of Israeli Jews returned to the West Bank as consumers and sightseers, their routes made possible by the sense of security that Oslo had delivered. Most such travel would cease with the outbreak of the second Palestinian uprising in 2000.

Figure 2. Regional routes before nation-states. Jewish travelers from Palestine camping in Aqaba (Jordan), 1929. PHOTO: AVRAHAM SOSKIN.

As a study of the interplay between travel and power, my investigation is by no means novel. Rather, it draws on a body of scholarship inaugurated by Edward Said's *Orientalism*, with its consideration of how travel practices have participated in Western imperialist projects. Scholars working in *Orientalism*'s wake have argued that we understand travel narratives as instruments of colonial conquest, discursive tools intimately related to the more violent projects of resource extraction, settlement, and colonial governance.[32] Postcolonial critics also have insisted on the ambivalent nature of such narratives, arguing that their ruptures can signal both the blind spots and the fragilities of colonial dominance.[33] They contend that reading such narratives against the grain with an eye to such ambivalences participates in a kind of decolonizing work, work this book will try to advance. In drawing on postcolonial criticism, I am advancing a historical argument about the colonial nature of the Israeli nation-building project. I am contending, as many other scholars have, that Zionism borrowed heavily from contemporaneous colonial movements by sharing settlement tactics, forms of land acquisition, economic structures, and cultural ideologies and that many of these colonial institutions persist in the Israeli present, although in altered forms.[34]

As should be clear, I employ the rubric *tourism* a bit unconventionally

SOCIETY FOR THE PROMOTION OF TRAVEL IN THE HOLY LAND

FOR, LO, THE WINTER IS PAST; THE RAIN IS OVER AND GONE; THE FLOWERS APPEAR ON THE EARTH; THE TIME OF THE SINGING OF BIRDS IS COME, AND THE VOICE OF THE TURTLE IS HEARD IN OUR LAND

COME TO PALESTINE

Figure 3. Courting Western Jews. Poster produced by the Society for the Promotion of Travel in the Holyland, 1929. ARTIST: ZE'EV RABAN.

in this study to designate a wide array of Israeli traveling practices, leisure cultures, consumptive desires, and market discourses of the Oslo period. Together, I argue, they form a distinct cultural field. A comprehensive study of Israeli tourism of this decade is, however, well beyond the scope of this inquiry. Numerous itineraries and traveling practices have been excluded, many of which have been intimately involved in the production of national intelligibility. These include postarmy travel to third world countries by which tourism functions as catharsis for the military project; the annual visits by Jewish high school students to Holocaust memorial sites which suture Holocaust memory to Jewish Israeli identity; political journeys of both Jews and Palestinians with Israeli citizenship to former Palestinian villages destroyed during the course of the 1948–49 War, journeys that commemorate the dispossession; and Mizrahi pilgrimage and homecoming travel to Morocco, routes that frustrate state interdictions on Mizrahi memory.[35] I leave these Israeli itineraries to other studies.

Yet I include other itineraries in their stead, ones infrequently grouped under the rubric of tourism. At the heart of this inquiry is an investment in what I'll call *discrepant mobility*—a term that refers to the broader regimes and histories of mobility and immobility in Israel, Palestine, and the Arab Middle East in which, I argue, Israeli tourism is situated. These histories include the Zionist migration to Palestine beginning in the late nineteenth century and the forms of Palestinian dispossession that it generated; the flight and expulsion of some seven hundred thousand Palestinians in the course of the 1948–49 War; the Military Administration to which Palestinian residents of Israel were subjected in the early decades of state formation (1948–66), with its violent restrictions on Palestinian movement; the 1950s mass emigration to Israel of Mizrahi Jews from the Middle East, North Africa, and the Levant and the state-sponsored discrimination that followed; the numerous journeys of the Israeli army to Arab places in times of espionage, incursion, occupation, and war; and the strictures on movement to which Palestinians in the Occupied Territories have been increasingly subject since the onset of the Oslo process.[36] I am interested in the ways that Israeli tourist cultures have historically intersected with these routes, with these histories of both movement and spatial incarceration. In other words, I contend that Israeli tourist and leisure practices have been historically enabled by the journeys of soldiers, immigrants, and refugees.[37] Such convergences among seemingly dissimilar itineraries are at this project's core.

Borders and Crossings

As a study of Israeli political culture, this book has numerous scholarly precedents. I draw heavily on the tradition of new Israeli historiography and sociology that has emerged over the course of the past few decades, with its commitment to rethinking foundational Israeli myths about national history, demography, geography, and state formation.[38] In turn, my attention to Israel's Palestinian population is made possible by decades of anticolonial scholarship on Palestinian history and society—a scholarship that has boldly refused the dominant account of Palestinian absence from both land and modernity alike.[39] Although this anti-colonial literature has made my study possible, its goals are different from my own. While it has endeavored to restore Palestinians to the histories from which they have been so systemically foreclosed, my project, by contrast, concerns the mechanisms of their foreclosure in the dominant Israeli context. It follows that while Palestinians with Israeli citizenship are at this study's core, I am principally interested in their discursive function within prevailing Jewish Israeli imaginaries, their status as tourist commodities and objects of desire. My attention to Jewish Israeli tourist cultures is delimited by a related logic. I focus on elite tourists of European descent (Ashkenazim), the population most prominently involved in Arab commodification, and the population that has dominated Israeli political and social life since the early years of Zionist settlement in Palestine.[40] In these ways, this study seeks to advance a very different kind of progressive research agenda, arguing that serious attention be paid both to the terms of Israeli dominance and to the everyday Israeli cultural machinery of Palestinian dispossession.

This book is also proposing a relational approach to the study of Israeli cultural politics. As others have argued, scholarship about both Israeli and Palestinian society has traditionally been hampered by a national logic, a logic manifest in disinterest in "mutually formative interactions" between Jews and Palestinian Arabs, interactions that span borders, checkpoints, and national ideologies.[41] Traditionally, both Middle East studies and Israel studies have been party to this disinterest. Scholars working within the former rubric have, for their part, largely avoided sustained engagement with Israel, save its legacy as a Western colonial outpost. Avoidance was thought to perform radical critique, effectively removing the Jewish state from the region. Scholars working within the Israel studies paradigm have, in turn, focused principally on Jewish Israeli culture and society within the national borders, therein neglecting Israel's relationship to its regional context. In these ways, both traditions reproduced the fiction of Israeli spatial and cultural insularity within the Middle East, frustrating efforts to consider mutual formation across national borders and ideologies. A relational approach, by contrast, conceives of Israel differently, placing questions of cultural interdependence at the scholarly core.[42] I attempt to work in this relational mode. Indeed, I suggest that Israel's relation to the Arab Middle East structures the terms of national intelligibility itself.

Chapter 1 analyzes the regional routes enjoyed by Israeli travelers of the Oslo period through a reading of the mainstream Israeli print media. I focus on two distinct itineraries: Israelis traveling into the Arab Middle East and regional Arabs voyaging into the Jewish state. The figure of the tourist was a locus of both possibility and anxiety during this era. Jewish Israeli routes through the Middle East illustrated the promise of this peace process, even as incoming Arabs in tourist guise, often figured as threatening subjects, suggested its dystopic possibilities. Through attention to the colonial archive on which these narratives drew, this chapter considers how stories about tourists enunciated normative Israeli anxieties about the status of the Jewish state in the New Middle East that Oslo was poised to deliver.

The next chapters study the growth of an ethnic tourism market within Palestinian villages of the Israeli Galilee during this period. Chapter 2 considers how these tourist spaces, producing unusual forms of intimate contact between Palestinian and Jewish citizens of Israel, could generate contest over the terms of national intelligibility. In an effort to secure market viability, most Palestinian entrepreneurs fashioned their tourist offerings according to state-sponsored protocols, protocols that sought to regulate the kinds of histories and politics that such offerings contained. Yet these protocols were plastic forms, providing Palestinian hosts with the tools to narrate the Israeli nation-state in ways that challenged the very foundations of national intelligibility. This chapter is also an investigation of normative Israeli notions of cultural value and how such notions were being reworked amid the political changes of the period.

Chapter 3 turns to the politics and production of space. I argue that the Oslo process can usefully be understood as a rescaling project which enabled Israel's insertion into both regional and global marketplaces in some relatively unprecedented ways. Rescaling was a cause of both celebration and concern for the Israeli state. Even as it welcomed multinational capital investment, the state feared that a newly transnational Middle East would weaken the Israeli nation-state and bring its internal Arab population into threatening contact with neighboring states. This chapter posits the ethnic tourism market as a symptomatic instance of these anxieties. Through a study of the everyday practices of state planners and architects, I consider the ways that the Israeli state labored to remake Palestinian space for Jewish Israeli tourism in the midst of rescaling processes. I argue that the state responded to these processes with a fantasy of bounded Arab space, producing blueprints for tourist development that effectively fortified the scale of the village as a spatial container. This study of spatial production and everyday statecraft is thus an attempt to consider the link between regional and intranational processes during the Oslo era.

Chapter 4 moves to a very different political terrain. Here I consider forms of Jewish Israeli culinary tourism in the Palestinian village of Abu Ghosh, a village known for its history of collaboration with the Israeli state and Zionist institutions. While much ethnic tourism in the Palestinian Galilee occasioned a contestation of national intelligibility, Abu Ghosh entrepreneurs in the restaurant sector struggled to fortify its terms and therein secure recognition by the state and dominant Israeli society. This study of restaurant culture provides an occasion to reconsider the "romance of resistance" that frequently attends scholarship on Palestinian political culture, pointing to some of the histories, subjects, and structures of feeling that this approach has obscured.[43]

Although politically transformative, the Oslo process was relatively short-lived, declared a dead letter in 2000 following the diplomatic failures at Camp David. The outbreak of the second Palestinian uprising in 2000 precipitated a dramatic political realignment in Jewish Israeli society: a popular shift to the political right that provided the government with political authority to suppress the uprising at virtually any cost. Chapter 5 concludes with a reading of Oslo's demise through the lens of Jewish Israeli leisure practices. Returning to the dominant Israeli print media, I study political events in Israel during the spring of 2002, when Palestinian suicide bombings terrorized Jewish Israeli cities and the Israeli military administration launched a massive incursion into the West Bank. I am interested in how narratives of Jewish Israeli leisure under attack were used to represent this political crisis.

The *itinerary* to which my title refers has multiple resonances. In part, it gestures to the theoretical literatures on which this study draws, the ways that tropes of mobility have been deployed in poststructural theory to figure the transitory route of the signifier, its "detours" and "wanderings," and the potentially disruptive effects of these routes.[44] Michel de Certeau, for example, takes the "itinerary" of the urban pedestrian to elaborate the logic of performativity. De Certeau's "walker in the city" is a subject who makes the city through perambulation, giving meaning to the urban landscape in the act of traversing space. These traveling practices are polyvalent in their effects, both securing and reconfiguring the spaces made available by urban planners. "Pedestrian enunciation," as de Certeau coins this spatial practice, simultaneously "affirms, suspects, tries out, transgresses, respects, etc. the trajectories it 'speaks.'"[45] Posited as the counterpart of the map, with its panoptic vision, the itinerary designates a critical analytics rooted in contingent knowledges and polyvalent readings.

The tourist forms discussed in this volume are itinerant in similar ways. They are "many sided, resilient, cunning and stubborn," in de Certeau's words, generating contradictory trajectories.[46] At moments, they affirm national norms and logics of intelligibility. At other moments, they enunciate national space, identity, and culture differently, calling these logics into question. Nation-states are also itinerant—they are performative forms, constantly being reproduced, adjusted, and refashioned within the everyday practices of national communities and institutions. Tourism, I contend, plays a critical role in this performative process. To read Israel as itinerant is to consider the transgressive potential of its perambulating norms and intelligiblities. To read Israel as itinerant is to imagine its alternative futures.

1

Israeli Tourists in the New Middle East

In the summer of 1994, several days before Israel signed a peace treaty with Jordan, one of Israel's most popular newspapers documented the "first" Israeli visit to Petra. This prominent article, featured in the newspaper's front section, recounted the clandestine voyage of two Israelis who had illegally crossed into Jordan with their European passports. "I Got to the Red Rock!" the headline proclaimed. A first-person narrative described the travelers' mounting anticipation as they neared Petra in a taxi, their fear of detection by the Jordanian authorities, and thrilling arrival at a site with mythic status in the Israeli popular imagination. "And then it happened. Suddenly, between the crevices of the giant stones, 100 meters from us, [we caught our] first glimpse of the red structures hewn in rock. Tears came to our eyes. . . . 'Photograph me,' we said to each other in the same breath."[1]

Israeli voyages into neighboring Arab countries received extensive coverage in mainstream Israeli newspapers of the 1990s. This wasn't for reasons of human interest alone. The figure of the Israeli tourist and the grammar of a tourist imagination were crucial tools by which the Israeli media represented the Oslo process to mass publics. That is, stories about tourism were important vehicles of translation. While the intricacies of diplomacy could be difficult to convey in popular vocabularies, tales of leisure travel were not. The highly legible figure of the tourist was deployed to illustrate the effects of regional reconfiguration. This mobile figure, crossing borders made porous by diplomatic advances and economic liberalization, was offered to Israeli readers as Oslo's allegory.

In this chapter I discuss dominant Israeli imaginations of the Oslo process as enunciated through tourist stories in the national media.[2] For the state and private sector, Oslo was thought to hold tremendous promise. Israeli market analysts argued that diplomatic and economic agreements with the Palestinians and neighboring Arab states would enable Israel's integration into global economies. State officials trumpeted Oslo's value as a security arrangement by which the Palestinian Authority would participate in the work of the Israeli occupation. Yet for many Jewish Israeli publics, particularly those on the political right, regional reconfiguration was an anxious prospect that threatened the integrity of the nation-state, challenging normative institutions. Stories about tourism echoed these conflicting Israeli responses to the Oslo process. They illustrated both popular Israeli fantasies and fears about the course of regional reconfiguration.

Two stories were particularly ubiquitous in the Israeli media of this period. The first was an iconic tale of first contact, in which the Jewish Israeli traveler was cast as a heroic discoverer of the Arab Middle East.[3] The second was a phobic narrative about incoming Arab tourists from neighboring countries whose itineraries required vigilant regulation by the Israeli state and Jewish public. While the former celebrated the new forms of Israeli mobility through the region that Oslo had generated, the latter contended with its threatening flows of Arab persons, cultures, and things. Citizenship was supremely at stake in these stories. In both accounts, the identity of *the tourist* was harnessed to that of *the citizen*, although in variable ways. Stories about Israeli travel into the Arab Middle East figured good Israeli tourists as good Israeli citizens in highly normative terms. That is, despite the diverse populations of Israelis traveling throughout the Middle East during this period, Israeli tourists were perpetually cast as Jewish citizens of European descent (Ashkenazim), a move consistent with the Ashkenazi bias of the popular media.[4] Stories about incoming Arabs had an opposing logic. These travelers were marked as tourists only when differentiated clearly from potential Israeli citizens. The designator was a comforting one. It reassured readers that these traveling subjects were temporary visitors who did not seek residence in the Jewish state, therein threatening national demographics.

Tourism, I argue, was a crucial player on Oslo's political stage. As a market, it was both a product and progenitor of Israel's integration into regional economies. As a field of representational practices, it was an important tool by which Israelis contended with the status of the nation-state in a regional age. In part, then, I am suggesting that the figure of the tourist can be read as a surrogate, an image that stood in for something else. This is not to discount tourism's material importance in the Oslo process, but to suggest that its significance as a body of signs in the popular print media exceeded the terms of political economy. Stories about tourism tried to stabilize the nation-state at this moment of geopolitical flux, to consolidate the borders around normative national culture even as Israel's territorial borders were becoming porous in new ways. These narratives reasserted the prevailing terms of national intelligibility, insisting on Israel's Jewish and European identity amid a regionalizing process that threatened Israel with Arabization, or so some Israelis feared. They provided a popular grammar for understanding the Oslo process even as they grappled uncertainly with maps and meanings of Israel in a newly regional age.

The New Middle East

Diplomatic negotiations between Israel and neighboring Arab states have been openly pursued since the 1967 War. Nonetheless, the Oslo Accords of 1993 were celebrated in the Israeli and international media as the first significant breakthrough in Israeli-Palestinian talks. The Accords stipulated mutual recognition between Israel and the Palestinian Liberation Organization (PLO) and the beginning of Israeli withdrawal from Palestinian territories occupied in 1967. Signed by Yasser Arafat in an attempt to secure his regime in a time of crisis, the Oslo Accords reconfigured the terms of Israeli power in the West Bank and Gaza Strip through a new partnership with the Palestinian Authority.[5] They offered the Palestinians the symbolic trappings of statehood, such as postage stamps, passports, and uniformed immigration officers. However, the Palestinian governing entity and its territorial borders remained "legally subordinate to the authority of the [Israeli] military government."[6] In its Occupied Territories, Israel remained in control of land, security, the economy, and all matters pertaining to the Jewish settlements. Oslo offered Israel the economic and political gains of an internationally recognized rapprochement with the Palestinian people without requiring significant territorial or political compromise.

For Israel, Oslo's economic yield was substantial.[7] Peace with the Palestinians paved the way for Jordan and Israel to sign the Washington Declaration in July 1994, thereby ending the official state of war between the two countries.[8] Following the dismantling of the Arab boycott, Israel increased its trade with North African countries, particularly Morocco and Tunisia, and opened trade offices in Qatar and Oman.[9] The Israeli private sector pursued joint ventures with Jordan, Egypt, and the Palestinians in such matters as tourism, transportation, water, and the environment. Israel had been largely ignored by European and Asian multinationals prior to the 1990s, yet this changed following the dismantling of the Arab boycott's secondary and tertiary tiers banning third-party dealings with the Jewish state.[10] Total foreign investment in Israel increased to $19.6 billion in the first two years after the Oslo Accords, and several U.S. high-tech corporations, including Intel and Microsoft, announced major new investments in the country, made possible in part by a large workforce of Russian immigrants trained in science and technology.[11] Israeli companies also began to work through regional channels, as the example of the Israeli textile industry illustrates.[12] In the 1990s, raw cotton was being purchased in Egypt, sent to Turkey for spinning and weaving, to Israel for designing, to Jordan for sewing and packaging, and finally shipped for sale in the United States.[13] Israeli capital was also flowing to Asia as never before, as Israeli companies explored markets in Malaysia, India, Vietnam, and Indonesia.[14] Government ministers described Israel as the future "Singapore of the region," a hub between Asia and Europe.[15] Although the Israeli state and private sector described such trends in the language of regionalization and globalization, trumpeting Oslo's economic benefits on both sides of the Israeli border, such characterizations tended to obscure the highly uneven economic landscape that Oslo was generating. Short of economic regionalization in any comprehensive terms, Oslo enabled the

Israeli private sector to mine the Arab Middle East for new markets, sites of production, and labor pools in ways that tended to fortify the pre-Oslo balance of regional power.[16]

For the Israeli state, economic growth and liberalization depended on concurrent processes of containment, chiefly of its occupied Palestinian territories.[17] The policy of military closure was foremost among Israeli containment strategies, by which the West Bank and Gaza Strip were effectively sealed from each other, the Jerusalem area, and Israel proper.[18] At the same time, the state dramatically reduced the number of work permits granted to Palestinians for labor inside Israel, defending such policies in the language of security.[19] Due to a history of Palestinian dependence on the Israeli economy, closure and visa restrictions produced high rates of unemployment in the Occupied Territories, vastly reduced levels of Palestinian trade and production, and heightened poverty.[20] In keeping with the terms of the Oslo Accords, Israel maintained control over the perimeters of Palestinian areas and prevented Palestinian access to Israeli markets while ensuring Israeli access to Palestinian ones.[21]

This period also witnessed numerous changes within the nation-state that compounded the sense of political transformation. During the tenure of the Rabin-led Labor administration, many minority populations were recognized by the state in relatively unprecedented ways, including Ethiopian Jews, gays and lesbians, and Palestinians with Israeli citizenship.[22] Jews of North African and Middle Eastern descent (Mizrahim) gained greater political power and popular visibility, culminating in a major parliamentary victory at the decade's end.[23] Israel's Christian population grew substantially following the mass immigration from the former Soviet Union, as did Israel's population of blue-collar foreign workers, imported to supplant the Palestinian workforce from the Occupied Territories.[24] By the turn of the millennium, these legal and illegal laborers composed one-sixth of metropolitan Tel Aviv, living in its impoverished peripheries. Birthrates in Israel's Arab community were also rising, and right-wing demographers warned of an Arab majority in the combined area of Israel and Palestine by the early decades of the twenty-first century.[25] When coupled with the pace of regional integration, these social trends generated considerable anxiety. Some Jewish Israelis, particularly those on the political right, feared for the very future of the Jewish state.

Oslo's effect on the tourism sector, both in Israel and the broader Middle East, was equally substantial. This sector was the locus of some of the most significant joint national projects of this period, and these were projected to expand considerably in the context of a comprehensive regional peace settlement.[26] In 1995, Israeli state and private representatives began to coordinate joint marketing of tourism packages with Turkey, Egypt, and Morocco. Concurrently, Israel and Jordan embarked on a series of joint developments, including coordinated airport facilities in Aqaba and Eilat, a "Peace Road" connecting Haifa and Irbid, and a Dead Sea recreational park spanning the border.[27] Spurred by the consumer confidence that Oslo had generated, the number of incoming visitors to Israel peaked at 2.2 million in 1995, generating $3.1 billion in revenue.[28] Some analysts predicted a 250 percent increase in Israeli sector earnings as a result of regional marketing, air links between Israel and Asia, newly opened and eased border crossings, and political stability.[29]

The itineraries of Israeli travelers were also in flux during this period, as diplomatic and economic agreements made the Arab Middle East both newly available and attractive. Jordan was the first new Israeli destination in the region. Some sixty thousand Israelis visited in the months following the peace treaty with Jordan, and one hundred thousand would visit annually over the course of the next three years, making the route between Israel and Jordan a locus of tourism industry advertising and investment (see figure 4).[30] Israeli tourism to Morocco increased following low-level diplomatic relations with Rabat in 1994, as did Israeli travel to Egypt and the Sinai Peninsula.[31] The imaginations of Israeli armchair travelers were also being rerouted as a new set of regional sites became available as objects of popular fantasy. While talks between Israel and Syria progressed in 1995, the Hebrew press began to prepare its readers for their future trips to Damascus, Beirut, and Tunis, describing the local food, historic sites, and codes of propriety in the idiom of the tourist guide. At the same time, Israeli tourist agencies prepared their clients for travel across a Middle East without borders. Galilee Tours solicited potential clients with an imaginary map of the region, illustrating the Israeli tourist who moved effortlessly through the Arab Middle East without territorial impediments

Figure 4. Peace and Tourism. Depicts Israeli Prime Minister
Yitzhak Rabin and Jordanian King Hussein signing the Washington
Declaration, 25 July 1994.

or political obstacles. Such maps represented a substantial shift in dominant Israeli imaginations of regional geography. Prior to Oslo, Israel's
very proximity to its Arab neighbors had been largely viewed as a measure of threat. In the 1990s, these proximities were being revalued, indeed,
celebrated, in tourist terms. Israelis were being encouraged to view the
Middle East as a unified geography of leisure.

The Israeli Ministry of Tourism was even more expansive in its future
vision, imagining a region in which the differences between nation-states
would be replaced by the transnational flows of a liberalized economy.
State literatures designed for foreign investors spoke of Jewish-Israelis
traveling freely to Morocco, Tunisia, Lebanon, and Syria, and "Muslims
com[ing] by the thousands to Israel" to pray in Jerusalem.[32] Maps issued

Figure 5. Changing geographical imaginations. SOURCE: GALILEE
TOURS, 1995.

by the Israeli Ministry of Tourism illustrated the Middle East as a single
field of tourist opportunities, interrupted only by the occasional topo-
graphical obstacles (see maps 2 and 3). Beaches, ski resorts, and nature
reserves were sketched as recreational spaces that spanned borders. At the
same time, the state told a story of unconstrained mobility for all regional
actors, regardless of their provenance:

> We [i.e., the Israeli state] envision the emergence of a network of
> regional contacts. It will begin with . . . highways, flight paths, and
> seaways, water pipelines and electricity grids spread out in a web
> uniting us from east to west and from north to south. . . . Inhabitants
> of the region will live a life of freedom—freedom from obstacles,
> ostracism, and political coercion, free from the threat of violence

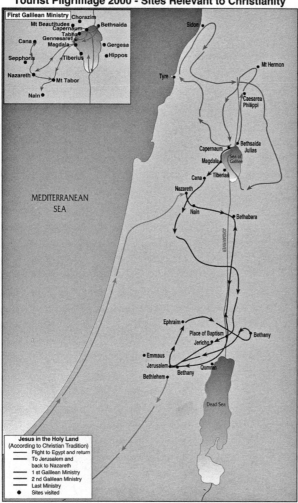

Tourist Pilgrimage 2000 - Sites Relevant to Christianity

Map 2. Tourism without borders, I. SOURCE: ISRAELI MINISTRY OF TOURISM. *REGIONAL TOURISM COOPERATION DEVELOPMENT OPTIONS*, 1995.

and terror. They will be free to travel and to trade, to develop joint ventures and to utilize together the potential of the region, to the benefit of all.[33]

This was a strategic discourse, designed for export, which depended on the disavowal of the highly uneven regimes of mobility that Oslo was generating.[34] Even as the voyage between West Jerusalem and Amman was

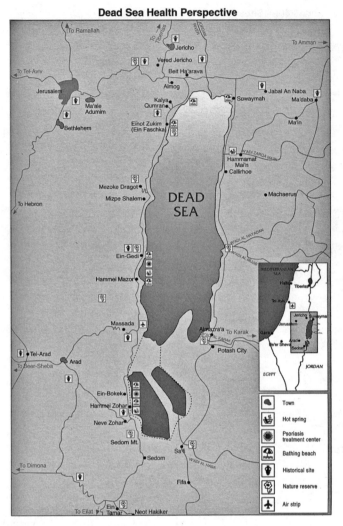

Dead Sea Health Perspective

Map 3. Tourism without borders, II. Projected development spanning the Israeli-Jordanian border. SOURCE: ISRAELI MINISTRY OF TOURISM. *REGIONAL TOURISM COOPERATION DEVELOPMENT OPTIONS*, 1995.

increasingly possible for most Jewish Israeli tourists, the ten-minute drive between East Jerusalem and Ramallah was obstructed in new ways for Palestinian travelers. Contra state discourse, regional mobility was highly contingent.

Tales of Discovery

Let us return to the account of the "first" Israeli tourists in Petra with which this chapter began. The Israeli arrival in Petra could only be imagined in heroic terms. Petra was a place long immortalized in Israeli myth, the subject of collective longing, popular song, and children's stories. Beginning in the 1950s, clandestine travel to this Nabatean city had been a virtual rite of passage for young Israeli men who risked their lives in enemy Jordanian territory for a glimpse of the city's red sandstone cliffs.[35] By the mid-1990s, the Israeli desire for Petra was firmly embedded in the national imagination.[36] In the Israeli press of this period, the tourist was installed to consummate that desire:

> Now we are here, descending on foot on the donkey path, and my heart is beating wildly. When no one is around, we speak in Hebrew — certainly the first conversation that has been heard here, in this language, for many years. Suddenly, standing out from two sides of the narrow path, the giant red rocks rise proudly, casting a menacing glance on the small figures that move between them. . . . And then it happened. Suddenly, between the crevices of the giant stones, 100 meters from us, [we caught our] first glimpse of the red structures hewn in rock. Tears came to our eyes. . . . "Photograph me," we said to each other in the same breath.[37]

This text rehearses many of the standard tropes and narrative devices of the colonial travelogue: the ardor of a clandestine voyage, the mounting anticipation as they approach the site, and victorious testimonial upon arrival. The thrill of arrival depends on secrecy and disguise, on hushed Hebrew tones within earshot of local persons whose presence is implied but never thematized, lest they threaten the discovery claim. To forestall this threat, the arrival scene is staged in an insistent present tense that belies any prior claims: *"Today, at this moment*, [Petra] is being discovered by two Israeli journalists with the excitement of children. I pinch myself to confirm it"* (italics added).

Discovery claims were substantiated by a photograph (see figure 6).[38] Like the televised images of this scene that were aired on Israeli news, the quality of the photograph was poor. The image was grainy and overexposed, and its composition weak. The Israeli tourist stood squarely at its center, posing before Petra's mythic landscape with a compact camera worn around his neck like a medal of honor. Poor quality and composition played a crucial role in this discovery discourse, authenticating the moment of arrival. Moreover, the very amateurism of the image rendered

דורות של ישראלים גדל על מיתוס פטרה. שליחנו לירדן גד ליאור הגשים את החלום

הגעתי אל הסלע האדום

המשטרה הירדנית מצידה: חקירה נעימה

Figure 6. "I got to the Red Rock!" Depicts the "first" Israeli tourist in Petra (Jordan), published in *Yediot Aḥaronot* on 18 July 1994.

it legible as a tourist snapshot, one that faithfully inhabited this quotidian genre.[39] The heroic valence of the scene depended on this inflection, on this common portrait of everyday tourists crossing state lines. The tourists were thus recognizable to readers as Israeli everymen. As such, they were able to consummate the national desire for Petra metonymically, on behalf of the Israeli nation-state. The photograph's prosaic nature also enabled acts of recognition by which readers were hailed as tourist-discoverers in kind. Thanks to the narrative's present tense, interpellation was perpetual ("Today, at this moment, Petra is being discovered"). Through consumption of this text, and many others like it, Israeli readers discovered Jordan over and over again.

This story line was not unusual. Indeed, it was merely an instance of a narrative about Israeli "first times" in Jordan that would proliferate over the months that followed, despite the narrative's manifest claims to temporal novelty. The scene of discovery would be restaged less than one month later. On August 12, 1994, three days after the Israeli-Jordanian border opened to third-party passport holders, images of "the first Israeli tourists to return from Jordan" appeared again on a newspaper's front page.[40] The same scene recurred in November, when the border was officially opened to all Israelis regardless of passport.[41] Indeed, over the course of the months that followed, the press documented numerous first-time tourist events: the first private Israeli vehicles in Jordan, the first flights between Tel Aviv and Amman, the first direct bus service to the Jordanian capital.[42] Some of these accounts were celebratory, such as Israeli tourists speaking Hebrew in certain Jordanian towns "for the very first time," while others were cautionary tales, such as "the first time since [peace] that a Jordanian newspaper printed a racist article against Israeli tourists."[43] As the scope of Israeli-Jordanian relations expanded, the first-time narrative was extended beyond the tourism arena. Newspapers described the first agreement between Jordanian and Israeli telephone companies, enabling the first direct dialing, and plans for the first joint Israeli-Jordanian college.[44] Some firsts were highly quotidian, such as the first Jordanian dance troupe to perform in Israel, the first performance of the Israeli national anthem in the Jordanian capital, and the first Israeli hairdresser to enter a Jordanian contest ("The 31-year-old Israeli will represent his country after winning the local championship last month in a peace festival in Tel Aviv").[45] The power and credence of the first-time narrative relied on its sheer proliferation. And yet, in proliferation, the story of newness was perpetually undone. Each successive first required the forgetting of its antecedent.

As the Oslo process progressed, as Israeli diplomatic and economic agreements with neighboring countries proliferated, the story line was retooled for other regional contexts. At moments it was used to celebrate cultural forays between Jewish Israelis and Palestinians in the Occupied Territories, as in the "first joint Israeli-Palestinian film" and the "first Israeli singer to perform in the [Palestinian] Autonomous Zone."[46] This rhetoric was also used in a more anticipatory register, as when newspapers mused about "the first Israeli visitors to the Gulf" and proposed a "combination weekend of Qatar-Oman–Abu Dabi."[47] Similar stories anticipated future Israeli routes to Syria and Lebanon and the Gulf States.[48] While not all anticipatory narratives employed the first-time vocabulary, most repeated the story of an uncharted Middle East. It was in this vein that articles introduced Israeli readers to Damascus, as Israel pursued negotiations with Syria.[49] Some offered tips on shopping, museum going, and proper ways of bargaining.[50] Another presented "Thirty Things You Didn't Know about Syria," with lists of useful facts and attractive vistas.[51] North Africa and the Arabian Peninsula were also entering this imagined tourist cartography. As early as 1994, Israeli journalists were pondering a future "express train to Saudi Arabia."[52] On the occasion of Shimon Peres's first visit to Qatar in 1996, the press introduced its readership to "The Qatari: Our New Friend in the East" through an imagined encounter with Israelis "in the world of tourism."[53] In the spring of that year, newspapers announced "Yemen: Starting to Open to the World" and featured Tunisia as an "Oasis in the Sahara."[54] When snapshots of first contact were unavailable, they had to be anticipated. The tourist potential of Tunis was illustrated with a photograph of an empty marketplace above the caption "Soon to be a center of Israeli tourism."[55]

The first-time narrative had a companion story about geography. While Israeli firsts in the Middle East were themselves astonishing, the spatial relations that they illuminated were no less wondrous—wondrous for the ways that they rewrote dominant geographical imaginations of the nation-state and the fiction of Israel's physical distance from the Arab Middle East. Articles about Israeli tourism to Jordan frequently remarked on the surprise of proximity.[56] They announced that Jordan was "Closer Than You Think!" or "closer than Turkey . . . or even Egypt."[57] Stories about future Israeli travel to Syria spoke in similar ways, stressing Damascus's negligible distance from Israeli urban centers: "An Hour and a Half from Tiberias."[58] In these accounts, proximity itself was represented as an effect of regional realignment rather than as geographic truism. Indeed, in the terms of what I have been calling national intelligibility, this rendering was accurate. In decades prior, spatial and temporal indices of proximity were primarily intelligible as measures of threat. Oslo was altering the ways these indices could be narrated and understood within prevailing Israeli discourse. Both the distance and the difference between Israel and its Arab neighbors was becoming thinkable in new ways.

Yet not all proximities were in flux. Nor were all deemed cause for celebration. Many were actively obstructed by the Israeli state and feared by Jewish Israeli publics. Israel's growing intimacy with the Arab world generated considerable concern among the Israeli right, particularly the settlement movement, who feared for Israel's security and Jewish identity.[59] And most Jewish Israeli tourists, even self-proclaimed leftists, embraced regional proximity in highly selective ways. Even as they visited Jordan for leisure weekends, few traveled the considerably shorter distance into the West Bank for tourist purposes, continuing a trend that began with the first Palestinian uprising (1987–93).[60] In keeping with the highly discrepant terms of the Oslo process, its uneven flows and mobilities, proximity had no absolute value.

Historic Routes

The regional itineraries enjoyed by Israelis during this period were by no means unprecedented, despite the implication of the first-time narrative. Their precursors can be traced to the early decades of the twentieth century when Jewish settlers in Palestine traveled through a Middle East not yet interrupted by the borders of nation-states. Most preferred routes within Palestine or what they termed the Land of Israel (*Eretz Yisrael*) and considered their ancient homeland, favoring walks through the Judean Desert and around the Dead Sea (see figures 7–9). They were favored for reasons of both feasibility and ideology, as travel within Eretz Yisrael was deemed a crucial practice of Zionist nation making, a means of conquering the homeland with one's feet.[61] Yet many Jewish settlers also embarked on routes beyond Palestine's borders, particularly during the British Mandate period. They traveled into Jordan, Lebanon, Syria, Egypt, and Iraq by motor convoy, bus, and train. Their travel diaries from this period, sometimes illustrated with photographs, describe voyages to Cairo, Beirut, Damascus, Baghdad, and Petra (see figure 10).[62] These routes were often risky and arduous. During the Mandate, entry into Lebanon and Syria required a visa from the French consulate in Jerusalem, a lengthy and often unsuccessful venture, and many travelers were required to negotiate their passage with border guards and police who frequently denied their entry.[63] For these reasons, and despite attendant dangers, some opted to surreptitiously cross into neighboring territories. Such acts of disobedience were themselves nationally inflected, articulating with the Zionist ideology of heroism through defiance.[64]

These regional itineraries came to a temporary end following the creation of the Israeli state in 1948 — that is, save episodes of clandestine Israeli travel across the new national border. Petra was the most celebrated clandestine destination of the immediate postwar period.[65] Between 1953 and 1957, many Israeli youth risked their lives in enemy Jordanian territory on voyages that soon acquired mythic national status. When twelve Israeli travelers were killed on this route by Jordanian forces, their losses were

Figure 7. Jewish travelers from Palestine on the Dead Sea, 1933. PHOTO: DAVID SERRY.

Figure 8. Jewish travelers from Palestine on the banks of the Dead Sea, 1933.
PHOTO: DAVID SERRY.

Figure 9. Jewish travelers from Palestine in "Samaria" (West Bank), 1924.
PHOTO: DAVID BENVENISTI.

Figure 10. Regional routes before nation-states. Jewish travelers from Palestine camping in Petra (Jordan), 1929. PHOTO: AVRAHAM SOSKIN.

mourned as a national tragedy.[66] Smaller numbers of adventure travelers crossed into Lebanon, Syria, and the Jordanian-controlled West Bank, yet these itineraries never acquired equivalent national stature.[67] The fact that Petra trumped biblical sites within Jordanian territory as a preferred clandestine destination suggests a substantive shift in the Zionist symbology of travel from the early decades of the twentieth century, when travel through the Land of Israel was granted nationalist primacy. After state formation in 1948, the national stature of the itinerary depended at least as much on the potential danger incurred by the traveler as on the route's location within an explicitly Zionist landscape.

Regional routes changed considerably in the wake of the 1967 War, a war which resulted in the Israeli occupation of the West Bank, the Gaza Strip, the Golan Heights, and the Sinai Peninsula.[68] Occupation and the dismantling of borders generated a massive and almost immediate flow of Israeli hikers, sightseers, and consumers into territories that had been off-limits to Israeli passport holders since state formation.[69] Hundreds of thousands of Israelis visited the Old City of Jerusalem during the first week after the war's end.[70] Within several weeks, large Israeli tourist crowds would be reported in Bethlehem, Ramallah, and other West Bank sites, to be followed by what the Israeli press termed a tourist "invasion" of the Gaza Strip and Golan Heights.[71] For Palestinians with Israeli citizenship, the occupation enabled reunions with families from whom they had been separated since 1948, even as it occasioned Palestinian travel from the Occupied Territories into Israel in search of family and former homes.[72] Israeli leisure and consumption within the newly Occupied Territories continued through the next two decades, although with less urgency. Sinai was a particularly popular Israeli destination during the 1970s, made possible by the opening of a highway from Eilat to Sharm el-Sheikh in 1971.[73] Tens of thousands enjoyed its affordable beachfront accommodations, mythic landscapes, and celebrated "Bedouin hospitality," a trope borrowed from Orientalist discourses of the prestate period.[74] When the Sinai Peninsula was returned to Egypt in 1982 per the Camp David Accord, many Israelis mourned its loss through the language of tourist nostalgia. Yet Camp David also made new itineraries possible, opening Egypt to Israeli travelers, Egyptian Jews among them. In the immediate aftermath of the accord, tales of "exhilarating" travel across the Israeli-Egyptian border proliferated in the Israeli press.[75]

Most Jewish Israeli itineraries in the Palestinian territories ended with the outbreak of the first Palestinian uprising in 1987.[76] Some would resume after Oslo, but in highly limited forms and magnitude.[77] Security was only one part of the equation. The forms of recognition that Oslo had conferred on Arab places, persons, and cultures within the greater Middle East did not apply to the Palestinian territories. Their exclusion from the New Middle East as imagined by the Israeli state, save as objects of regulation, was fundamental to the new regional order.

Historical Fictions

The first-time narratives of the 1990s made little mention of these histories of Jewish Israeli travel. Few noted that many of the regional routes enjoyed or anticipated during the Oslo period had been traversed by Jewish settlers in Palestine in the decades prior to state formation.[78] To the contrary, such narratives depended on their absence. That is, they were predicated on the erasure of remembered histories of contact between Israel and its Arab neighbors that would undercut the narrative's claim to temporal primacy. This is not to suggest that all first-time narratives were fictions. But together, the very prevalence and repetition of this story line fashioned a historical fiction about Israeli newness in the Arab Middle East.

The stakes in this fiction were considerable. First and foremost, the notion of newness monumentalized the Oslo process by installing a history of noncontact between Israel and its Arab neighbors that regional diplomacy had bridged "for the very first time." But the fiction had a more important ideological function. It worked to consolidate Israel's difference from its Arab neighbors at precisely the moment that Israel's borders were becoming porous in new ways. Thus, even as these narratives ostensibly celebrated border crossings, they also labored to stabilize the Israeli border as both a geographic and a cultural divide. Hence the missing history of regional travel. Prior routes through the Middle East before nation-states thematized the fragile and perhaps arbitrary nature of the nation-state itself at precisely the moment that its consolidation was required.

The fiction of noncontact was also sustained through the biography of the Israeli tourist. In most media accounts of the 1990s, encounters between Israeli guests and Arab hosts were figured as scenes of cross-cultural contact. In other words, the Israeli tourist was represented as both Jewish and European (Ashkenazi), principally through accounts of linguistic confusion in Arab places. In this vein, articles about Israeli tourism to Jordan suggested that visitors adopt muffled Hebrew tones in case of anti-Israeli sentiment, as tourists were not credited with Arabic language knowledge, but reassured readers that Jordan's waiters and hotel keepers were often conversant in Hebrew.[79] Nor were tourists credited with knowledge of the daily cultural landscape of the Arab Middle East. "Thirty Things You Didn't Know about Syria," a media exposé of Damascus, presumed a population of Jewish Israeli travelers lacking knowledge of Syrian and Arab culture more broadly. The fiction of Israeli firsts in the Arab world depended on this story of cultural ignorance.

The facts about Israeli tourism were otherwise. Contra the media portrait, diverse communities of Israeli citizens were traveling through the Middle East during the Oslo period, and many lacked the cultural illiteracy that the press presumed. Unprecedented numbers of Israeli Jews of Moroccan descent were touring Morocco during this decade thanks to low-level diplomatic agreements with Israel. Nor were most of them tourists in any strict sense; rather, their travels were frequently fashioned as homecomings, including visits to family tombs and former places of residence.[80] Palestinians with Israeli citizenship were also traversing the region. In fact, notwithstanding media presumptions, they represented the decided majority of the Israeli passport holders who traveled to Jordan following the peace accord of 1994.[81] As with Mizrahi travelers to Morocco, they were not conventional tourists, as most went to Jordan to visit family members who had fled or been expelled from Israel during the course of the 1948 and 1967 wars. Because neither of these Israeli populations was new to the Arab Middle East, they were banished from the first-time account. That is, they were not afforded the right to represent the Israeli nation-state within this discourse of national consolidation.

Palestinians from the Occupied Territories were also missing from Israeli accounts of regional travel. Or rather, they were introduced in highly selective ways. Consider the following compendium of travelers' tips, amassed from Palestinian residents of East Jerusalem:

Nasir Al-Din Nashashibi . . . recommends a visit to the Jirash festival. . . . He discourages hitchhiking. . . . Sagu, an employee in a camera store who requested anonymity, often travels to visit his family. He recommends the Jabri chain of restaurants, especially the one with American-style [food]. . . . Da'ud Ma'uli, a cook at the Munatin restaurant, recommends a visit to the King's castle.[82]

This account adopts the standard rhetoric and narrative form of the tourist guide, replete with restaurant reviews, tips on sightseeing, and notes on everyday behavioral norms. In this case, the genre enacts a form of historical revision, crediting Palestinian knowledge of the Jordanian national landscape to tourism rather than to the history of Palestinian exile that made these routes necessary. This kind of revision was a standard feature of Israeli travel narratives about Jordan, narratives that struggled to circumvent the history of Jordan's Palestinian majority, comprised of populations exiled from Palestine during the 1948 and 1967 wars. Nonetheless, these threatening histories sometimes surfaced through a trope of sameness, often enunciated with considerable surprise, by which the press registered the legacy of cultural sharing between Jordan and the Palestinian territories. "The food in Amman is not that different from that in the Old City . . ."; "indeed, most souvenirs look strikingly familiar."[83] The discourse of surprising similitude functioned to elide the history of Palestinian exile, attributing cultural resemblance to chance.

Histories of military travel were also elided. The fact that many Jewish-Israeli men were familiar with Beirut's landscapes, markets, and restaurants from the invasion of 1982 was not remarked on in most Israeli newspapers, allowing the city to be celebrated as a new Israeli destination. A similar set of erasures enabled the press to anticipate first-time visits to Tunis, a city that had been navigated by Israelis during histories of espionage directed against the PLO leadership in exile. Such memories were infrequently brought to bear on ways that tourism was narrated. To do so would rupture the first-time narrative and its function of national consolidation.

Tourists and Citizens

Regional travel during the Oslo era was not unidirectional. In the mid-1990s, Arab tourists from neighboring states were beginning to appear in Israeli cities and their itineraries to garner media attention. Jordanian nationals represented the largest incoming Arab tourist population. Some twenty-five thousand visited Israel in 1994 after the peace treaty with Jordan. By 1995, their number had risen to over eighty thousand.[84] The demand for tourist visas greatly surpassed the number granted to applicants due to rigid screening by Israeli state officials who endeavored to sort tourists from migrant laborers, terrorists, and those seeking permanent residence.[85] In 1994, as the Israeli media celebrated Israeli discoveries in Jordan, it anticipated the beginnings of incoming Arab tourism with considerable unease: "They Are Coming to See Eilat."[86] Two years later, the press predicted "A Million Arab Tourists Will Visit Jerusalem and Bethlehem."[87] Small numbers of Muslim travelers from neighboring countries had visited Israel before Oslo, often illegally or through third-party passports.[88] Israeli market analysts predicted untold numbers in the aftermath of a regional peace settlement.

Israel faced this prospect with some ambivalence. The private sector eagerly anticipated "the wealthy of Amman" and the Gulf States, "tempted by Eilat's nightclubs and the availability of alcohol" and destined for Tel Aviv's malls.[89] More frequently, these prospective tourists were depicted as an underclass mob, and Oriental menace replete with "black clad women from Iran . . . thronging the streets of Tel Aviv."[90] This ambivalence was shared by the Israeli Ministry of Tourism as it endeavored to articulate policy in this arena. In 1995, the Ministry announced that Israel was open to "all Muslim and Arab travelers," yet such statements were recanted in the Hebrew press shortly thereafter, when Ministry spokespersons "clarified" that Muslim tourism to Jerusalem would not be "encouraged" at a time when the political status of the city was so fiercely contested.[91] They argued that the unprecedented nature of the market was to blame. "We don't know yet how many people will come, from where, and what will interest them," I was frequently told in interviews. "It just isn't known."[92] Many argued that they were unable to assess Arab needs for accommodations, restaurant facilities, and informational literature.[93] Like the specter of "black clad women," bodies hidden from sight, these prospective tourists were unintelligible figures, and uncomfortably so.[94]

Incoming Arab travel also took other forms. Residents of neighboring countries were beginning to populate Israel's illegal workforce, gaining entry with tourist visas. True to the terms of their visas, these workers often spoke in tourist idioms: "I'm meeting a lot of girls. It's interesting for me here, because it's another country."[95] Incoming Jordanian nationals were of particular concern.[96] Newspapers began to document the Jordanians who "came to visit and stayed," noting the large numbers of Jordanian men who worked in construction and the growing numbers of Jordanian women selling sex in northern Israeli towns. Headlines warned of "Arab Towns [in Israel] Being Used as Hiding Places for Illegal Tourists."[97]

Indeed, the problem of illegal Jordanian labor was frequently enunciated through stories about tourism. Articles noted that these Jordanians bore little resemblance to tourists in any conventional sense, despite the terms of their visas. They lacked the requisite tourist props, itineraries, and desires. This concern with resemblance framed one newspaper's discussion of a typical scene at the Israeli-Jordanian border. The alleged Jordanian tourists crossed the Israeli border together, the article noted, only to disband on the other side: "Immediately after the border crossing, they separate and each one travels to a different place. There are some who come with mattresses and equipment, and it's clear that they aren't exactly tourists that are coming to tour and then return to Jordan."[98] A crime is being documented here, that of traveling subjects who try to pass as tourists. Their fraudulence was fully evident: "It's clear that they aren't exactly tourists." Crime could be deduced from material artifacts that didn't bear the standard markers of leisure travel: mattresses and kitchen implements rather than cameras and tourist guides.

Although unacknowledged in the mainstream media, these visitors had little need to conceal themselves. Indeed, this was precisely their threat. Most illegal Jordanian laborers were also Palestinian. Their ability to "hide in Arab towns" rested in a history of familial and national ties to the Palestinian communities in which they sought refuge. Their bodies could look at home in Israel. They could pass in ways that the state could not easily control. Their alleged criminality was thus complex, as it rested both on their failure of resemblance as tourists and their threat of likeness as citizens. These stories inverted the logic of the first-time narrative, in which tourist and citizen were produced as isomorphic terms. As such, they produced a coupling which deviated from the prevailing national imaginary in which citizens are implicitly figured as Jews. Suspicion arose in the Israeli media when these travelers began to look at home, when Arab tourists began to resemble Israeli citizens.

Although politicians and market analysts could predict Israel's economic future, the social and political effects of regional reconfiguration and economic liberalization were uncharted. Even as Oslo promised to globalize the Israeli economy, or so many Israelis hoped, it also mounted a set of cultural and political threats. The first-time narrative responded to this imagined threat by shoring up the borders of the nation-state, demarcating clear parameters around Israeli identity and the subjects that could claim it. Fantasies about Israeli tourists were normative and not descriptive accounts that sought to stabilize the terms of dominant Israeli identity at a moment of political upheaval and potential threat. They struggled to preserve Israeliness as both a Jewish and a European domain. These stories spoke in two temporal registers, fashioning a historical fiction about Israel's past even as they endeavored to protect its national future.

But stories about incoming Arab tourists did a different kind of work. Although manifestly phobic in nature, they told another set of stories when read against their grain. The scene of border crossing described earlier is a case in point. These alleged tourists threatened in their resemblance to Israeli tourists. But their likeness posed an additional threat as well. Burdened with household goods and fleeing in haste, these travelers raised the specter of an unpleasant past that was coming into national consciousness in new ways.[99] These alleged tourists recalled the mass flight of Palestinians during the course of the 1948–1949 War, travelers similarly burdened with mattresses and kitchen implements as they fled with their homes on their backs.[100] Indeed, in the 1990s, this Israeli nightmare was beginning to materialize. As Israeli newspapers documented, Palestinians with deeds to Israeli property lost during the course of the 1948–49 War were beginning to explore legal restitution. Some were arriving on West Jerusalem doorsteps to reclaim what was theirs.[101] In the midst of the Oslo process and enabled by its political advances, the history of dispossession was reemerging — a history that the state had long endeavored to repress — and tourism was a key player in this process.

The tourist narratives of this period had multiple functions. They provided a popular grammar through which the Oslo process could be told.

They provided an allegorical terrain on which fears and fantasies about regional reconfiguration could be negotiated. Their ideological function was neither single nor secure. Some narratives fortified the terms of national intelligibility. Others challenged its terms, bringing repressed subjects and histories to the fore.

Enjoying the Arabs Within

D ror and Gila Sheffer are spending a holiday weekend
in the Palestinian city of Sakhnin in Israel's Galilee
region.[1] They've driven north from their Tel Aviv home
to enjoy Arab culture in its most daily forms and private
spaces, filling their days with guided walks through the
village center, tours of working homes, and late-night
conversations with their bed-and-breakfast proprietor in
his modest living room. For the Sheffers, these cultural
landscapes are by no means novel. They have been to the
Arab Galilee many times before, attending the wedding of
workers and enjoying occasional lunches at village restaurants, favoring those on village peripheries that could be
easily accessed and rapidly exited should political threat
ensue. Indeed, Dror remembers the streets of Sakhnin
from late-night army patrols during the 1970s and 1980s,
decades when the internal Palestinian population was
deemed a particular threat and Israeli soldiers were sent
to "keep the peace." "I came here in a soldier's uniform
and with a weapon. The Arabs would invite you to join
them for meals, but you'd never know how to interpret
their hospitality. It's more comfortable as a guest."

Yet comfort is contingent. Sitting in the courtyard of
his bed-and-breakfast, enjoying a home-cooked meal,

Dror confesses a "recurring nightmare that somebody is going to pull out a gun." The thought, he said, is perpetually on his mind. At this unwieldy intersection of cultural consumption and political fear, where the routes of soldiers are being refashioned as leisure itineraries, an Israeli tourist market is being forged.

This chapter explores this intersection, this process of refashioning. I consider the emergence of an ethnic tourism market within the Palestinian communities of the Galilee during the mid-1990s and the consumptive practices of the Jewish-Israeli tourists who were its target population. As the previous chapter has suggested, the consumption of Palestinian culture by Jewish-Israeli populations was by no means unprecedented, its history traceable to the early decades of nation-building by Jewish settlers in Palestine.[2] Yet in the 1990s, such practices sought different objects, inhabited different spaces, and were attended by a new set of political discourses that emerged as a byproduct of the regional diplomatic process. This decade marked the first time that sizable numbers of Jewish-Israeli civilians spent organized leisure time in what the Israeli state designated as the rural Arab sector, and the first time that this sector was officially sanctioned as such by the Israeli Ministry of Tourism. In the 1990s, Palestinian villages inside Israel that had once been marked as sites of enmity were being reconfigured as Jewish-Israeli leisure destinations. I argue that this remapping altered the terms of Israeli intelligibility in significant ways. Arab places, persons, and cultures within the borders of the nation-state were being marked by the state and Jewish private sector as consumable in new ways. I contend that this reconfiguration of the Israeli tourist landscape was concurrently a recalibration of the terms of symbolic inclusion within the nation-state. The nation-state was becoming thinkable, becoming perceptible, in different ways. In the contact zones where Jewish Israeli tourists met their Palestinian hosts, the terms of Israeli identity, history, and geography were being revised.

Like Jewish-Israeli tourism to Jordan as explored in the previous chapter, the emergence of this ethnic tourism market was enabled by the Oslo process, made possible by the commodity desires, cultural interests, and geographical imaginations that regional diplomacy had catalyzed. Yet a certain logic of belatedness was at play. Initially, Jewish Israeli populations focused their desire for Arab culture on sites within the broader Middle

Figure II. Tourism as contact zone. Guide David Benvenisti holds the map, 1923.

East, beyond Israel's borders. It was only in the wake of such regional fantasies that these desires were extended to places within the borders of the nation-state. Regional Arab culture was a relatively safe object of consumer intrigue, posing little challenge to the integrity of the Jewish state. Yet Arab culture within the state raised national histories and civic questions of a far more threatening kind.

This turn to what we might call the Arab interior was also made possible by changes in domestic state policy. As I suggested in the Introduction, the state began to recognize its Arab citizenry in new ways during this decade, both materially and symbolically. Spurred by the course of regional politics, the state extended an invitation to its Jewish citizens to "coexist" with their Arab conationals. Something akin to a discourse of multiculturalism was at work, whereby the state and the private sector were inviting Jews not merely to tolerate but to enjoy Arab cultural difference.[3] Such invitations were posed in a comparative vein: if Jewish citizens of the state could make peace with their Arab neighbors in the broader region, then surely they could make peace with the Arabs living inside Israel's borders. And if they could enjoy the Arabs abroad, why not also at home? By 1996, a small population of elite Jewish Israeli citizens began to accept the state's invitation and venture into internal Arab villages as tourists.

Figure I2. Jewish travelers, Bedouin guide. Negev, 1928. PHOTO: DAVID BENVENISTI.

Consumer desires took several forms. Most tourists sought the canonical markers of cultural authenticity. As the market developed over the course of the decade, an increasing percentage deviated from these templates, seeking access to daily Palestinian cultural practices and forms. In either form, consumer desire was cross-cut by a set of political demands. Most Jewish Israeli clients sought Arab culture stripped of recognizably Palestinian histories and sentiments. And while many Palestinian entrepreneurs, guides, and shopkeepers complied with these directives, explicit or otherwise, others used tourism as an occasion to educate the Jewish-Israeli public about Palestinian histories of underdevelopment and disenfranchisement within the Jewish state. In turn, a small percentage of the tourist population departed from dominant protocols and used their visits to educate themselves about a population with which they had few occasions for exchange outside the highly stratified contexts in which Jews typically encountered Palestinians within Israel's borders. At stake in these encounters, I argue, were the terms of national intelligibility itself. At moments, tourism enabled a reinsertion of Palestinian-Arab citizens into national space and history in ways that substantively altered hegemonic accounts of the national. At other moments, tourism provided a stage for the reassertion of prevailing national logics, as the tools of cultural performance and consumption provided another idiom by which to dispossess Israel's Arab citizenry of their history, agency, and symbolic stature within the nation-state. As a site of political meaning making; ethnic tourism was a highly variable domain.

This chapter is an ethnographic exploration of the early years of market development within the Palestinian Galilee. My ethnography focuses on the politics of Jewish-Israeli patronage and pleasure, particularly on the forms of cultural value that Jewish visitors sought in Palestinian places. I argue that we can understand tourist pleasure as an instance of the broader shifts in national intelligibility that were engendered by Oslo and attendant national processes. Tourist practices, to put this another way, reveal the ways that prevailing Israeli imaginations were being reworked within the sphere of cultural consumption in response to the politics of the moment. This chapter also considers some of the creative ways in which Palestinian workers in the tourist market negotiated consumer demands and discourses of cultural value. In so doing, they exposed the gap between consumer pleasure and state practice, between their ability to be recognized as objects of Jewish desire yet their inability to achieve full political recognition within the terms of Israel's inequitable democracy.

Touring the Arabs Within

Jewish-Israeli tourism to the Palestinian Galilee was largely nonexistent in the early 1990s. Nor did it contain anything resembling a tourism infrastructure, save a handful of informal eateries and a modest museum serving a predominantly local Palestinian clientele.[4] A small number of Bedouin and Druze villages within Israel's borders had been state-sponsored tourist destinations since the 1950s and 1960s, including the villages of Pik'in, 'Isfiya, and Dalyiat al-Karmil.[5] But the Palestinian Galilee had not been conceived in analogous ways. While Jewish residents from neighboring towns paid occasional visits to its restaurants and inexpensive markets on their trips between Jewish towns, most avoided these places for fear of politically motivated hostility.

The onset of institutionalized cultural tourism in the Palestinian Galilee can be traced to the spring of 1994, when a music festival sponsored by a Jewish regional council expanded its purview to include several Palestinian villages as musical venues within the festival schedule. Their inclusion proved enormously popular. In subsequent months, the first substantial Palestinian efforts to develop a local tourism market built on the Jewish consumer demand unleashed by the festival. The initial stage was modest in scope and offerings. Several families in the area converted spare rooms into bed-and-breakfast facilities, residents began to lead occasional tours through village centers, and local restaurants began to expand in anticipation of a growing Jewish consumer base.[6] Over the course of the next year, the market expanded to include numerous home-based attractions, including informal restaurants, fortune telling, and art displays—most of which were launched within the private homes of Palestinian proprietors.[7] By the spring of 1996, five local councils in the Palestinian Galilee had hired a tourism official to manage village affairs, a position that had not existed in their governance structures heretofore.

The popular Israeli press began to cover these developments in the spring of 1994 in articles that registered considerable surprise at the willingness of Jewish Israelis to visit Palestinian areas that long had been deemed sites of internal enmity. "Best wishes from Sakhnin!" read an ironic headline from the period, coupling a popular tourist idiom with a village long associated with anti-Israeli sentiment.[8] Interviews with aspiring Palestinian entrepreneurs surveyed the emerging tourist landscape and assessed the willingness of village residents to participate in coexistence efforts. Citing testimonials from bed-and-breakfast guest books, articles chronicled the growing numbers of enthusiastic Jewish clients, the same population that "was once afraid of wandering, even by mistake, into Arab villages." As the Hebrew press remarked, the very villages beginning to host Jewish Israeli tourists were "the same blots on the landscape that until now we have only glanced at from a distance behind the closed windows of the air-conditioned car."[9]

While the fact of Jewish Israeli tourism to these places was virtually unprecedented, state backing for such tourist ventures was equally novel. In the summer of 1994, the Israeli Tourism Ministry began exploring potential development options in the Arab sector with the aim of modeling ethnic tourism on examples in Turkey and Greece. By 1995, the Ministries of Tourism and Infrastructure had approved budgets for planning and development in a number of Galilee locales, including Sakhnin, 'Arrabeh, Kawkab abu al-Hayja, and Dayr Hannah. The criteria for selection were varied: Some had particularly picturesque vistas and historic quarters, while others were home to ambitious entrepreneurs whose initiatives found favor with the Ministry. Perhaps most crucially, all had populations which were deemed friendly to the incoming Jewish tourist. By 1996, with the Jewish tourist population growing, the Tourism Ministry attested to daily entreaties from village entrepreneurs seeking fiscal assistance for home-based tourist developments.

To understand the political significance of this emerging tourist market, and the initial surprise that it generated among Jewish publics, one must consider the political history of the Palestinian Galilee and its figuration in Jewish Israeli imaginations. In the aftermath of the 1948–49 War, the Galilee region was the area of densest Palestinian settlement within Israel's borders, despite a massive decline in its Palestinian population due to wartime flight and expulsions.[10] These demographics provoked considerable Jewish anxiety.[11] "The problem of the Galilee is a Jewish problem," noted the Hebrew press in 1965. "[It] is an Arab empire within our borders."[12] "'Our Galilee?' Maybe on the map. In reality, over 120,000 Arabs . . . live in this area and a total of about 10,000 Jews, that is—only about eight percent."[13] In 1963, the state announced plans for development of the first Jewish urban settlement in the Galilee—plans that met with considerable opposition from the Arab villagers from whom such land would be confiscated.[14] These efforts constituted initial implementation of the so-called Judaization of the Galilee (*Yihud ha-Galil*), which had been in planning stages since the 1950s.[15] Through Judaization, the state sought to undercut Palestinian power within Israel's borders by means of massive land confiscation and to woo Jewish settlers to isolated population centers in the midst of Palestinian settlement.[16] The goal, simply put, was "stem[ming] the hold of foreigners on state lands," in the words of Ariel Sharon.[17] Judaization efforts escalated considerably in the period from the mid-1970s through the late 1980s.[18] By 1993, over 80 percent of previously Arab-owned land had been lost to expropriation.[19]

Chief among Judaization efforts of the 1980s was the establishment of the Misgav Regional Council in 1983 with the aim of uniting disparate Jewish Galilee settlements under a single administrative umbrella.[20] The council's map of jurisdiction was intentionally noncontiguous, excluding Palestinian population centers even as it incorporated their reserve lands, therein alleviating the burden of servicing their communities.[21] By the early 1990s, the nearly 7,000 Jewish residents of Misgav enjoyed grossly disproportionate landholdings when compared with those of adjacent Palestinian communities, at a ratio of approximately 25:1.[22] Under the Labor administration of the mid-1990s, state budgets for the Misgav remained exponentially larger than those provided to neighboring villages. The council's growing industrial district, which employed many of the area's Jewish residents, continued to bar Palestinian employees through discriminatory hiring practices, while state-mandated building restrictions prevented Palestinian villages and cities in the region from being zoned for industry.

Judaization has not gone unchallenged. The history of this challenge can be traced to 1976, when communist-backed village committees in the Palestinian Galilee organized a general strike and a day of protest in response to government plans to expropriate vast tracts of Palestinian-owned land in the area. This resulted in a series of violent clashes with the Israeli army that left several Palestinians dead and hundreds more wounded and under arrest.[23] "Land Day" was commemorated in subsequent decades by popular demonstrations and strikes throughout the Palestinian Galilee, and, in the years following the outbreak of the first Palestinian uprising (1987–93), functioned as an occasion for solidarity with Palestinians under occupation.[24] The reassessment of Israeli state policy vis-à-vis its Arab minority that followed the clashes of 1976 focused on the question of how the Arab population might be more effectively controlled.[25]

Tourism's emergence in the Palestinian Galilee was intimately tied to these histories of land expropriation, uneven development, and struggle. Many of the Palestinian communities in which tourism flourished during the 1990s (e.g., Sakhnin, 'Arrabeh, and Dayr Hannah) had been victims of expropriation and centers of Land Day activism.[26] Many had lost land to the establishment of the Misgav Regional Council and were prey to the discriminatory zoning and economic policies that affected the Palestinian communities excluded from its jurisdiction.[27] Popular politics in these communities had shifted considerably during the early 1990s, as issues of civic identity and equity began to mute the radicalism of the 1970s and 1980s.[28] Such shifts were crucial, enabling Jewish Israelis to feel comfortable visiting sites once deemed dangerous. In turn, the allure of financial success in the tourism market encouraged would-be Palestinian entrepre-neurs to distance themselves from radical politics and demonstrate their identification as dutiful Israeli citizens—at least, within visitor earshot. Tourist dollars were at stake.

Touring Tradition

In the spring of 1996, in the midst of the Passover holiday, I join a group of Israeli Jews on their walking tour through the Galilean village of 'Ilabun. We are a group of thirty-seven, including families, young couples, and one American Jewish researcher, lingering in 'Ilabun's narrow streets in sunglasses, baseball caps, and video cameras. Our local Palestinian guide, Akram, has led a tour once before at the first annual Olive Festival held in the Galilee during the previous fall. At twenty-seven years of age, he is studying to be a dentist and hoped that occasional work as a tour guide would augment his income.[29]

We are participating in the Music and Nature Festival, sponsored by the Misgav Regional Council with funds from the Israeli Ministry of Tourism and held in the Galilee every spring since its inception in 1988. In 1996, as in the two years prior, visitors have a choice: They can enjoy the festival's unique three-day combination of concerts and nature walks through the area's Jewish settlements and adjacent national reserves, or they can join an organized tour through an Arab, Bedouin, or "mixed village." Such is the language of ethnic differentiation employed by festival organizers. In 1996, the village of 'Ilabun was added to the itinerary, joining the villages of Dayr Hannah, Kawkab, 'Arabbeh, and Sakhnin, which had participated in previous seasons. In addition to walking tours led by Palestinian youth, this year's festival board had approved a children's folkdance troupe from Kawkab village and had added the Sakhnin Museum of Palestinian Folk Heritage to the festival program. Indeed, festival organizers had encour-aged all Palestinian locals with cultural talents to apply for inclusion.[30] These shifts were enormously significant for a festival initially imagined as part of Judaization efforts, whereby Jews who visited Misgav as tourists would return as residents.[31]

The group makes its way into the central room of a small one-story house, opened for several hours daily during the festival weekend. We sit on the floor on mattresses, as Akram lectures in a halting but enthusiastic

Hebrew: "This is an example of the traditional Arab living room. During my grandfather's generation, the entire village would gather here, in the home of elders."

Save for a number of distracted children, his audience is attentive and interested in the social history he provided, stopping him frequently to ask for clarification: "What I'm holding here is called a *jurn*, an instrument used for making coffee." Sitting on the floor, Akram demonstrates the traditional art of coffee grinding, how beans are pounded rhythmically like a musical instrument as a way of welcoming guests. It's an ad hoc performance, he assures his guest. Many comments ensue.

"Was that a traditional *debke* rhythm?"[32]

"Whoever wants to play, can try," Akram offers. There are no immediate takers.

"Rafi," a woman jokes to her husband, "next time you make me coffee, make it musical." Questions of cultural preservation arise with commentary about the need to record such traditions for wider distribution.

The group is engaged. Many questions arise. They ask about Akram's family, burial customs, and the number of local students pursuing higher education. Women's role in the community is of particular concern.

"That's big progress," whispers the woman to my left, as Akram describes the aerobics classes for girls that are now offered locally.

Outside again, we continue our tour. "This looks just like Jaffa," says a woman to her daughter, walking a golden retriever in streets nearly empty of residents, still unaccustomed to tourist crowds. Akram narrates the history of the village, the significance of prominent structures, which religious groups live where, and why houses were built as they were. He points to a residence that has recently been converted into bed-and-breakfast facilities for weekend tourists and offers its phone numbers to interested parties. We ascended to the top of someone's roof to look out over the valley. Akram tells the story of the expulsion of 'Ilabun villagers to Lebanon in 1948 following the massacre of twelve village youth by the Israeli Defense Forces despite the village's surrender at the time of occupation. Yet unaccustomed to guiding, he speaks too softly. Much of the narrative is lost.[33]

"It's a big performance," says a woman in her mid-forties, eager to be interviewed. Like many festival visitors, she lives in a neighboring moshav.

"They don't really drink out of one cup." She refers to the shallow cup of bitter coffee Akram had offered in the living room in the tradition of welcoming guests. Everyone shares one cup, he had said, as a symbol of togetherness. "It's just less dishes that way," she insists. "In Arab houses, when they come to visit, everyone gets their own cup." From a hill above the small commercial center, we gaze down on the premium agricultural land that used to belong to the village for farming and development reserves. "They just do it," she adds, "for tourists."

The Politics of Patronage

In the early stages of market development, the Israeli tourist population in the Palestinian Galilee was relatively homogeneous. The majority were middle-class Jews, largely of European descent.[34] Most were residents of Haifa and the adjacent Jewish communities in the Galilee. Many were professionals with extensive history of travel through Europe and Asia. As the market grew in renown it would attract a wider Jewish demographic, although elite visitors remained predominant. While most had spent leisure time in other Palestinian places in Israel, primarily Druze and Bedouin villages designated for tourism, most described this as their first tourist experience in an Arab village inside Israel's borders.[35]

Their visits took several forms: as festival tourism, which brought from twenty to two hundred tourists to participating villages during designated weekends; as independent weekend visits, made possible by a growing number of bed-and-breakfast facilities; and as organized tours.[36] The first such tours were rather general in their focus, introducing Arab culture in rather broad strokes. They became more specialized as their popularity grew. Despite a growing number of Palestinian guides, some of whom were formally trained, most visitors opted for a Jewish guide with specialization in the minority sector, a form of expertise that was growing in commercial value during this period. Jewish guides were typically positioned as cultural mediators, tasked with translating Arab, Bedouin, or Druze practices into more recognizable Jewish idioms.[37]

Although many used the rhetoric of coexistence to describe their visit, few visitors framed their presence in explicitly political terms.[38] When pressed, most aligned themselves with left-wing political parties such as Labor or Meretz, although this affiliation by no means guaranteed support for local struggles. Indeed, many visitors chided the history of political activism in these places, with little tolerance for critiques of workplace discrimination and inequitable resource allocation. Most had little patience for a discussion of local land claims: "They have no end of land, they just never developed it, and that isn't the Jews' fault." Many argued that because Arabs didn't serve in the Israeli army, they had no right to demand equitable treatment. Others spoke of the corrupt practices of village officials. "They are always claiming that they don't get enough money from the government. But it goes places we don't know about." Very few were versed in the history of the Land Day protests, and still fewer were prepared to articulate an integrated critique that linked histories of inequity within the state to histories of repression in its occupied territories. Occasionally, however, such a critique would surface: "Look, inequity exists, and it will always exist because we have a situation of rulers and ruled. I know why the Intifada happened, even if I don't agree with it."

Although enthusiastic, these visits to the Palestinian Galilee were always contingent. Israeli Jews came without trepidation during periods of political stability within Israel and on its borders, but many retreated during times of political crisis. In the wake of a bus bombing in Tel Aviv or Jerusalem, of which there was an increasing number during this period, the sector emptied of tourists for days and even weeks at a time. These shifts in tourist practice were attended by a discursive shift. In times of peace, the villages of the Galilee were enjoyed as explicitly "Arab" places. At moments of crisis, their threatening status as "Palestinian" came suddenly to the fore. The state-sponsored fiction of a denationalized Arab minority, a population stripped of its Palestinian identity and history, often collapsed under the weight of political crisis.[39]

For most Palestinian entrepreneurs in the Galilee, tourism's appeal was largely attributable to its financial promise for rural populations that had been subject to decades of forced underdevelopment, massive land confiscation, and explicit state policies of neglect and containment. Despite the growth in state budgets for infrastructural development in the Palestinian Galilee during this period, many villages still lacked sewage systems, and numerous roads were dangerous and unpaved. For some entrepreneurs, tourism also was valued as a means of furthering coexistence between Jews and Palestinians in the spirit of the Oslo process. Those who vocally advocated this line were keenly aware of its economic yield. The market value of a coexistence ethos encouraged a muted critique of state policy, reserved for the private spaces of Arabic-language conversations.[40]

Orit and Gal Avidor typified the elite client base which the market drew. They had arranged for a bed-and-breakfast in the Palestinian city of Sakhnin during the festival weekend in 1996, and I joined them for a lavish dinner prepared by their host and set on folding tables outside the family home. Dressed casually in sweater and jeans, Orit, a middle-aged Jew from the prosperous community of Kfar Shmariyahu, spoke about her patronage in an Oslo-inflected account: "We didn't have this feeling of freedom a few years ago, that we could come to an Arab village. It all changed with the peace process. Of course, there's still plenty of apprehension. A friend of mine said to me, 'What, there aren't enough places in the Jewish sector? You have to go there?'" While demographically typical, the Avidors' political rhetoric was exceptional. Orit met her husband at Columbia University in 1969 when they were studying for advanced degrees. As we concluded our meal he shared his memories about student demonstrations against the Vietnam War, police brutality, and the emergence of the civil rights movement. In their construal, the Palestinian Galilee partook of an analogous history. "You feel a deep hurt here when the Arabs talk about how they've been discriminated against," he said, as coffee was served. "They're polite, but you can feel it."

The daughter of our local host, on vacation from her studies at the University of Haifa, cleared our plates as we continued our discussion. "She may not know how to wait tables," Orit noted when she passed, "but it's more authentic that way."

Belated Routes

The impact of the Oslo process on this emerging market was also spatial in kind. As I have suggested, Israel's peace accord of 1994 with Jordan catalyzed a shift in dominant Israeli conceptions of regional space, and these new geographical imaginations were crucial in making the Arab Middle East attractive to Israeli Jews as a potential tourist destination. The same was true of domestic cartographies. Like the distance between Tel Aviv and Petra, the short drive between the Jewish community of Yodfat and the neighboring village of 'Arrabeh was once an abstract proposition for most Israeli Jews, overwritten by the political and ethnonational alterity, a proximity that was ascribed to Israel's Arab population.[41] The discourse of peace and coexistence made it possible for many Jewish Israelis to reimagine these distances, to recalibrate the geographical relationship between Jewish places with the nation-state and Arab ones.

Yet these new geographical imaginations, at the regional and national scale, respectively, did not emerge concurrently. Most Jewish Israelis were able to rethink national space only after they had reimagined the region. The same was true in a tourist idiom. The Palestinian Galilee became intelligible as a tourist site only after the emergence of the Arab Middle East as a potential Jewish-Israeli destination. It was only after Israeli visits to Jordan, for example, that Arab villages within Israel could appeal to Jewish consumers, only then could the desire for Arab things that Oslo catalyzed seize on internal Arab spaces, cultures, and subjects. In part, this belatedness was a manifestation of the structural invisibility of Palestinian citizens of Israel within the Oslo process—a process that entirely overlooked their status as political actors within the Arab-Israeli conflict.[42] But belatedness was also an index of threat. For most tourist populations, the commodification of regional Arab culture was politically benign, posing little threat to Israel's well-being. Indeed, as the previous chapter argued, it sometimes functioned to consolidate the Israeli sense of territorial and cultural security as a nation-state. The same could not be said of similar processes within Israel's borders, however. By enjoying Israel's Arab population for their Arabness, Jewish tourists were engaged in a dramatization of Israeli heterogeneity that threatened to disturb the prevailing fiction of "one Israeli people" (read: one Jewish people). Put in spatial terms, the political consequences of internal tourism stood in inverse proportion to the geographical distances involved. Making short journeys to Arab villages in northern Israel involved substantial political steps.

The Logic of Value

"It's not about high politics," noted a middle-aged women who walked with her husband through the streets of Dayr Hannah on a festival-sponsored tour:

> It's spring, I'm on vacation, and I wanted to leave the house. Besides, this area is a part of us [helek mi-shelanu].

Have I visited Arab villages before? Not really. We've been to the Bedouin [in the Negev] and we used to visit the Old City [of Jerusalem] before the Intifada. But we stopped when the violence started. Here, it's clean and quiet [*shaket*], and you get something authentic.

As I have argued, the ethnic tourism market borrowed a cultural logic from the regional tourist market that had emerged as a result of the Oslo process. Yet the domestic market also pivoted on its own grid of value and pleasure. On the broadest level, Jewish Israeli tourists came to enjoy something that they identified as authenticity, that is, "authentic" Arab culture. The Hebrew term *otenti* circulated constantly through this market, proliferating in the narratives of guides, tourists, local entrepreneurs, and state planners as a means of identifying and prescribing value. The criteria for authenticity were various and changed over time. In the early years of market development, as the client base was being established, Palestinian entrepreneurs and Jewish planners sought to build authenticity into the market in iconic ways, investing heavily in recognizable ethnic signifiers such as Arabic coffeepots, traditional clothing, and Bedouin tents often in the absence of Bedouins after a history of forced relocation from the Western Galilee.[43] Authenticity was palatable only in the absence of Palestinian-inflected politics. As the tourist quoted above suggested, these villages had to be manifestly "quiet" (*shaket*) or lacking in radical politics in order for authenticity to signify.

By the spring of 1996, as the market was expanding, the locus of pleasure was beginning to shift. Tourists were placing a rising premium on the culture of the everyday. Authenticity was being reassigned to quotidian forms: a walk through the village center, tours of a working home, and late-night conversations with the bed-and-breakfast proprietor in his private living room. Palestinian entrepreneurs, festival organizers, and tour guides also began to focus their attentions here. The popular Jewish-led tour of local healers, for example, began to guide visitors into the private courtyards and living rooms of local residents, where an older generation of Palestinian men and women demonstrated their medicinal work. Many spoke broken Hebrew at best, and few wore ethnically marked clothing, and these absences were crucial to the forms of market value that were emerging at this moment. Visitors increasingly sought to indulge in cultural forms that were neither explicitly performative nor spectacular in their mode of delivery. Indeed, the presence of spectacle threatened to disrupt the value of the cultural offerings. Thus it was that the market began to turn on a refusal of ethnic iconicity, at least, in its most recognizable forms. This is not to suggest a symbolic economy suddenly stripped of either performance or icons. Both were still available to tourists in the form of Bedouin tents, folk dance troupes, and other ethnic signifiers, but their centrality was being undermined by a new tourist investment in the day-to-day: the personal encounters, home-cooked meals, and private spaces of daily living.

The temporal modality of authenticity also began to shift. In the early stage of market development, consumers and developers were heavily invested in a story of cultural pasts. This discourse, which built on iconic colonial narratives, was prevalent in the language of Jewish guides and state planners and was backed by Palestinian entrepreneurs eager to ensure financial success. Brochures marketing the Palestinian Galilee emphasized tourist access to "a taste of the past" (ta'am shel pa'am), by which villages were marked as places outside of time, unsullied by modernity or the marketplace. The forms of infrastructural development initially sponsored by the state also obeyed this logic, favoring the renovation of sites that could deliver an appropriate past: tombs and cemeteries, mosques and churches, traditional architecture. The value of the past generated multiple and sometimes contradictory discourses, both configuring tourism as an act of despoliation that threatened authentic Arab culture with the sullying influences of the marketplace ("How long will it be before the Arabs of the Galilee discover the irresistible call of tourism, and lose all the authenticity, the openness, and the hospitality that emanates from within them?"), and casting tourism as a redemptive practice that could restore forms of cultural value that had been overlooked by ignorant locals.[44]

The onset of daily value in the latter half of the 1990s altered this temporal register. The tourist desire for quotidian forms and narratives translated into an investment in real time. For many Jewish visitors, authenticity now cohered primarily in the marks of the present. This temporal shift was particularly visible in the prevalent demand for autobiography. In their conversations with Palestinian hosts, many visitors now asked about family life and communal practices. History was of secondary concern. This new regime of value generated new storytelling strategies among Palestinian Arab guides, restaurant owners, and bed-and-breakfast proprietors. Tourists asked them to narrate themselves, that is, their own life stories and those of their communities. Such stories had more impact when told without the assistance of a translator, but were frequently requested even when translation was unavoidable. By the second half of the decade, such narrative had become one of the market's most authentic commodities.

This temporal shift was not matched by a spatial one. That is, tourists were not equally invested in geographic locality, in forms of Arab culture tied to particular villages. Rather, many understood the Palestinian Galilee and its cultural offerings in a broad geographic context, a context which conferred intelligibility on Arab villages. Many cited visits to other Palestinian places as important precedents for Galilee tourism, such as prior trips to the Druze villages of 'Isfiya and Dalyiat al-Karmil in the Galilee, to Bedouin heritage centers in the Negev, and the Palestinian territories before the first uprising. Many relied on geographical analogy to explain the local landscape — as in, "This looks just like Jaffa." Others spoke comparatively about prior visits to "the Far East" (ha-mizrah ha-rahok). "Why should they go to Nepal," remarked a Jewish guide, "when they can find this stuff in their backyard?" Or, as a popular Hebrew daily newspaper puzzled: "Because all of these Arab and Druze villages . . . [possess] the smells of the East and its characteristic hospitality, the question arises, why go as far as Thailand?"[45] These comparative narratives emptied the Palestinian Galilee of its geopolitical specificity. But in so doing, they conferred a certain kind of value on the Arab villages in question. Geographical analogy rendered them both safe and newly intelligible as sites of leisure rather than enmity. What emerged at the intersection of Jaffa, Petra, and Nepal was a composite portrait of Oriental allure that the Palestinian Galilee was asked to reference if not mimic. In this way, regional Arab places conferred value on Arab places within Israel's borders, this being yet another index of the market's belatedness. The discourse of analogy accorded with prevailing Israeli logics in the ways they stripped Arab places of their Palestinian specificity. Yet these analogies also had counter-hegemonic resonances. Even as they rewrote Israeli geography in ways palatable to mainstream imaginations, they also linked Palestinian places across national and ethnic lines in ways that challenged state interdictions on Palestinian connections.

Analogy was also at play in the ways tourists evaluated the veracity of the everyday in tourist sites. While most sought access to genuine Arab dailiness, "the genuine" was a rather malleable notion. Most were savvy to the presence of a certain degree of performance or simulation in the tourist site. They anticipated an uneven field of cultural veracity and were satisfied with precisely that. Cultural inaccuracies or perceived fabrications did not necessarily diminish tourist enjoyment, although they sometimes elicited comment, as in the suggestion that Arabs "don't really drink out of one cup." Moreover, as in the mobile Oriental geography that conferred value on the Galilee by way of analogy, "the genuine" did not depend on a strict geographical mooring of the cultural object or subject to a given place. In the incitement to autobiography, Palestinians were not necessarily asked to *be themselves*, but only to be somebody *like themselves* — that is, to perform as a figure who was recognizably Arab or Eastern, according to a broad geography of Arabness. Most tourists were invested less in the quotidian practices of any particular community than in quotidian practices per se.

Impromptu Memorials

The April 1996 tour of 'Ilabun continues in the late morning sun, turning its attention to home-based attractions. We visit a beekeeper who harvested honey for medicinal purposes and an artist who specialized in Syrian-style bronze works. We walk through the living room and courtyard of a historic home, as its owner describes plans to open an informal restaurant. At every stop, wares are available for purchase, although most Palestinian entrepreneurs complained of slim financial gains from poor sales. In a few months' time, the same itinerary will be enjoyed by Jewish Israeli tourists on a weekly basis.

We conclude our tour at the courtyard of the local church, where brightly colored plastic chairs are arranged for a concert by village musicians. Akram explains that the traditional Arabic wedding music they play is experiencing a renaissance in the Galilee. We follow the lyrics on photocopied Hebrew translations. A middle-aged man from Tel Aviv gets up to dance, joining a young woman from the village in her T-shirt and jeans. Soon she sits down, to be replaced by several women from our group who wave their arms above their heads in a rendition of traditional Arabic movements as local Palestinian teenagers watch from the sidelines. The history of this courtyard is not narrated by our guide. Here, during the course of the 1948–49 War, Jewish soldiers of the Golani Brigade executed twelve residents of 'Ilabun before expelling the remaining villagers to Lebanon.[46]

There is a proposal from the audience: someone from the tour wants to sing. The musicians pass the microphone to a woman from the affluent suburb of Kfar Shmariyahu, north of Tel Aviv, who begins "Shir la-shalom" (The Song of Peace). The song has a long political history in Israel. Written as a political protest in the wake of the 1967 War, it was banned from Israeli radio by the army for its subversive potential, then adopted by the Israeli peace movement as a peace anthem.[47] In the spring of 1996, the tune has the familiarity of a national anthem, recalling its feverish repetition on the radio through seven months of public mourning for the former Israeli prime minister Yitzhak Rabin. This was the song Rabin had sung from the political podium in Tel Aviv moments before his assassination by an orthodox Israeli Jew several months prior.[48] Some tourists join her in song while others sit quietly. The Palestinian musicians on traditional folk instruments try to strum along, but their labors are unsuccessful. Having acquired the status of a national anthem, this memorial defies efforts at Arabic translation, efforts to reinvent it in a minority tongue.

This scene of impromptu memorializing, staged six months after the assassination of Prime Minister Rabin, carried a considerable symbolic burden. In mourning Rabin, Israelis lamented not only the loss of their leader but also the dissolution of Jewish unity within the nation-state, shattered by a Jewish assassin, and the pending dissolution of the regional peace process of which Rabin was popularly understood as architect. The song also functioned as a patriotic rite within this broader memorial context, one of many public vigils, bumper stickers, and graffiti-inscribed testimonials of grief and outrage. Public sites of commemoration were deemed exalted national places. To mourn from a place was to mark it as a national site. To be witnessed publicly in one's grief, to be recognized as a subject in mourning, was to be marked as an authentic Israeli.

The musical tribute in 'Ilabun intervened into this symbolic landscape by extending its geography. By staging a memorial in the Palestinian village of 'Ilabun, Jewish Israeli tourists marked the village as an explicitly Israeli place, that is, not merely as a place within the nation-state, but one included within the national consensus and worthy of intelligibility as such. In keeping with the expansive spatial logic of the tourism market, this gesture was a broad one that implicitly inscribed the entire Arab sector onto the sanctioned map of the nation-state. Indeed, this remapping was a popular strand of the memorial discourses that followed Rabin's assassination. The Hebrew press assured its readers that the nation's grief knew neither party lines nor ethnic divisions. Ethnically explicit photographs of Arabs and Druze mourning for their fallen prime minister were granted prominence in the Israeli press, as they helped illustrate a multicultural nation united in sorrow.

The ritual practices and emblems of nationalism were not foreign to western Galilean villages in the mid-1990s, brought in by tourists from the outside. Many Palestinian restaurant owners, shopkeepers, and families experimenting with bed-and-breakfasts in their homes adorned their public spaces with some of Israel's most familiar national artifacts, rendered uncanny in these incongruous spaces: photos of Jewish Israeli statesmen, Hebrew posters endorsing the peace process, emblems of Zionist parties. Because of the political history of the Palestinian Galilee, these artifacts played a critical role in the market and were, at times, its very condition of possibility. Familiar artifacts of national allegiance helped to overwrite the history of presumed internal enmity, marking rural locals as loyal and safe and readying the ground for Jewish clientele.

The centrality of such artifacts points to the contingent nature of tourist pleasure in this marketplace. While consumers sought Arab dailiness and identified value here, they also required a visible display of Israeli allegiance and explicit disaffiliation from radical, Palestinian politics. The use of geographical analogies helped make this possible by locating the Galilee within a desituated geography that was stripped of explicitly Palestinian markers. The incitement to autobiography also centered on this logic. When tourists demanded personal stories or those of the local community, they forestalled something much more threatening: the political biography of a nation. Value cohered at this awkward intersection where daily Arab culture met a set of implicit political demands, namely, the demand for Israeliness. These semiotic systems did not compete for symbolic primacy but were enunciated through each other. A viable market emerged at this messy intersection.

Performative Authenticity

In the spring of 1996, I join Adnan Abu Raya in the crowded room that serves as both exhibition hall and office for the Palestinian Heritage Museum in the city of Sakhnin, the only museum in the Palestinian Galilee during this period. Behind us, arranged according to date of use, are shelves of historic cooking implements gathered from Palestinian-area families and labeled with handwritten Arabic placards. Upstairs are cases of embroidery, women's jewelry, and traditional dresses whose patterns varied according to city of origin: Ramallah, Nazareth, Jericho, Beersheba. There is no Hebrew here, and little English, save the return address on the museum brochure. It's an issue of fierce contention among local Jewish guides and tourist agents who organized visits to the museum as part of their Galilee tours. "There are no Arabic explanations at the Israel Museum in Jerusalem," Abu Raya argues. "Why should there be Hebrew here?"[49]

This museum has a history of rapid growth. At the time of its founding in the 1990s it was housed in three dilapidated basement rooms and catered largely to Sakhnin residents; advertising was limited to word of mouth. In 1996, Abu Raya boasts of six rooms and has profited from prominent advertising in Hebrew-language Galilee guides. Leafing through the meticulous, handwritten log of museum history, Abu Raya notes a sixfold rise in visitors since 1990, its growth aided by local festivals and the general expansion in rural tourism. Yet the shift in visitor demographics was even more dramatic, still. Over the course of 1995 alone, the museum has hosted an increasing number of Jewish Israelis on educational visits, including students from major universities, elementary school pupils from the Misgav region, high school teachers seeking to improve their knowledge of Arab culture, kibbutz residents on holiday weekends, and visitors on privately organized tours led by both Jewish and Palestinian guides. By 1996, Jewish Israeli visitors constituted 85 percent of the museum's client population, up from 30 percent in 1993. Palestinian Israelis were the new minority visitor population. Palestinians from the West Bank and Gaza have yet to arrive.

Like most Palestinian residents of Sakhnin from his generation, Abu Raya has a history of active participation in the Land Day demonstrations of 1976. He was a teenager at the time and recalls the sight of Israeli tanks and their violent encounter with unarmed demonstrators. He takes many Jewish Israeli visitors to the Land Day memorial that stood in Sakhnin's center.[50] Here he describes the ongoing expropriation of Palestinian land and explains how the state rhetoric of Judaization has given way to a euphemized narrative about national development, even as expropriation continued.[51] Some visitors are acquainted with this history; others hear it for the first time. During our interview, Abu Raya describes the legacy of state surveillance in Sakhnin and neighboring villages in an effort to monitor anti-Israeli activity, the interrogations and arrests, and the residual local fears of speaking openly about politics with strangers. He insists on the ways such fears constrained the local Palestinian encounter with Jewish tourists, despite the Israeli rhetoric about a new era of coexistence.

Over coffee and cigarettes, Abu Raya speaks a Hebrew that was rapid and intricate:

> What are the political implications of being seriously introduced to Arab culture, tradition, customs, tools? You can find these in many places in Israel. If the Israeli public wants to see *authentic* tools, they can go to any moshav with a museum of [Jewish] settlement. . . . But these tools are Palestinian. That is what we are trying to introduce into their consciousness, even though it makes some visitors shudder with discomfort. It was very worrisome to hear the word *Palestinian* five years ago. Today, with normalization [e.g., the Oslo process], it has become natural.[52]

He describes constant provocations over the past few years from Jewish tour guides and Misgav officials who challenge his insistence on a Palestinian descriptor. They seek to replace it with the denationalized term Arab Israeli, still the state's terminology of choice.

While he concedes that tourism threatened to primitivize the local population, Abu Raya believes in its possibilities as an important avenue for cultural education. He begins each organized visit with a lecture on Palestinian culture, history, and contemporary politics:

People are coming to learn about Arab culture, not just to spend leisure time. They sit, listen to every word they hear, and ask a lot of questions. There is a gap [in their knowledge]. They've always heard those stereotypes about Arab culture—that Arabs are screwed up, uneducated, underdeveloped. But the tourist that comes here hears the truth. I expose all of the pain that exists after land confiscation, even though it hurts. Because the confiscation of my land happened for your good, and today you visit as a guest.

Itineraries of Struggle

The Palestinian Heritage Museum was an anomalous tourist institution in this emerging market. It was the only museum of any kind in the Palestinian Galilee, and grew increasingly unrepresentative as a Jewish Israeli destination as the locus of market value shifted from cultural display to daily practice. In 1996, Abu Raya was invited to join the Music and Nature itinerary by Misgav Council officials. By the end of the decade, having refused to temper his political message, the invitation was no longer extended. Although infrequently articulated within tourist earshot, Abu Raya's political analysis was shared by most residents of Sakhnin and neighboring communities. Privately, many Palestinian guides and proprietors would willingly speak of their Land Day memories and activist histories, their encounters with discrimination and Jewish racism, and their personal histories of lost land. A small percentage shared these histories with their Jewish guests. Some took their visitors to the roof of the family home, from which they pointed to the vast fields their families used to farm, prior to expropriation.

Abu Raya educated his Jewish Israeli guests through the labor of defamiliarization. Most Jewish Israeli visitors to the Palestinian Heritage Museum had seen Sakhnin before: through a car window, as they drove through the Palestinian Galilee on a shortcut between Jewish towns, or for emergency shopping on Shabbat, when most Jewish shops were closed. Many male tourists over fifty remembered the village streets from dark evening patrols, recalling years spent monitoring Land Day demonstrations during the first Palestinian uprising, arresting those responsible for political leaflets and Palestinian flags. These were uncanny memories that carried uncomfortable histories of violence and hatred that couldn't necessarily be narrated during tourist visits if consumer pleasure was to be maintained. For most of these men, the pleasure of their visit depended on the erasure of these histories, on envisioning the place anew.

The cultural artifacts Abu Raya presented to his visitors were also familiar. Many Jewish Israelis had seen them preserved in their grandparents' homes, for sale in Israeli boutiques, and on display in kibbutz museums of early Jewish settlement. What was different in the Palestinian Heritage Museum was their context: "If the Israeli public wants to see *authentic* tools [*kelim otentiyim*], they can go to any moshav with a museum of [Jewish] settlement. . . . But these tools are Palestinian." Through the medium of cultural display, Abu Raya turned the discourse of authenticity against itself, insisting that the adjective "authentic" modify a cultural artifact marked explicitly as Palestinian. In turn, he played tactically with the incitement to autobiography by educating visitors not about himself but about the political history of his community.

Abu Raya's insistence on the Palestinian provenance of his artifacts was a substantive challenge to prevailing Israeli imaginations of regional geography, a challenge to the selective proximities and spatial intimacies of the Oslo era. Regional diplomacy had modified the perceived relationship between Tel Aviv and Sakhnin and between Petra and Tel Aviv. That is, it had enabled new Israeli spatial relations with some "Arab" places inside the nation-state and some beyond its borders. But places marked explicitly as "Palestinian" had not been similarly reimagined. To the contrary, the perceived distance between Israel and the West Bank and Gaza Strip had been elongated by a state eager to contain its occupied population and prevent the emergence of an independent Palestinian state. Abu Raya responded with a countermapping that linked Ramallah, Nazareth, and Beersheba, with a geography that dramatized forms of Palestinian kinship and cultural sharing across borders and checkpoints in ways that refused Oslo's spatiopolitical terms. In so doing, he exposed the fiction of an Arab citizenry stripped of its Palestinian markings.

Abu Raya staged his political intervention at the site of an open secret. The performances of patriotism in which many Palestinian hosts engaged at the implicit bequest of their Jewish guests did not afford them full inclusion within the Israeli nation-state, a fact that few Jewish visitors would deny. This was an implicit social contract between hosts and guests. Palestinians were asked to perform as authentic Arabs and as loyal Israelis but without contesting their highly conditional status as nationals, that is, their status as Arab Israelis rather than Israelis per se. They were asked to mimic and perhaps exceed the Jewish Israeli tourists in their performative fidelity to the state, but not in their symbolic or juridical demands as citizens. The market teetered perpetually on this axis, threatening to collapse in the potential slippage between mimicry and presumption, a slippage that, for many visitors, would unsettle their pleasure in Arab things.

This reading of the Palestinian Heritage Museum suggests the blasphemous potential of the ethnic tourism market, even in the midst of its normative injunctions. I have argued that the commodification of Arab culture in the Oslo period was typically premised on dominant Israeli logics. As such, it often functioned to fortify Israeli fictions about its Arab citizenry, strengthening a discourse of Arab primitivism, bolstering their peripheral status within the nation-state. Yet the tourist marketplace was a highly variable political field, producing multiple and at times conflicting effects. In some spaces of contact between host and guest, the commodification of Arab culture had an unsettling potential. At moments, that is, the cultural performances and displays staged by Palestinian hosts had the capacity to undermine state logics and terms of inclusion. The Palestinian Heritage Museum was one such instance. Abu Raya told Israeli history differently, departing from state-sponsored accounts about the nation-state through an insistence on Palestinian cultural circuits and legacies of dispossession. His six-room museum challenged the fictions on which the coexistence discourse was predicated, exposing the gap between the Arab as an object of Jewish enjoyment and as a subject of Israeli political recognition. Here, through redeployment of a set of familiar cultural props and rhetorics of value, the prevailing terms of Israeli history and identity were being contested and refashioned. Here, within a tourist marketplace predicated on dominant Israeli cultural logics, the nation-state was becoming intelligible in new ways.

The Israeli State and the Production of Palestinian Space

Representatives from the Israeli Tourism Ministry were frequent visitors to the Palestinian Galilee during the 1990s. Lower-level officials would meet with Palestinian mayors to discuss local development options, and planners and architects employed by the Ministry would inspect villages on foot, evaluating market viability. Arabic speakers were subcontracted to catalogue the cultural practices of particular village populations. They traveled door-to-door with surveys, querying residents about their willingness to welcome an incoming tourist population and assessing cultural talents that might be mined for a tourism market. Surveys read, "Is there someone in the family with knowledge of folklore and/or arts (metal work, weaving, embroidery, baking, or other)? Is there somebody in the family who knows how to dance or play an instrument? Would he/she be willing to perform?" But while the Tourism Ministry was interested in the quality of Palestinian cultural offerings, it was equally invested in the nature of Palestinian space, both the geographical particulars of individual villages and their private interiors. Surveys were particularly focused on the latter: "Is there a room in your house for hosting guests? Would you be interested in hosting tourists in your home?"[1]

The ethnic tourist market in the Palestinian Galilee was primarily a local venture, fueled by Palestinian entrepreneurs from participating villages. But it was also a state production, a market financed and developed with state aid and assistance. This chapter considers the state's role in this process. More specifically, I investigate the everyday practices of lower-level state officials and their private sector affiliates in their efforts to develop ethnic tourism. In some regards, this was a strictly commercial venture, aimed at generating new opportunities for Jewish Israeli consumption and at bolstering local Palestinian economies. Yet this venture signaled a significant shift in the state's relationship to its rural Palestinian citizenry. Through the development of these rural tourist infrastructures, Palestinian populations within Israel's borders were becoming new objects of state scrutiny and regulation. This is not to suggest the onset of a regulatory regime where there had been none before. To the contrary, the Palestinian Galilee had been carefully monitored and controlled since Israel's founding, particularly in the decades after state formation, and regulation continued with varying degrees of intensity through the 1990s.[2] Yet tourism development marked the onset of a different kind of regulatory regime, one that seized primarily on Palestinian culture, intimate spaces, and daily practices as its objects of control. Unlike prior regimes, this one was motivated less by the desire to maximize Jewish Israeli security than the desire to maximize Jewish Israeli leisure.

Space was at the core of this regime. Planners, architects, and consultants employed by the Tourism Ministry labored to remake Palestinian villages as particular kinds of geographies, and as particular kinds of scales. One spatial modality reigned supreme during the course of market development: *interiority*. State officials and their private sector affiliates imagined a tourist market predicated on concentric interiors or nested small scales.[3] In the course of the planning processes, interiority was identified as the organic locus of Palestinian life within Israel's borders. That is, planning discourses posited Palestinians as naturally at home in these confined spaces, in these small scales. These scales did not precede state involvement, or not strictly so. They had to be nurtured and produced in the course of tourist development.

The stakes in this scalar template were considerable. I argue that we can read the state's investment in interiority as a response to the Oslo process itself, a response to the porous borders and transnational flows that Oslo was beginning to deliver. As I have suggested, these transnational processes were predicated on concurrent forms of regulation and containment, particularly within the occupied Palestinian territories. This chapter argues that the Palestinian tourist market was an additional site of containment, albeit of a far less violent kind. More pointedly, I suggest that the market was a realm in which the state's fantasy of spatial regulation was being enacted, a realm in which the spatial controls exercised in the Occupied Territories were being translated into development priorities within Israeli territory. In chapter 1, I argued that political processes at the regional scale produced a substantive shift in Israeli spatial imaginations, altering prevailing perceptions of Israel's very proximity to its Arab neighbors. Space making by lower-level state officials can be understood as a response to these new spatial imaginaries, to this shift in the geographical terms of intelligibility. Regional proximity, or the emerging intelligibility thereof, was the cause of both celebration and concern among dominant Israeli publics. The scalar templates on which tourist development was predicated responded to the concerns, to the fears, that the very perceptability of proximity had instigated. The production of Palestinian interiority in the course of market development was a tool by which to fix Palestinians in space, therein diminishing their perceived threat in the era of a newly transnational Middle East. As such, the spatial investments of the state in the midst of tourism development suggest the highly contingent ways in which Israeli geographical imaginations, or spatial modalities of intelligibility, were being reworked during this period.

In what follows, I consider the ways that lower-level state officials and their private sector affiliates endeavored to produce Palestinian space and scale in the course of market development and I consider the political ideologies in which such scalar productions were rooted.[4] It should be stressed that the state's interest in the Palestinian Galilee as a tourist market was relatively short-lived. While planning was extensive during the mid-1990s, only a small percentage of state-sponsored development blueprints would be implemented in subsequent years. Some were discarded during the course of the planning process, while others failed to acquire sufficient state funding. When the Likud Party took power in 1996, development priorities shifted radically and many Arab sector projects were abandoned for lack of government interest.[5] My analysis won't fall on such outcomes, however. Rather, my goal is to illustrate the set of spatial fantasies at work during the period when Oslo was at its height.

Producing the Rural

While the history of Israeli efforts to regulate Palestinian space can be traced to the early decades of Zionist settlement,[6] the 1948–49 War, with its dramatic transformation of Palestinian Arab society and geography, is perhaps the most decisive moment in that history.[7] The vast majority of Palestine's educated and urban classes fled during the course of the war, convinced of their imminent return, leaving those who remained without their prior leadership base, urban economies, and bourgeois classes. Their flight from cities such as Haifa, Jaffa, Ramla, and Jerusalem brought a virtual end to the institution of the Palestinian city within the new state.[8] Those Palestinians who remained were located in largely agrarian communities in rural areas.[9] As a result of the war and the waves of land expropriation that followed state formation, these populations were converted into a landless proletariat living in villages on Israel's geographic peripheries.[10] Without its agricultural base, the community's sociospatial form was now indeterminate: "Village society became neither rural nor urban."[11]

Although Israel did not orchestrate the de-urbanization of Palestine during the 1948–49 War, it labored to preserve this rural geography in the decades that followed.[12] The severe constraints on mobility to which Palestinians were subject under the military government (1948–66) fortified the process of de-urbanization by frustrating travel between villages and cities, effectively confining most Palestinians to the rural areas of their residence.[13] In turn, the waves of land confiscation which began immediately following the war had similar effects; the seizure of Palestinian reserve lands prevented their expansion and urbanization, even as it disrupted spatial contiguity between communities. For the state, the stakes in this geography were considerable: confined in rural spaces, Palestinians were easily controlled by the military apparatus and were separated from Israeli Jews, for whom they posed a perceived security threat. In the terms of state discourse, this geography of separation helped keep Israel's urban core predominantly Jewish and modern.[14]

Discriminatory land-use planning was another means of fortifying this geography, a strategy most clearly exercised in the drafting and enforcement of highly restrictive "outline plans" for village development in the Palestinian Galilee and in the outright failure to provide rural localities with such plans.[15] In villages lacking plans, all construction was deemed illegal and was subject to demolition, while plans that were provided by the state typically failed to adjust for natural growth.[16] Given high birth-rates in Palestinian communities in the decades after state formation, these restrictive plans resulted in overcrowding and hazardous density, in abundant unauthorized construction subject to demolition, and in a lack of proper infrastructure, as no buildings without permits could be legally provided with services.[17] In an effort to prevent the emergence of urbanized Palestinian communities that might compete with Jewish cities for economic prominence within the nation-state, few villages were zoned by the state for industrial development, a policy that forced Palestinian residents to seek work outside their communities and yielded decades of high unemployment. The production of such discriminatory land use policies was also made possible by the exclusion of Palestinian Arabs from the planning stages and appeals process.[18]

Yet the Judaization project was not merely territorial in nature, bent solely on the gross accumulation of land. It also had a substantive spatial dimension that pertained to the ways that expropriated lands and settlement projects were managed, designed, and distributed. Beginning in the 1970s, the state favored the construction of Jewish settlements on mountaintops that overlooked Palestinian villages and thus could provide surveillance.[19] That such settlements were sparsely populated did not frustrate state designs.[20] Explicitly referred to as "Lookouts" (*Mitzpim*), these new settlements were designed to fulfill a military function, tasked with "prevent[ing] unauthorized Arab agriculture, residential or grazing activity."[21] This discourse of Arab illegality and implicit criminality was a vital component of the Judaization project that effectively justified and retroactively naturalized the state's claims on Palestinian land.[22] At the same time, while state policies were remarkably effective in controlling Palestinian space and preserving Israeli cities as predominantly Jewish locales, the state could not entirely prevent a Palestinian presence in urban areas; this presence would grow progressively.[23]

Yet in some regards the state was remarkably successful. What resulted from land use planning and policy in the Palestinian Galilee were densely populated, poorly serviced, nonindustrialized villages that lacked spatial contiguity with others—villages that, following the loss of many Palestinian urban centers in the 1948–49 War, functioned as the central institution of Palestinian life in the poststate period. In turn, through spatial planning, the state was able to limit Palestinian Arab territorial growth and power in the nation-state. Through such spatial practices and tactics of localization, Israeli urban populations were secured as predominantly Jewish ones insulated from the Palestinian Arabs they feared. What this history suggests, then is that the Arab village was not an organic artifact of Palestinian history, as subsequent Israeli state and academic discourse would contend. Rather, it was predominantly an effect of Israeli spatial control.[24]

The Accidental State

I am driving to the Palestinian village of Dayr Hannah in the aging car of Ruti Shalev, a middle-aged Israeli Jew and advisor to the Rural Development Branch of the Israeli Tourism Ministry. Since the early 1990s, building on her personal history as a long-time Galilee resident, Ruti has traveled through the region's Palestinian villages, looking for ways to develop a tourism market. When I first met her in 1994, she was trying to sell her vision to an incredulous Tourism Ministry. By 1996, she was on the Ministry payroll. We are traveling to the village of Dayr Hannah on this spring afternoon in 1996 at the behest of a Palestinian family from the village who wants to develop a bed-and-breakfast unit in their home. Ruti is going to assess its feasibility.

Ruti's history in the Galilee is considerable. In 1959, as a personal commitment to the Judaization project, she moved to the region and helped establish the Jewish collective settlement of Yodfat, subsequently incorporated into the jurisdiction of the Misgav regional council. Over the course of many conversations, she has described her younger years hiking through the region, meeting its Bedouin residents, developing strong friendships, and acquiring a serviceable Arabic. She describes herself as a cultural insider, equipped with intimate knowledge of local Palestinian customs, and contends that this intimacy is crucial for tourist development.

In Ruti's assessment, Ministry officials in Jerusalem have little under-standing of the Palestinian Galilee and its emerging market. They aren't familiar with the private lives of its residents, the quarrels between fami-lies, its picturesque back streets and touristic possibilities. Her role as intermediary with local Palestinian publics is critical in her position as Ministry consultant. As a result of this insider knowledge, she is invited to all the important Jerusalem meetings, and is the Ministry's primary contact in the field, called upon to evaluate the viability of proposals, to consult during local festivals, and to introduce national officials to poten-tial Palestinian entrepreneurs and influential local figures who might have an impact on state-sponsored development. Ruti doesn't have an office, and sometimes not even the use of a car. Her salary is meager. She works mostly out of a kitchen cluttered with handwritten papers, brochures, and unemptied ashtrays. But for both the state and Palestinian residents of the Galilee, she is the Ministry's local proxy.

When we stop for gas, Ruti offers a ride to two young Palestinian women who wait for the infrequent local bus. "Where are you going?" she yells out the window in Hebrew. They are also traveling to Dayr Hannah and shyly accept the ride, sliding into the backseat. "I wanted to ask, but I was embarrassed," says one, in a hesitant Hebrew. "If you don't ask, you don't get," Ruti replies in her signature tone as we drive on.

"Where are you from?" Ruti asks the women in the backseat. "Dayr Hannah," says one, as her friend sits silently. Ruti presses for details, and the woman describes the location of her family home, just off a dead-end lane that tourists often enter by mistake. Many are forced to make a noisy three-point turn under their window. Ruti knows the spot. "I am work-ing with the local [Music and Nature] festival committee," she explains. "How would you feel about having tourists come to your home? You could serve them coffee, talk to them about the village, and be paid for it." The woman seems interested: "But they wouldn't have to pay. They would be our guests." Here Ruti is insistent: "No, no. Business is business." At Ruti's request, they exchange phone numbers before we drop them off. "I've met most of them from hitchhiking," she notes as we drive on.

I present this scene to illustrate the everyday practices of lower-level state officials and consultants as they assessed market viability in the Pales-tinian Galilee. This portrait of what I'm calling the accidental state is meant to suggest the haphazard nature of state involvement in daily Palestinian life during the course of such assessments, an involvement that sometimes bordered on threat for the Palestinian residents involved, but which was largely tolerated due to its fiscal promise. As the Ministry's local representative, Ruti worked often inadvertently and unsuccessfully, reliant on chance encounters and polite promises that were frequently unrealized. Yet her labor was critical to the Ministry as it formulated policy for this emerging market, determined its central cultural icons, and allocated development budgets.

Ruti's presence in the Palestinian Galilee signaled a significant shift in state policy. Since the time of state formation, very few Palestinian villages had been granted government aid for tourist development, save a small number of Bedouin and Druze villages.[25] State support in these exceptional cases accorded with the terms of ethnic favoritism; that is, they rewarded Israel's "good" minorities (Bedouin and Druze), favoring villages with a strong history of political allegiance to the state.[26] Yet in the wake of the Oslo Accords, the logic of development began to shift. In 1994, the Ministry of Tourism began preliminary discussions about tourism development in Palestinian villages with very different histories. Indeed, it began to consider Palestinian places with quite radical political legacies, villages like Sakhnin, 'Arrabeh, Kawkab, and Dayr Hannah that had struggled actively against discriminatory state policies in prior decades.[27] In 1995, when the first substantial state budgets were committed for integrated and broad-based infrastructural development in these places, the Ministry was explicit about the ways such policy shifts had been enabled by "the peace era" [edan ha-shalom].[28] It should be stressed that although state investment was growing, funding for the Palestinian sector still composed a small fraction of Ministry budgets. The significance of state involvement is not, however, reducible to such numbers. Rather, it should be evaluated on the basis of the dramatic shift in political logics that such involvement represented. Palestinian places historically perceived as internal dangers were being actively refashioned by the state as Israeli tourist destinations, as sites of Jewish leisure.

These changes in tourism policy were linked to broader shifts in the state's relationship to its Palestinian minority.[29] State budgets for Arab sector development increased significantly between 1992 and 1996—particularly in the areas of education, health, and tourism—climbing from

New Israel Shekel (NIS) 141.2 million in 1992 to NIS 480.1 million in 1996, an actual growth of 240 percent.[30] Under the previous government (1989–92), the sector had been virtually ignored, with infinitesimal budget allocations for planning and development.[31]

In tandem, the Ministry of Tourism was exploring development prospects in Palestinian cities and waterfronts. Nazareth was granted top priority in this category, with an $80 million project to renovate its Old City and expand its tourism infrastructure in preparation for the millennial anniversary of the birth of Christ and the magnitude of expected pilgrimage, this in a city crippled by a history of underdevelopment and land expropriation.[32] Simultaneously, but with more modest budgets, the government pursued renovation projects in the Old City of 'Akka, of which the development of the Jaffa seaport was imagined as precedent.[33] The Jisr al-Zarka' beachfront was also targeted for development during this period, hailed by the government as the first state-sponsored tourism project designed for an internal, Arab clientele.[34]

This interest in Palestinian places as tourist destinations was accompanied by a cautious interest in encouraging the tourist practices of Israel's Palestinian citizenry, a population that had been granted little attention of this kind before. Like incoming Arab travelers from the broader Middle East (see chapter 1), the prospect of Arab-Israelis as tourists was, for the state, a perceived enigma. Many Ministry officials argued that they would be most at home in Arab locales: "The most comfortable place for Muslim tourists is somewhere where people speak their language, where there's a mosque, and a lifestyle with which they are familiar."[35] But in 1996, when the Ministry of Tourism published its first official survey on the subject, based on interviews with the target population, it concluded otherwise: "Participants conclusively rejected the notion of vacationing in an Arab village. . . . From their perspective, there was no reason to vacation in a site similar [to] . . . their place of residence."[36] Although the study avoided political questions, they emerged clearly in the interviews included in the study's appendix: "In Jordan, it's close and it's cheap, and [unlike in Israel] you're not always forced to show your identification to the police . . ."[37] By 1995, the Ministry of Tourism had abandoned this line of inquiry.

But the Ministry of Tourism was also exploring development possibilities in Israel's so-called rural sector (ha-migzar ha-kafri), imagining a market in country hospitality that might compete with the metropolitan centers that had historically monopolized government budgets: Eilat, Tel Aviv, Jerusalem. Initially, it focused its attention on Jewish collective settlements (*kibbutzim* and *moshavim*), many of which were turning to tourism after a gradual decline in agricultural revenues.[38] It bears noting that most initial Ministry discussion of the rural sector made no mention of Palestinian places.[39] It was only after the success of development efforts in rural Jewish locales that the ministry reconsidered Palestinian villages as targets of "rural sector" investment.[40] Indeed, the state's belated interest in Palestinian villages was linked to its highly delimited construal of the rural (*ha-kafri*)—a term which, despite its etymological roots in the Hebrew word for village (*kfar*), had long been used adjectivally in the dominant Israeli lexicon to denote something like "country style," modifying such commodities as potato chips and interior design. The rural, then, was intelligible only insofar as it had been debased, dehistoricized. It was a sign stripped of any reference to Palestinian places, to the fact that villages are the primary centers of Palestinian dwelling inside the borders of Israel.[41] In colloquial Hebrew usage, rural comes to mark precisely that absence: a pastoral aesthetic dependent on the emptying of the actual territory itself. Historically, then, the term has functioned as a means of symbolic deterritorialization that has removed Palestinians from the imagined Israeli countryside. But in the 1990s, fueled by the discourses of the Oslo process, this geography was being rethought. In turning its attention to Palestinian villages as potential tourist destinations, the state was repopulating or re-Arabizing the rural imaginary.

Making Village Space

In late February 1996, I return to Dayr Hannah with the Jewish Israeli architect Betsalel Rinot whose firm has been employed by the Ministry of Tourism to draft plans for tourist development in several Palestinian villages in the Galilee. At the time of our visit, Rinot and his associates had already prepared initial blueprints and awaited approval from state officials before implementation could begin.

I meet Rinot in the Dayr Hannah local council, where a meeting with the mayor and village deputy for tourism affairs is under way. Rinot leads the proceedings, unfurling an aerial photograph of the village and discussing its intricacies in animated Hebrew. Using the photograph as guide, he delineates the village's most impressive structures, stressing the need to work with vernacular aesthetics rather than importing styles from outside. The political demographics of this scene of planning are typical of many I had witnessed: Jewish professionals designed and planned while Palestinian representatives from the area consulted and approved when necessary. The Jewish professor of archeology from the University of Haifa, consulting on historic preservation, had already come and gone.

"We'll focus our energies here," Rinot explains, pointing to the center of the village, where most of its historic structures are concentrated.

"First we'll renovate the periphery, where the old walls used to be." He leads our eyes with a pencil to illustrate the path of a proposed walkway. "Then we'll guide the tourist into the heart of the village [*gar'in ha-kefar*]."

The mayor is enthusiastic, envisioning an integrated market built in stages and expanding alongside its client base. He had appointed the village's tourism deputy only two months before to address the promise of a vibrant market.

After the meeting concludes, I join Rinot and his assistant on a tour through prospective renovation sites. We walk briskly through the narrow alleys of the village center, winding past low stone houses built in close proximity, occasionally flanked by small gardens. Rinot carries his plans and occasionally marks them with notes and drawings.

We follow Rinot through backyards and into courtyard interiors to examine spots of architectural interest that will figure centrally in his plan. We climb staircases and peer over walls to examine sites that might have escaped prior notice.

"I'd put a drinking fountain here, and a shop for local crafts in that alcove." His assistant concurs, scribbling onto a pad as Rinot describes his vision.

Walking through a private garden and behind a small housing compound, Rinot discovers a portion of the ancient village wall he hasn't seen before, identifying places where cement has been applied as fortification and suggesting methods for restoration.

"We could put a restaurant on this side, and illuminate the whole thing at night," he continues aloud, sketching as he walks. "Most mayors want their villages to look like Tel Aviv and everybody wants a McDonald's," he explains to me, pausing to examine the ancient cistern. "But I try to work with the local elements."

In 1996, at the time of our visit, Israeli Jews were still infrequent visitors to Dayr Hannah, and our party elicited stares and muffled commentary from residents who observed our expedition from their second-floor windows. Still fresh in people's minds were other histories of state regulation, whereby the sight of state officials or Jewish Israeli civilians wandering through village centers often represented orchestrated efforts to manage and survey the Palestinian population in the interest of national security. The visible presence of Israeli state planners was overlaid by these regulatory histories.

Remapping the Village

The development of the tourist market required the production of space. Village courtyards had to be remade as restaurants and alcoves as cafés, a labor of reinvention that was clearly illustrated in the sketches that accompanied Rinot's development blueprints (see figure 13). Through such spatial processes, these villages were made intelligible and consumable for Jewish tourists who had long regarded them as dangerous geographies, requiring vigilant regulation.

In Dayr Hannah, as in the vast majority of villages targeted by the state during this period, tourist development focused on the village's historic center or core: *gar'in ha-kefar*, in the Hebrew lexicon.[42] The term was both a historical and a spatial designator, referring to the original village center around which residential and commercial expansion had grown. In Israeli planning and academic discourses about the Arab village, it represented the spatial anchor of Arab culture and tradition. Indeed, spatial and cultural designators were often conjoined in such discourses through the notion of the "traditional core."[43] It was in this spatial domain that state-employed developers, following Ministry dictates, centralized their efforts. In addition to the cosmetic renovation of façades and public spaces, the Ministry of Tourism typically worked in conjunction with the Ministries of Housing and Infrastructure to improve or install sewage systems, street lighting, and pipelines in core neighborhoods. But the highly limited geography in which the state focused its energies meant that many

Figure 13. Lower caption reads: "Courtyard of the oil press, touristic application." Detail from an architectural plan for Dayr Hannah. SOURCE: BIRNACK INVESTMENTS. *DAYR HANNAH: PROGRAMAH LE-FITUAḤ TAYARUT.*

neighborhoods were left untouched during the course of development, often despite severe infrastructural needs. These limits were also enabled by a perception of underdevelopment as picturesque, as if landscapes of neglect could authenticate a village for incoming tourist populations. Moreover, state officials often attributed underdevelopment solely to histories of internal social disarray within the village, a construal that helped to alleviate the perceived need for infrastructural improvement.

In keeping with the state typology of ethnic difference, planners insisted on the difference between village cores in the Druze and Arab sectors. Indeed, the Ministry of Tourism maintained a separate administrative apparatus to govern the management of each. Nonetheless, belying state logic, development plans for both tended to follow a relatively standardized blueprint that favored a stable set of architectural elements—stone walkways, ancient walls, and domed roofs—and a stable set of cultural ones, including ethnically marked restaurants, open markets, and home-based attractions.[44] Thus it was that ethnic signifiers were frequently the only terms that substantively differentiated development plans in these sectors (e.g., "*Druze* market").[45] At the same time, developers modeled their blueprints for rural tourism on Western European markets in rural hospitality,

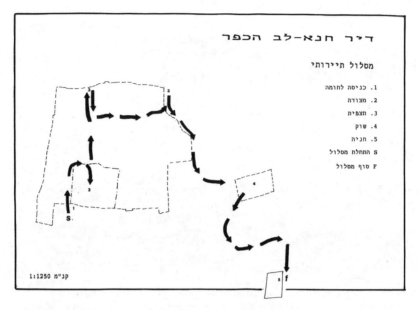

דיר חנא-לב הכפר

מסלול תיירותי

1. כניסה לחומה
2. מצודה
3. חצפית
4. שוק
5. חניה
S התחלת מסלול
F סוף מסלול

נק"מ 1:1250

Figure 14. The geography of intimacy. Reads: "Dayr Hannah: Heart of the Village. Tourist Path." Detail from an architectural plan for Dayr Hannah. SOURCE: BIRNACK INVESTMENTS. *DAYR HANNAH: PROGRAMAH LE-FITUAH TAYARUT.*

a precedent betrayed by the Hebraized German name *zimmerim* used to denote bed-and-breakfast facilities.[46] What resulted was a doubly referential model, by which planners, architects, and policymakers sought to develop a village core that would be recognizably Arab *or* Druze, even as it mimicked a rural, European landscape.

The locations of these historic cores differed. In some villages, they were at the geographic center of present-day Palestinian settlement and economy. In other places, modern construction and commercial centers had usurped the geographic centrality of historic neighborhoods. But in all cases, the core was squarely within the village and still inhabited by residents, and was neither accessible nor necessarily visible on a drive around the village periphery. The maps included in Rinot's plan for Dayr Hannah illustrate this clearly (see figure 14, above). The village's proposed tourist path was designed to take the visitor through its dense residential neighborhoods and into the heart of the center, rather than along its borders. This was a radical departure from the spatial logic that had guided the small numbers of Jewish Israeli tourists who had ventured into Palestinian villages in prior decades. For most, the value of the site previously had been directly proportional to its spatially peripheral status, and therein its ability to be easily accessed from the main road, or rapidly exited should threat ensue. In the mid-1990s, a new set of Palestinian geographies were acquiring tourist value. Planners and policymakers were setting their sights on intimate spaces within the rural interior.

Close Encounters

In the spring of 1996, sixteen people gathered in the Palestinian city of Sakhnin for a meeting of the Israeli Small Business Development Center (sbdc), a joint state and private sector effort that was tasked with supporting small entrepreneurial ventures. In 1996, it began work in (what it termed) the non-Jewish sector and invited Palestinian entrepreneurs to apply. Most Palestinian applicants sought funding for tourist projects, and most employed Jewish-Israeli consultants to do their bidding before the board.

The meeting begins with a set of Tel Aviv–based consultants who represent applicants from the Druze village of Horfeish. The literature they have prepared for the meeting outlines the village's history, assesses its tourist potential, and describes the anticipated difficulties which will be faced by developers. The consultants express multiple frustrations, complaining about Horfeish entrepreneurs unfamiliar with development protocol; they don't understand that they "can turn their grocery store into a restaurant, or take their parent's former house and convert it into café."

The representative from the Ministry of Tourism disagrees: "Maybe it's not in a family's best interest to turn their grocery store into a restaurant?"

The consultants hold their ground: "Part of the authenticity [*otentiut*] is that these are living places and the tourists are in the middle of it all."[47]

When the proposal is tabled for lack of consensus our attention moves to consultants representing a Palestinian businessman from Kawkab. Their client has been denied government loans for expansion because his kitchen does not meet national health standards. His restaurant was originally fashioned "in the style of a Bedouin tent," with patrons seated on the floor. But lacking proper building permits, it wasn't connected to the national electricity grid and relied on a generator. The consultants refer to a problem of cultural incommensurability: how can their client preserve the authenticity of the place *and* comply with state regulations? "The restaurant is doing well and the owner wants to expand, but there are no clauses in the health regulations that provide for kitchens in tents."

The Ministry's representative requests clarification: "So it's a problem of putting a modern kitchen into a Bedouin tent?"

"I've heard about a Bedouin tent in Rahat [in the Negev] with a full kosher kitchen," somebody interjects, "approved by the Rabbinate."

The consultants agree to present the case to the Ministry of Health.

I dwell on this forum as a way to illustrate the micropractices by which tourist sites in Palestinian villages were conjured into being by low-level state officials and their private sector affiliates. The scene above is in many ways unremarkable, rehearsing a rather predictable template of tourist value, one grounded in the imbricated markers of tradition, authenticity, and the local. But its spatiocultural logics merit attention. I want to suggest that the tourist market envisioned by the Israeli state and its affiliates in this meeting, as in many others, was predicated on a very particular spatial logic, a logic that departed from prevailing Israeli epistemologies, even as it rehearsed familiar cultural ones. Consider two of the spaces favored by consultants and Ministry representatives in the scene above: the village core and the former residence to be remade as a restaurant or café. Both are instances of what I'll call *interiority*—a spatial modality which the state and private sector was increasingly favoring during this period in its efforts to develop the rural Palestinian market. Indeed, the village core was merely the outer limit of a *geography of interiority* with multiple tiers. Architects and planners aimed to develop villages as bundles of consecutive insides of increasingly smaller scales.[48] Within the core, they set their sights on the intimate spaces of Palestinian living behind gates, inside courtyards and backyards, within kitchens and living rooms. They sought to transform these interior spaces into cafes, shops, places of leisure, or sites of tourist production. Their aim was to open private spaces for Jewish consumption and to afford tourists with heightened degrees of proximity to everyday village life. Authenticity was located here.

The emphasis on consecutive interiority recurred within the development blueprints produced by state-employed consultants, architects, and planners. These documents favored a form of infrastructural development that would yield close encounters with locals, a closeness garnered on the basis of spatial intimacy with village life. In chapter 2, I argued that Jewish tourists in the Palestinian Galilee sought access to the truth of Arab culture, a truth that increasingly cohered in the semiotics of daili-ness. Yet dailiness also had a crucial spatial modality. The daily cultural forms favored by tourists and subsequently by state planners were insis-tently interior ones that brought tourists into the heart of private Pales-tinian dwellings. This was the perceived locus of value. The state sought to maximize its availability.

The following survey of viable development projects in the Druze vil-lage of Yerka, as catalogued by a Tel Aviv firm, is suggestive of the prepon-derance of this spatial logic:

> *Salon*: [The client plans] to enclose his courtyard and convert it into a shop at a later date. At the present stage, it is possible to convert the courtyard into a salon that could seat between 8 and 12 people; includes grape-leaf trellis and view.

> *Guest Houses and Kiosk*: The client . . . is planning to turn [his] store into a kiosk and gallery. Immediately adjacent is an apartment of 140 square meters that the client intends to convert into guest rooms.

> *Guest Garden and Tea House*: The client plans to construct a guest area in his large courtyard, surrounded with greenery. Guests will be served cold drinks, Druze snacks [*hatifim druzim*], and green tea from herbs grown on the premises.[49]

The spaces just enumerated include private exteriors such as courtyards and gardens, semipublic commercial spaces (e.g., the store), and residen-tial interiors. Most are restricted domains within limited square footage in close proximity to others: stores back onto small apartments and court-yards closely border private homes. All of these spaces are enclosed; all afford varying degrees of spatial intimacy. All were ensconced within the lives of village residents and thus able to provide tourists with highly prox-imate encounters with local culture, bodies, and everyday life, marked by the requisite markers of ethnocultural authenticity (e.g., Druze snacks).

The geography of interiority that interested the state was comprised of various scales: the village center, the narrow streets of the village, the courtyard, the enclosed garden. In the discourse of planners, each succes-sive scale seemed to promise a greater degree of cultural value. After the courtyard or garden, the next consecutive interior favored by planners was that of the home, chiefly the living room. This space had already been established as a central feature of the rural Palestinian tourism market by the time state development began, thanks to the institution of bed-and-breakfast facilities. Surveys conducted by the private sector were often explicit in their queries to residents about the availability of such interior spaces within the family home. They asked residents, "Would you [plural] be interested in hosting tourists in your home?" and "Is there a room in your house for hosting guests?"[50] State officials feared that because most would-be entrepreneurs were relatively inexperienced, proper standards and regulations would not be met. As a result, they recommended education by means of "courses and written materials" and the strict regulation of home-based attractions.[51] The following "recommended criteria for guest units" in the "Arab and Druze sector" was an instance of this regulatory effort:

1. Each holiday unit should include private bathroom facilities.

2. Each unit should have its own entrance, separate from that of the family house.

3. Hosts and the guests can share components of the meal. The eastern mentality [ha-mentaliyut ha-mizrahit] welcomes shared meals, conversations in the living room, etc.

. . .

10. In the case of a family unit, there should be a division between the parent's room and children's room.[52]

Although these recommendations promoted the spatial proximity of host and guest, they also regulated these distances, providing clear dictates on spatial allocation and division, recommending walls separating children from parents and signs designed to produce a clear demarcation between guest and host. The document also suggests the cultural presumptions that attended such regulatory practices. Here, shared meals and living room conversations are described as a natural component of the host's cultural milieu, his "eastern mentality." In this instance, a hospitality ethic is valorized. More frequently, it was perceived by state officials as evidence of ignorant business practices, that is, of Palestinians who privileged a symbolic over a material economy.

The forms of spatial intimacy sought by planners and policymakers were not invented for the scene of tourism. Their interest in small spaces and semiprivate domains was partially due to the market's material constraints. Because of the sheer density of Palestinian dwellings in many village centers, there were numerous possibilities for acute spatial intimacy between host and guest. Indeed, it was largely unavoidable in many village settings. At the same time, many Palestinian entrepreneurs had limited capital and land available for development, and Jewish planners were forced to work within these limits and imagine a market predicated on small scales. Policymakers from the Ministry of Tourism also aimed to avoid overdevelopment in areas that lacked the infrastructure to support massive tourist traffic. Yet what interests me are the ways these preexisting spatial forms and standard regulatory protocols were marshaled by planners to create the village as a particular kind of geography: a *geography of intimacy*. Issues of interiority, proximity, and small scale came to monopolize the development imagination in ways that radically delimited the meanings attributed to the Palestinian village, its cultures, histories, and place in the nation-state.

Jewish Interiorities

To a certain degree, rural tourism in the Arab and Druze sectors was modeled on its Jewish predecessor; the success of the latter was required before a Palestinian market could be explored by the state. Yet the development norms that governed these markets were remarkably divergent.

Nature was at the heart of the Jewish sector market: planners and entrepreneurs prioritized the natural world as tourist commodity. Market surveys conducted during the mid-1990s suggested that the vast majority of Jewish tourists chose to vacation at kibbutzim and moshavim, with their proximity to hiking trails, national parks, and bodies of water.[53] Culture in the form of museums or historical and archeological sites was of peripheral concern. By the second half of the decade, the Ministry of Tourism was deploying the rhetoric of environmentalism and ecotourism and encouraging entrepreneurs to focus their energies here.[54]

Consider, by way of comparison, the growing demand for alternative medicine within both the Jewish and the Palestinian rural tourism sectors. Jewish Israeli visitors in these sectors increasingly were seeking tours and vacations structured around this theme.[55] In the Palestinian market, the allure of such offerings was often premised on the forms of spatial interiority described above. The Jewish Israeli guides administering such trips invited tourists to visit Arab medical practitioners in their private homes. Tourists typically entered the living room or courtyard of the practitioner, where they were invited to witness traditional practices. In the Jewish sector, alternative medicine as tourist attraction was reliant on the natural world. The commercial literature produced by alternative medicine centers in Jewish locales stressed their proximity to natural sites, places deemed crucial to market value. In the Palestinian sector, nature was only marginally for sale.[56] Of much greater value was the nature of the Arabs themselves, their daily practices and life history.

Thus, in sharp contrast to the Palestinian market, rural tourism in the Jewish sector trafficked in exteriority and spatial expansiveness in both literal and figurative senses, stressing both outdoor leisure and spiritual awakening. Indeed, many tourist facilities in the Jewish sector were established in the Mitzpim or "Lookout" settlements, constructed on hilltops as a means of monitoring the Palestinian villages below, thereby offering tourists the vista as an additional spatial expanse.[57] This is not to disregard the sector's indoor services, the massages and meditation sessions that were a staple of the alternative medicine market. But interiority was incidental to their market value. Indeed, it was avoided by planners and entrepreneurs when possible.

Other Interiorities

In October 1995, I join Ruti Shalev on a visit to 'Ilabun. She had been contacted by a Bedouin family who wanted to offer meals to tourists during the Music and Nature Festival season and had contacted Ruti for informal consultation.

We park in the village and walk toward the entrance of our host's two-story home, where several men sit smoking cigarettes and talking. Two are clad in Israeli army uniforms. Ruti introduces us and asks where they serve.

"My son's in the same unit," she says. "Do you know him? David Shalev?"

They weren't sure but it's possible: they compare stories about the difficulties of army service.

Amin Aburaya is our host, and he guides us behind his cement house to a spectacular site overlooking the neighboring valley. Ruti has many ideas: "Why not set up a tent here? You could serve coffee the traditional way, put in Bedouin style mattresses or have people sit on stools."

Amin agrees on the tent, but isn't interested in the traditional goat-hide weave. "We are thinking of buying a plastic one. There's less smell that way."

Ruti objects. "What is important is the atmosphere. It should be Bedouin." She suggests applying for a small-business grant from the SBDC.

As Ruti tours the site, Amin complies with my request for a political history, recounting his family's forced relocation by the Israeli government in 1979 when the state "resettled" the Galilee's Bedouin communities within a small number of towns, therein easing the burden of governance and advancing Judaization efforts. The move resulted in massive loss of land for the Palestinians involved. Amin's account rehearses the dominant state narrative about a primitive people remade as civilized through state assistance: "If you were smart, you agreed to move. We are more advanced now, and this is a good time."

This scene of planning was, as others have been, unremarkable. That is, Ruti's endeavors to dictate the market's cultural terms and Amin's strategic performance of political acquiescence, aimed at maximizing market potential, proceeded along rather predictable lines. In this scene, cultural value is scripted by the Israeli state at the rather fragile, but essential, intersection of Orientalist tropes and performances of state allegiance: the history of Israeli army service effectively authorizes the Bedouin cultural wares, giving them not merely ethnic but also national intelligibility, and enabling Jewish-Israeli tourism in this otherwise suspect site.

But it is the highly spatialized blueprint through which Ruti's colonial imaginary enunciates that concerns me here—a blueprint which, in fact, makes this seemingly familiar scene anything but. The space at issue is "the Bedouin tent," yet another interiority that the state sought to both regulate and encourage within the Palestinian marketplace. In the broader geography of interiority on which the market turned, the tent was a complex spatial form. It was highly changeable: enclosed and permeable, inside and outside, therein partaking in both the natural world and the presumed nature of the Bedouin it housed. State efforts to manage this interior were far-reaching, including regulation of its cultural contents and literal fabric (goat hide preferred to plastic), all in an effort to assure Jewish Israeli visitors access to legible Bedouinness.

The interiority of the Bedouin tent has a long Israeli history, one traceable to the early years of Zionist settlement in Palestine and the Orientalist fantasies in which many Jewish settlers participated.[58] In the discourse of this community, Bedouin were both romanticized for their nomadic lifestyles, which seemed to mount little threat to Zionist territorial claims, but credited with racial similitude to the ancient Hebrews. Thus it was that they disproportionately populated Zionist imaginations in the pre-state period. Travelogues written by members of the Yishuv during the 1920s and 1930s were frequently decorated with stories of Bedouin encounters, many of which occurred within the spatial intimacy of the tent.[59] Some travelogues written for publication provided detailed instructions on how to replicate such interactions, schooling readers in the proper way of entering the tent and greeting the sheikh, how and when to drink the ceremonial coffee, what to discuss in fireside conversations, and how to distinguish friendly from hostile tribes on the basis of visible signs.[60] In subsequent decades, when the so-called Palmach generation engaged in the emulation of Arab cultural practices as a means of performing their indigenousness, many quasi-Bedouin tents appeared on the landscape.[61] Yet this Jewish romance with the Bedouin was highly ambivalent: They were perceived as sites of both cultural value and potential threat alike. Both idioms could be accommodated within Zionism's highly flexible deployment of Orientalism, fluctuating with the demands of Jewish nation making.[62]

Because of the ways that Bedouin culture has been incorporated into a Zionist cosmology, Bedouin tents have long been available to Jewish Israelis in either real or phantasmatic form. Indeed, they constituted the primary Palestinian interior enjoyed by Jewish-Israelis tourists in the decades prior to the emergence of the rural tourism market. Most of the tents in question, however, were radically delocalized and ahistorical forms, erected in Jewish locales and tourist facilities and often staffed by paid performers. Yet the Bedouin tents encouraged by state planners during the 1990s differed from these models, and primarily in geographic ways. That is, in the context of the emerging market, Bedouin tents were being erected within the very heart of Palestinian population centers, often densely populated ones. They were being removed from Jewish-Israeli geographies and hence from Zionist cosmologies in ways that were generating a shift in Israeli cognitive mapping.

Portraits

I have argued that the geography of interiority was structured in tiers, moving inward within the village core from courtyard to living room, and that the degree of market value seemed to accord with the depth of penetration into these interior zones.[63] In this concentric progression, the ultimate and most intimate site was the Palestinian body. Amateur photographs of village inhabitants, shot by architects and planners, were often included in the appendixes of development documents. Most were portraits featuring a single Palestinian subject; most were posed. Some featured only faces, while others included entire figures. All were offered as evidence of a village's tourist potential, appearing alongside architectural sketches or population tallies. The iconography of such portraiture was repetitive and predictable, inscribed with the ethnic markers on which state development was founded. The sitters tended to be dressed in the community's traditional garb, framed by the local landscape. Traces of nonrural modernity such as cars, cement façades, and billboards were typically expunged. Because of the desire for an iconography of the traditional, such images tend to feature an older generation of rural Palestinian men and women among whom traditional clothing was still worn. Posed against a picturesque wall or with a historic farm implement, they reiterated the colonial narrative of a premodern place outside of time.[64] Stripped of proper names and any identifying information, these portraits were offered to readers as synecdochic snapshots of an ethnocultural community whose phenotypes were interchangeable. Placed alongside architectural sketches, such photographs were rendered analogous to them: typical and picturesque instances of the larger village on which development plans focused. Positioned more as bodies than as subjects, these figures betrayed a fantasy of a population stripped of its political claims.

The signs of premodernity employed by these texts were anything but novel. They functioned according to a familiar set of conventions governing ethnic portraiture. Indeed, their citationality was crucial, as it worked to empty these places of local particularity, inserting the portrait as metonym into a broader economy of traditionality, unfettered by Palestinian particulars that threatened to sully market value with the traces of this threatening national identity. Stripped of locality, these images thus functioned as instances of typicality itself. These portraits were also intimate forms. The camera's close-up mimicked the forms of spatial proximity that planners sought to orchestrate in courtyards and living rooms. Although placed at the end of planning documents, these images and the subjects they represented were by no means extraneous. For the state and its private sector affiliates, the value of spatial interiority was dependent upon these subjects. The intimacy that planners sought to construct required their human presence in the tourist site. The small scales envisioned by planners had market value only insofar as they contained Palestinian life conceived of in these iconic, ethnically marked ways. Indeed, in the discourse of development, life and space frequently merged. Spatial intimacy within the small scale was often deemed synonymous with the human intimacy it afforded. Palestinians and their small scales were one.

Most documents tended to abbreviate the history of the village in question. Unsurprisingly, most ignored the larger history on which the rural market depended: that of the 1948–49 War and its destruction of the Palestinian city; of state efforts to prevent the emergence of Palestinian urban formations in the decades after state formation; of discriminatory zoning and land use planning in the rural formations that remained; of the unwanted forms of spatial proximity through overcrowding that were generated by such policies. In the absence of these and other histories, development discourse produced an ontology effect, suggesting that Palestinian Arabs were naturally at home in the village core, the courtyard, and the living room — that is, within rural places and small scales.[65] In these ways, planning discourses also naturalized the legacy of the Palestinian dispossession in 1948–49 and the underdevelopment that followed, practices that secured the status of the village as the central institution of Palestinian daily life within Israel's borders.

I have argued that planning discourses were engaged in the production of space. Yet, in the absence of history, they were also engaged in the production of scale.[66] Through normal planning processes, Palestinian social geographies that had long been forcibly confined to small scales were being both naturalized and fortified. In standard planning discourse, these scales were cast as found objects whose value had been rescued from obscurity by planners and policymakers. The inverse of imperial nostalgia was at work.[67] Rather than mourning spaces lost to modernization, development efforts implicitly celebrated the rescue of Arab villages from vertical expansion and urbanization.

Many histories were obscured in the midst of these naturalizing processes. Development discourses also obfuscated the numerous modalities of Palestinian culture and history that were not circumscribed by the coordinates of village, portraiture, and tradition—histories of places and communities that had been cosmopolitan, well connected, at the intersections of national and global flows of information, capital, and politics prior to the dispossession of 1948–49.[68] The naturalization of village scale was also an attempt to naturalize the scale of the Israeli nation-state and its history, obfuscating its emergence out of a vanquished Palestinian cosmopolitanism.

Interiority and the Oslo Process

The production of scale in the midst of market development can also be read as a response to concurrent politics in the national and regional arenas, especially that of the Oslo process. As I have argued in other chapters, Oslo promised to rescale the national economy, increasing Israel's involvement in regional and global networks of capital and labor.[69] Yet, for the state, rescaling also carried a degree of threat. Greater intimacy with the Arab Middle East also enabled flows of Arab things, persons, and cultures into Israel and flows of Palestinian things and persons from Israel into the region. To some degree, rescaling mitigated the internal Palestinian threat, as it lessened the importance of the nation-state as a spatial container. Yet rescaling also made Palestinian communities within Israel susceptible to insertion in regional, Arab networks. From the state's vantage, such processes threatened to destabilize the nation-state from within.

I want to suggest that the threats posed by national rescaling helped make the geography of interiority necessary. State anxieties about the course of the Oslo process generated an urgent need to freeze scale itself, to contain the Palestinian community living within Israel's borders and thereby forestall some of the unwanted transnational flows that economic liberalization enabled. We can thus read the production of village scale as a spatial fantasy that responded to concurrent political processes. By fortifying village scale, the state sought to quell Oslo's terrifying futures by fixing Palestinians in rural space, by containing Palestinian mobility. As such, development practices in the rural market constituted a discursive instance of what was occurring concurrently in much more violent forms within Israel's Occupied Territories by means of militarized checkpoints, curfews, closures, and travel restrictions. By insisting that Palestinian citizens of Israel were naturally rooted in rural places, the state betrayed its desire to freeze the transnational Arab networks that Oslo had enabled. State discourses about the ontological rootedness of Palestinians in rural places sought to mollify such fears.

At the same time, village spaces were mere instances of a scalar fear that was more national in character. The production of the village scale as discrete and natural, as a spatial container of populations and cultures, also betrayed an analogous fantasy about the Israeli nation-state as a spatial container. It was this scale that was deemed most at risk in the midst of the porous borders and transnational flows that Oslo had unleashed. Scalar production in the rural market revealed a desire to fortify Israeli territory, that of the nation-state as a whole, therein securing Israel's status as a Jewish space, now threatened by regionalization. In the era of a New Middle East, this geography was at risk. Villages were, then, spatial laboratories writ small.

Ethnic Restaurants and Melancholic Citizenship

Above the cash register at Abu Shukry's Restaurant, in the Palestinian village of Abu Ghosh, a photograph of two men is framed under glass. The restaurant's owner narrates its history as he rapidly prepares plates of *hummus* and *ful* in preparation for the lunchtime rush. "That's Prime Minister Moshe Sharett in 1954," he says, washing his hands before removing the photograph for closer inspection. "And that's my grandfather. He was the *mukhtar* [head of local government] of Abu Ghosh and they were like brothers, like close friends."

Parking is scarce on this warm Saturday in 1995 as Jewish Israelis stream into the restaurants for which the village is famous. Seven restaurants, three snack bars, and two bakeries compete for a population of middle-class Jewish Israeli consumers who wait in long lines for what they deem authentic cuisine at affordable prices. On most spring weekends, cars jockey for position in the crowded village center. With neither pedestrian sidewalks nor designated parking lots, traffic jams and accidents are frequent.

The photograph above the cash register is faded and its players unidentified. Indeed, many Jewish customers may overlook it altogether. Yet its function is critical, as it testifies to Abu Ghosh's historic alliance with the Israeli state—an alliance with which most clients are already familiar. At the time of my fieldwork in the mid-1990s, this history of alliance was constantly reiterated in restaurant spaces, through material artifacts and public testimonials by village residents that bore witness to enduring local patriotism. No less than the quality and affordability of the meal, these performances were critical to the market's success, ensuring its appeal among Jewish Israeli clients and safeguarding the very edibility of restaurant fare.

The growth of the Abu Ghosh restaurant sector, and the emergence of ethnic tourism in the Palestinian Galilee, occurred concurrently in the mid-1990s. Both markets were enabled by the cultural desires that Oslo had stimulated, by the reinvigorated appetite for Arab culture, particularly among elite Jewish Israeli consumers, that emerged during this period. Both markets staged an encounter—between Israeli citizens, Palestinian hosts, and Jewish guests—with highly discrepant histories within the nation-state and access to its resources. Yet the markets' political and symbolic economies were markedly distinct in ways that reflected the divergent histories of the villages that housed them. Abu Ghosh was famous (or infamous) for its political collaboration with Zionist institutions in the prestate period, particularly during the 1948–1949 War, and for its allegiance to the state in subsequent decades. The allure of its restaurants was vitally connected to these political coordinates, coordinates dramatized by local Palestinians in an effort to secure market success. This was in sharp distinction to ethnic tourism in the Galilee that took shape in Palestinian villages with histories of strident protest, sometimes enunciated in tourism spaces.

What follows is an ethnographic study of culinary tourism in Abu Ghosh during the mid-1990s.[1] I am interested in how the restaurant sector functioned as a political theater for the performance of what I have been calling national intelligibility. Much of my ethnography focuses on the ways Abu Ghosh residents staged their allegiance to Israel in restaurant spaces. I suggest that such performances be read as melancholic—that is, bespeaking a desire to be marked as normatively national in both juridical and symbolic terms within a nation-state that could not structurally satisfy this longing. I read these displays as performative ones that rehearse the grammar and gestures of dominant nationalism, but with a difference in ways that both dramatize the impossible desire for full Israeliness even as they suggest ways that Israeliness might be configured differently. I suggest that the very repetition of such performances dramatized their impossibility. This is also a study of the culinary coordinates of national intelligibility. I am interested in the shifts in Israeli culinary culture that occurred during the 1990s, particularly the ways that certain kinds of Arab food acquired heightened popularity among Jewish Israeli consumers. This line of inquiry turns on a notion of what I will call *edibility*.[2] The term attempts to demarcate the contingent nature of food and eating in any given context, how what is deemed good to eat within the terms of a prevailing social imaginary is implicated in situated histories, politics, and notions of geography. Edibility is thus the culinary analogue of intelligibility. The *condition of edibility* denotes not merely that a given food is or can be eaten in any literal sense, but that it is popularly considered worthy of consumption. Thus more than consumer taste, in any limited sense, is at issue.[3] Rather, edibility marks the ways certain culinary traditions and ways of cooking acquire social value at a particular moment. This chapter considers the conditions of possibility that enabled Abu Ghosh restaurants to acquire heightened edibility in the mid-1990s and the ways that edibility intersected with issues of nationalism, citizenship, and historical memory. As in prior chapters, this study of Israeli culinary cultures is also interested in the limits of coexistence and full civic equity at this moment in the history of the Israeli nation-state.

In many respects, Abu Ghosh is an atypical Palestinian village. Although it shares a history of disenfranchisement and state-sponsored underdevelopment with other Palestinian communities within the state, it has historically struggled to disidentify as Palestinian by linking its fate to that of the Jewish state. As such, this study of Abu Ghosh is an attempt to complicate the account of Palestinian politics provided in previous chapters. At the same time, it is a response to the resistance paradigm that has dominated scholarly work on Palestine produced over the course of the last few decades — a scholarship that often installs, however inadvertently, an isomorphism effect, whereby Palestinianness is rendered synonymous with resistance culture. This presumed isomorphism has enabled "the Palestinian" to be deployed in leftist scholarship as a sign of the counterhegemonic, broadly construed.[4] While I take seriously the politics of solidarity out of which such scholarship emerges, I am concerned about its homogenizing effects.[5] This turn from the study of resistance to the study of what might be termed *melancholic citizenship* is also an attempt to complicate the literature on performativity with its disproportionate investment in the resistive effects of iterative processes.[6] In Abu Ghosh, the stated project of iteration was different: to situate the iterating subject within the field of the hegemonic. I argue that the failure of this project dramatizes the aporias and disjunctures within hegemonic ideology itself, exposing the violent gaps between Israel's claims to democracy and its status as a Jewish state.

Histories of Patronage

According to village lore, the first restaurant was established on Abu Ghosh's eastern hill in the early 1950s. The number of village restaurants grew gradually over the next few decades, drawing a small but steady Jewish clientele. The market experienced its greatest growth as a result of the increase in Jewish Israeli consumer demand that followed the outbreak of the first Palestinian uprising (1987–93), and with it, the disruption of Jewish Israeli leisure and consumptive practices in the Palestinian territories that had been popularly enjoyed by many since the onset of the occupation in 1967. With the Occupied Territories now deemed too dangerous as a culinary destination, Jewish Israeli consumers sought other alternatives. In the late 1980s and early 1990s, Abu Ghosh emerged as a viable replacement. For Jerusalem residents, it was the closest Palestinian village within the borders of Israel, and its history of political affiliation with the state enabled Jewish Israelis to feel secure as visitors. Even after the formal cessation of the first uprising, coincident with the Oslo Accords of 1993, this replacement principle remained operative, as few Jewish Israelis felt safe returning to West Bank sites that they had frequented in prior decades. It was thus during the 1990s that Abu Ghosh's restaurant sector would enjoy its most precipitous growth.[7] In 1994, the Ministry of Tourism conducted its first survey of development possibilities with an eye to future investment.[8] In 1995, a popular Jerusalem newspaper declared Abu Ghosh "the new old" (*ha-atikah ha-ḥadashah*)—that is, the new alternative to Jerusalem's Old City. In the words of the press, Abu Ghosh had secured its status as the new "hummus empire" of the Jerusalem area.[9]

The Abu Ghosh restaurant sector has multiple histories, with roots that precede the arrival of Zionist settlers in Palestine. Due to the village's location along the historic roadway linking Jaffa to Jerusalem, its political allegiances were successfully wooed by centuries of successive government and local administrations that sought a political foothold in this strategic site, a point of political leverage that won Abu Ghosh the right to collect a tax on travelers crossing through their territory. Indeed, many foreign travelers passed through the village on their journeys between Palestine's major cities, as nineteenth-century travelogues confirm.[10] This history of allegiance between the village and successive administrations set the stage for Abu Ghosh's relationship with Zionist institutions in Palestine, beginning in the early years of the British Mandate in Palestine—a relationship that took the form of active collaboration between the village and Zionist institutions during the course of the 1948–49 War.[11]

The gains of wartime collaboration are difficult to assess.[12] Although Abu Ghosh was one of the few Palestinian villages in the Jerusalem area that was not categorically expelled or razed by the Israeli army during the course of the war (a fate that some scholars have attributed to an Israeli failure to carry out drafted expulsion plans) its history was still marked by dispossession. In July 1948, the army successfully "encouraged" village residents to flee with the promise of postwar resettlement. After the cessation of violence, however, the army actively worked to prevent the incremental return and resettlement of residents.[13] Those discovered on village lands were forcibly deported, and often violently so, for the crime of "infiltration."[14] In a final settlement with the village, most residents in exile were permitted to return, only to find Abu Ghosh's territory greatly diminished following massive state campaigns of land confiscation designed to benefit neighboring Jewish towns and enlarge national reserves.[15] Prominent village residents unsuccessfully appealed to the state on behalf of neighboring villages whose communities remained in exile and sought resettlement.[16] The complexity of this history is belied by its facile rendering in popular Israeli lore, rewritten as a didactic story about the rewards bestowed upon Israel's Arab allies within the national borders: "They supported us and hence made good."

The state's failure to meet its war-time promises did not substantively alter the political landscape in Abu Ghosh. Rather, the decades that followed state formation witnessed continued village identification with the state. Geography played a crucial role in fortifying such affiliations. The dispossession of Palestinians as a result of the 1948–1949 War left Abu Ghosh isolated from other Palestinian communities. Over the course of the decades that followed, the village was increasingly flanked by Jewish settlements: Ma'ale Haḥamisha and Kiryat Anavim, established on Abu Ghosh lands in the 1920s and 1930s; the Jewish community of Mevassert Zion, established in the 1950s and expanding into an affluent Jerusalem suburb in the 1990s; and Telz Stone or Kiryat Ye'arim, founded in 1973 by ultra-orthodox Jews from the United States.[17] This postwar geography catalyzed political disaffiliation from other Palestinians and active affiliation with the Israeli state and normative Israeli social institutions. In formal political terms, this has taken the form of village support for Zionist parties in both local and national elections. In more localized terms, this geography has produced regular contact between Abu Ghosh residents and neighboring Jewish communities. In the mid-1990s, many young male residents of Abu Ghosh sought work in these communities and sometimes patrolled their streets in the uniforms of the volunteer National Guard (*Sherut Leumi*), a role particularly attractive to those small numbers of Palestinian citizens who sought the symbolic and material rewards of army service but were refused by the state.[18] At the same time, female residents of Abu Ghosh frequently met their Jewish neighbors in the village grocery stores they used as inexpensive alternatives or when Jewish shops were closed for Shabbat. And Jewish and Palestinian neighbors in this district often traveled together in the cramped space of shared taxis on their hourly runs from Abu Ghosh, Telestone, and Ma'ale Haḥamisha to downtown West Jerusalem. Some left-wing Jews trumpeted these shared rides as evidence of coexistence on a local scale, a complement to the regional diplomacy of this period.

In the mid-1990s, Jewish Israelis constituted the decided majority of Abu Ghosh's restaurant clientele. Unlike the ethnic tourism market emerging concurrently in the Galilee, which initially served elite consumers with left-wing political leanings, the visitor population in Abu Ghosh was relatively diverse. Liberal politics was not a prerequisite, nor were elite cultural pretenses or pedigrees. Indeed, many Jewish clients actively distanced themselves from the coexistence politics of the Israeli left, noting their distaste for the forms of cultural tourism under way in the Galilee and their unwillingness to spend the night in Arab homes: "Too dangerous," they said. While many restaurants boasted of their celebrity clientele, including Israeli television personalities and prominent members of Parliament, the village's affordable restaurants also served a more modestly middle-class population. Although the majority of customers were residents of the Jerusalem area, the village's location just off the main Tel Aviv–Jerusalem highway also wooed many visitors from elsewhere who stopped for lunch on their drive between urban centers. Business was relatively slow during winter months but picked up in spring and summer on warm afternoons. Most visitors came on Shabbat and on national holidays and as residual traffic from the biannual music festival held on village grounds. On some holiday weekends, the number of customers reached the low thousands. For a village of some five thousand residents, these numbers were enormously significant, generating needed income for dozens of local families and converting Abu Ghosh's small geographic core into a place of cramped and constant interaction between Jewish and Palestinian citizens of the state. Even as culinary tourism flourished in the 1990s, Abu Ghosh continued to suffer from explicit state policies of underdevelopment and neglect: many roads were still unpaved and many neighborhoods lacked sidewalks, streetlights, and even adequate sewage systems, signs of underdevelopment that were typically read as markers of genuine rural living by restaurant patrons.

For many Jewish Israelis during the mid-1990s, the Abu Ghosh restaurant sector and the emerging ethnic tourism market in the Palestinian Galilee were perceived as radically discrepant entities. In part, the difference lay in their consumer offerings: Abu Ghosh was attractive for its food, particularly for its *hummus*, while the Galilee offered visitors cultural authenticity and intimacy in various forms.[19] Yet the substantive difference was of a more historical and political kind. Tourism in the Palestinian Galilee was predicated on a substantial shift in the political landscape, whereby Arab places once deemed dangerous were remade as sites of Jewish consumer pleasure. Tourism in Abu Ghosh was predicated on a very different political rationale. By contrast, it depended on the promise of political continuity in any Arab place whose allegiance to the Zionist project predated state formation. Jewish Israeli patronage hinged on it.

It's just after three o'clock on a Friday afternoon in late September 1995 and the streets of Abu Ghosh are already bustling with restaurant clientele. I am sitting on the porch of the Sweet Things Bakery in the crowded village center, where three modest restaurants, two grocery stores, and the mayor's office compete for space along a narrow road in desperate need of repair. On the hillside above the bakery, old stone houses cower under the weight of modern cement additions, built in the past twenty years to meet the needs of growing families. Scattered fruit trees in the valley below are all that remain of Abu Ghosh's once expansive orchards, expropriated after 1948 to build the growing state.

Abu Ra'id, the bakery proprietor, greets his Jewish clients in fluent Hebrew as they arrive to buy *baqlawa* for the weekend, carried away in Styrofoam containers.[20] Wearing sunglasses and carrying his portable phone in hand, Abu Ra'id addresses the regulars by name.

"Zvi! Zvi Mendel, . . . How are you?" He shakes the hand of a stocky man in yarmulke and blue jeans. In the absence of designated parking areas, his Volvo sedan blocks the entrance to the adjacent market.

"Fine, fine. . . . and *mazel tov*, congratulations."

"Thanks." Abu Ra'id's youngest son is getting married next month and he invited Zvi to the wedding, as he did most of his regular clients. "I like this place," Zvi tells me, walking out with half a kilo of *baqlawa* for the weekend. "It's quiet here. No trouble."

Sweet Things is one of two bakeries selling traditional Palestinian Arab sweets in Abu Ghosh: baqlawa, a rich pastry layered with nuts; *kanafe*, honey soaked and stuffed with a salty cheese; *ka'ak*, date-filled cookies; *mahlabi*, a corn flour confectionery with rose water. This bakery is the more central of the two and better able to attract first-time clients who wander through the village after meals at neighboring restaurants. Business from Abu Ghosh residents is strong during the Muslim festivals and feasts and during the celebration of weddings, births, and homecomings, when such sweets are traditionally consumed. But Abu Ra'id's business relies largely on the patronage of his Jewish Israeli clients who come in large numbers on weekends and holidays from nearby Jewish communities and towns in the Jerusalem area.

"They like it here because we aren't like other villages," he says, as we drink coffee on the porch that borders the parking lot. "Abu Ghosh is a quiet place, and has been since the establishment of the state." In the Hebrew lexicon on which he draws, "quiet" (*shaket*) connotes the absence of radical politics, describing a place that hasn't agitated against the state like those a mere fifteen miles away in the West Bank.

"Some residents serve in the army, and many volunteer for Sherut Leumi, the National Guard." Abu Ra'id pauses over the noise of honking cars, as visitors maneuver aggressively through the crowded village center. "We have rights just like the Jews and excellent relations with our neighbors." His family had forty dunams of land prior to 1948, the vast majority of which is now under the jurisdiction of neighboring Jewish towns. "There's no resentment here," he says. "We gave them our land by choice."

Inside the bakery, Abu Ra'id's twenty-four-year-old son, Kamal, is preparing a round tray of *kanafe*. He heats sugar and water in a two-quart can over the fire to make the syrup, adding lemon juice and the traditional red dye. Cook twenty minutes, he says, until the syrup thickens, then pour over the baked pastry. The job is usually done by the Palestinian workers they employ from East Jerusalem where labor comes cheaper, but they are out for the day. "We get our supplies from a Tel Aviv distributor because the quality is better," Kamal explains. "And we trust the Jews. With the Arabs, you're never sure."

After frequent afternoons in the Sweet Things Bakery, I have become accustomed to such testimonials and their stock vocabularies of allegiance. When business was slow, Kamal and his friends would cluster on the porch and describe the village's support for the Zionists during their prestate struggle in stories passed down from their parents, intended both for my ears and those of their Jewish clients. Over coffee and cigarettes, they spoke of the number of young men serving in the Israeli army, border police, and national guard; of their mistrust of Arab workers; of their disaffiliation from Palestinians. Some guests would respond to their narratives. But more often, their didactic tales constituted a kind of aesthetic backdrop to baqlawa and coffee, a constitutive part of the flavor of the place. Guests seemed to take comfort in the predictability, in the very repetition of this familiar discourse.

On an unusually warm day in late October, as I sit with Abu Ra'id over my tape recorder and list of questions, we are joined by a small group of Ashkenazi Israeli men in their late twenties who order coffee and baqlawa and light up their cigarettes. Abu Ra'id has greeted them in Hebrew, and they've answered in the Arabic slang that is a popular component of the Hebrew vernacular, modified to suit its sounds and grammar.

I ask them about their knowledge of the language.

"Arabic? We speak the kind of Arabic you use for bargaining over prices." They respond casually to my questions, as if among friends.

"We also speak Intifada Arabic. But that's what we used in the territories [ha-shtaḥim]. It's not for this place."

I'm not familiar with "Intifada Arabic" and I ask for clarification.

One answers willingly, in a dispassionate Hebrew: "You know, things like: 'Shut off your car' or 'Open your trunk.'"

Others from the group collaborate in the telling: "And words like 'curfew' or phrases like 'Get out of the car.'"

Their list builds slowly at first, like the recitation of phrases once committed to memory in a foreign-language class and now rather awkward on the tongue. Abu Ra'id interrupts, to remind them of expressions they've forgotten: "There's also 'Open the door.'"

Building on his suggestion, they begin to pick up speed, adding to the compendium: "And 'Give me your I.D.'"

"Or 'Hands above your head.'"

Over coffee and hot kanafe in Abu Ghosh's late afternoon sun, Jewish customers and Palestinian host rehearse these national lessons together.

Identifications

This scene, this collaborative chronicle of the daily violence of the Israeli occupation, was not unusual. The porches of bakeries and the cramped spaces near cash registers frequently functioned as intimate stages for the joint performance of national allegiance, spaces in which Palestinian hosts labored to situate their village within the Israeli political consensus. Through such practices, Palestinian waiters and restaurant proprietors established their familiarity with dominant Israeli lexicons and structures of feeling, marking their disaffiliation as Palestinians and loyalty to the

Jewish state. As I have suggested, these scenes were frequent and their grammar repetitive. Most returning clients had witnessed or participated in these rituals multiple times before. Although stale and lacking in spontaneity, they were nonetheless critical. Through the reiteration of these familiar narratives and nationalist gestures, Jewish patronage was made possible.

Such rituals were neither restricted to the Abu Ghosh restaurant sector nor unique to the 1990s. They had occurred in multiple forms and spaces since 1948: in the history of support for Zionist institutions and ideologies; in electoral allegiance to Zionist parties; in popular participation in secular Zionist commemorations, such as Israeli Independence Day;[21] and, conversely, in popular disidentification with Palestinian struggles and ideologies, at least in public forums. Many bakery and restaurant owners adorned their walls with some of Israel's most familiar national artifacts, such as photos of Jewish Israeli statesmen and emblems of Zionist parties, and recounted their intimate relations with some of Israel's most prominent political leaders. "Many prime ministers have eaten here," they would say, as Jewish clients waited within earshot for their orders. "Some of them even visited our home." Such artifacts and testimonials built consumer confidence, enabling Jewish guests to feel comfortable in Arab spaces they had been taught to fear in a visceral politics of the body.

Local fidelity to the Jewish state was perhaps most powerfully enunciated through rites of personal identification. In the 1990s, some Palestinian men from the village wore Jewish stars around their necks or adopted Jewish names for use outside the village, whereby Mohammad became Moshe. Such practices of passing were efforts to prevent police harassment and the surveillance of the Jewish public. They were also thought to carry an erotic charge, aiding young male residents in their efforts to attract Jewish girlfriends. Most men and women refused to identify publicly as Arab and especially as Palestinian. Some anchored this disidentification in history, tracing Abu Ghosh's ancestry to Yemen and Russia.[22] Because restaurants were the primary sites for contact with Jewish outsiders, such rites were often staged here. In turn, because most laborers in the restaurant sector were men, the women of Abu Ghosh were largely denied access to the symbolic capital that these rites conferred.

Such rituals of identification had limited efficacy, at best. Outside the space of the village, they were at odds with the ways local residents were marked by the state, with the official identity papers that marked them as Arab, and with the practices of the Israeli police, who rarely differentiated among Palestinians when security was at issue. In the mid-1990s, reports of police harassment were frequently relayed to me by Abu Ghosh residents as stories of mistaken identity: "I was in Jerusalem, and I saw these kids from the village being held against a wall by the border police. So I go over and say the guys are from Abu Ghosh, and that it's a different set of rules for us. But they asked me for my I.D. and forced me up against the wall, too." Such testimonials were frequent. Both the urgency that attended their telling and the detail with which they were recounted sought to expose what was perceived as a state error, their mislabeling as "Arab." At the same time, they suggested something of the intensity with which many Abu Ghosh residents experienced their identification with Jewish Israel. It was because of this identification that Abu Ghosh residents also faced possible retribution from other Palestinians, both residents of Israel and those of the Occupied Territories. More often than not, retribution took the form of shame rather than violence.

In the village's restaurant sector, Jewish Israeli clients participated in this discourse through their labors to rewrite the ethnonational identity of the village. This rewriting frequently happened through disavowal. Most responded with considerable incredulity when asked about the significance of their patronage as Jewish Israelis in an "Arab" village. "Arab village? I don't feel that it's an Arab village." "We just don't think of it that way." "I didn't come to see an Arab village," many said, "I just came to eat hummus." Often, the question was met with considerable rancor, as the terms of my inquiry had refused a founding Israeli logic about the place, and our interview would frequently end there. Those willing to continue our conversation often spoke, by contrast, of Abu Ghosh's insistently "Israeli" identity, thereby affirming the village's political location within the national consensus. "Abu Ghosh?" as one visitor queried, with considerable surprise. "It's not part of the Arab sector [*migzar aravi*]. They've been with the state since the independence war." These were complicated maneuvers, whereby the village's pro-Zionist history was translated into ethnonational markers and genealogies. Despite advances in the Oslo process during this period, many Jewish Israelis still understood "Arab" as a sign of enmity. The term "Palestinian" was not used in reference to this place.

At times, Jewish Israeli clients focused their labor of historical revision on religious rather than ethnonational terms. The following exchange with a middle-aged man from the Tel Aviv area as he waited in line for restaurant service during the Shabbat morning rush, was typical of many:

RLS: Can you identify the religion of this population?

CUSTOMER: Here? They are mostly Christians, with a small percentage of Muslims. You'll notice that you don't see them walking around with *kuffiyes* on.

RLS: [pause] Actually, it's a largely Muslim village.

CUSTOMER: Okay . . . but it's not a *Muslim* village, you understand? It's an Arab village with Muslims in it.

In this account, Islam rather than Arabness was identified as the locus of enmity, cast as synonymous with radical Palestinian nationalism, represented metonymically through the figure of the *kuffiye*, or traditional Palestinian head scarf.[23] This exchange also suggests something about the status of historical claims within this discourse of dis/identification. While such claims were marshaled as evidence of local fidelity, the rebuttal of such claims did little to shake Jewish perceptions. As with the ways "Arab" functioned as a sign of enmity, Abu Ghosh's perceived Israeliness was resistant to relabeling. Nor was this a political characterization, many patrons insisted; indeed, few wanted to talk politics during their lunchtime visit and greatly resented my invitation to do so. Instead, Israeliness was positioned as a virtually ontological fact about the place. It was naturally so.

As the exchange above suggests, Jewish consumer knowledge of local history was sparse at best. Few could recount the details of Abu Ghosh's collaboration during the 1948–49 War or the history of local exile and eventual resettlement. Recent history was easier to rehearse, even if only in vague terms. My questions about village identification frequently elicited narratives about the first Palestinian uprising or Intifada: "In Abu Ghosh, when the Intifada started, there wasn't anything bad [*lo beseder*] going on here: no terrorists, no Hamas members. I've always said, if you want a good example of coexistence, go to Abu Ghosh. Why do you think I've had connections with these people for so many years?" For others, it was Abu Ghosh's electoral history that was cited as evidence of its location within the national consensus: "They're part of the country, just like I am. They support the same prime minister. And they're doing well. They have a real economy, not like those agricultural villages. . . . They want to be Israelis, and it's good for them." This characterization was common. The need to substantiate the village's difference from other Arab places and constituents, and thereby make Jewish consumption and patronage possible, often yielded the fiction of village affluence, the account of a place well rewarded by the state for its nationalism. Interestingly, this story was radically at odds with abundant visual evidence: unpaved streets, broken roads, lack of sidewalks, streetlights, or public landscaping. Like the facts of religious demography, the details of visual evidence were overwritten by the desires of hosts and guests to inscribe the village into the national consensus.

The Condition of Edibility

What did such performances of allegiance work to secure? In the most basic terms, they enabled Jewish Israelis to feel comfortable patronizing Abu Ghosh eateries, establishing the village as a safe and appealing culinary destination. Yet the function of such rites was more particular still. By altering perceptions of the village, they also affected the ways its cuisine was understood. Such rites, particularly those performed within the spaces of restaurants, effectively inscribed local food with national value, conferring a kind of nationalist meaning on the act of consumption itself. These rites helped shape the edibility of restaurant fare, rendering the food intelligible in normative, national terms.

Yet the condition of edibility also relied on a long history of Jewish Israeli culinary desires and consumptive practices which established the precedent for Jewish patronage in Abu Ghosh. This history extends back to the early years of Zionist settlement in Palestine — notably, to the Orientalist imaginations that circulated within Jewish settler society of the 1920s and 1930s, particularly among immigrants of the Second Aliyah.[24] These imaginations included a robust culinary component, such as the emulation of Bedouin fireside cooking practices, coffee rituals, and cooking implements, glorified as instances of ancient Israeli culture and as tools for the production of the New Hebrew.[25] Jewish settlers were already visiting Palestinian eateries during the prestate period, save during times of political instability, as documented in numerous travel narratives from the period. And although Jewish Israeli travel beyond Israel's borders was no longer legally possible after 1948, the desire for Palestinian food could still be met. During the first decades after state formation, Israeli army officers were known to enjoy Palestinian food in villages governed by the highly restrictive military government (1948–66), to which all Palestinians inside Israel were subject. So prevalent was their consumption in cafés, restaurants, and private Palestinian homes (often forcibly so) in the very midst of military rule, that it was regulated by Israeli commanding officers who issued "strict orders on gatherings and meals in Arab villages."[26]

The Israeli landscape underwent multiple changes in the two decades following state formation, changes which made Arab culinary traditions intelligible in new ways. Although European food remained the Israeli norm during these decades, a norm fortified by institutions like the World Zionist Organization and the Israeli army, the Israeli national diet was heavily impacted by the mass emigration of Mizrahi Jews to Israel during the 1950s.[27] This process was complex and contradictory. On the one hand, state institutions sought to quell the "corrupted eating habits" of the "Oriental" population through reeducation.[28] At the same time, this shift in the Israeli social landscape had the effect of introducing Middle Eastern and North African culinary traditions into the mainstream Israeli diet, a process predicated on a disavowal of the Arab provenance of such traditions, whereby Mizrahi cuisine was marked merely as Jewish immigrant fare. One can tell a similar history about the growing popularity of *falafel* during these decades, a process enabled by an obfuscation of its Arab roots (see figure 15).[29]

Yet the condition of edibility in Abu Ghosh restaurants is also linked to histories of Israeli leisure and consumption in the occupied Palestinian territories, a history that can be traced to the immediate aftermath of the 1967 war, and one which Jewish patrons referenced with considerable nostalgia.[30] The impetus for travel into the territories was multiple. First and foremost, it was propelled by a desire to get a glimpse of territories and sites to which Israeli Jews had been denied access since 1948. While

Falafel — Israel's national snack

Figure 15. Culinary patriotism. A popular Israeli tourist postcard.

many visited sites of biblical importance, or hiked in landscapes they had enjoyed prior to state formation, large numbers were motivated by consumptive desires. Such desires were illustrated in the Israeli popular press a mere two weeks after the cessation of wartime violence:

> Irking visitors to the Old City yesterday [25 June 1967] was the fact that they were forbidden from purchasing West Bank goods. In the bazaars behind the Damascus gate, through which thousands of tourists wound their way to reach the Church of the Holy Sepulcher, the local populations scrupulously refused to trade against Israeli or foreign hard currency. The *Jerusalem Post* was the only item that could be bought with Israeli money. The magnificent figs and great variety of spices were "out of bounds" for Israelis and tourists. Mayor Kollek promised that this tourist problem too would be shortly overcome.[31]

Despite bans on Israeli consumption of goods in the newly Occupied Territories, and the punitive actions faced by violators, the press of the period reported shelves stripped clean of souvenirs and "cola and chocolate sold in large quantities."[32] "Most of the tourists went shopping with a vengeance in spite of the official ban," one paper reported, "buying up fruit, vegetables, glassware, jars, chewing gum and pencils with Israeli currency."[33] Initially, Jerusalem's Old City was the locus of the shopping frenzy, as "mass[es] of sightseers and bargain hunters surg[ed] through the narrow alleys."[34] Mass consumption gradually spread to other West Bank locales, as Israeli visitors "descended" on "statues, soap and the rest."[35] The Israeli media spoke of a "shopping invasion."[36] In the service of these shoppers, articles documented the best place to drink European-style coffee in the Old City, where to buy "Indian dates [Tamarind]" and Italian shoes,[37] and recommended restaurants in Hebron and Bethlehem, most of which were already mobbed with Israelis. "When we got to Bethlehem," one reporter noted, "we saw all of Dizengoff [Street in Tel Aviv] eating hummus and pickles."[38] Some journalists had already begun bemoaning the absence of "authentic" Arab goods, such as had been available in Palestinian markets prior to 1948.[39] Indeed, as one lamented, many of the goods now available in Jerusalem's Old City had been imported from China.[40]

Consumption took two forms, primarily. The early days of the Israeli tourist frenzy in the war's immediate aftermath saw a run on souvenirs, culinary delights, and luxury goods. Next came the demand for the household goods and appliances that could be purchased at a fraction of their Israeli prices. "First we bought transistors, cosmetics, straw baskets, and men's shirts," wrote one journalist, "and even English salt at a pharmacy. Today, the prices have already gone up a little, but you still won't find your friends at Israeli stores. They [the West Bank stores] are still tens of percentages away from the Israeli prices."[41] Although prices rose rapidly, and despite Israeli taxes levied on goods purchased in the Occupied Territories, the rush to consume was not tempered.[42] In mid-July, one month after the war's cessation, the "scope of Israeli shopping in the West Bank" was valued at 25 million Liras per month.[43] Jewish merchants and sellers complained that the magnitude of Israeli purchases in the territories was devastating their profits.[44] When Gaza City opened to Israeli visitors, headlines announced "Thirty-Five Thousand Israelis Spent a 'Shopping Shabbat' in Gaza." The article was vivid in its description: "The Israelis fell on the shops . . . and bought everything, almost without comprehension. The stream of buying mounted to such an extent that quickly one saw on the outskirts of town, porters traveling full of goods from the warehouses and apartments of the merchants."[45]

For some press commentators, the consumptive frenzy was a source of collective shame. "What kind of spiritual drive has pushed these men and women . . . to buy, buy, buy?" they mused. "I have no objection," another noted, "to a population denied the right to visit certain places for twenty years. But must we descend on every shop to buy things, whether we need them or not, as if we're a country in need or in hunger?"[46] In other accounts, mass consumption seemed to demonstrate the benign intentions of the Israeli nation vis-à-vis its occupied population: "For three weeks they [the Arabs] looked on as Israelis in increasing numbers flocked to [the Old City], and found them without the arrogance of conquerors, a nation of curious sightseers and seekers of modest bargains."[47] In this account, Israeli consumption was thought to undercut Palestinian fears of a repressive occupation. Indeed, taken together, the Israeli press's exuberant attention to the scene of consumption was guided by a similar logic, however implicitly. The sheer proliferation of such accounts worked to obscure Israel's relationship to the Palestinian Occupied Territories, recasting violence and repressive power through the language of consumption, leisure, and exploration. They functioned as anticonquest narratives, in which accounts of pleasure and consumer desires replaced those of violent incursion.

Israeli travel through the Palestinian territories continued through the 1970s and 1980s, although with lesser urgency. The popularity of East Jerusalem's Old City, which was increasingly marketed by the Israeli Ministry of Tourism as an "Israeli" site, remained strong among Jewish Israeli consumers, who flocked to its restaurants, cafés, and markets.[48] Smaller but still substantial numbers of Israeli Jews and Palestinians visited the markets and restaurants of major Palestinian cities, particularly those of East Jerusalem, Hebron, Bethlehem, Jericho, and Nablus.[49]

As I have noted, such itineraries came to a rather decisive end with the onset of the first Palestinian uprising in 1987. For most Israeli Jews, save territorial nationalists, consumption and leisure in the West Bank were now too dangerous to pursue. Such was the sentiment expressed in a popular joke of the period, a joke printed in the Israeli media in 1988, as the Palestinian uprising was gaining force and international visibility:

A : Where is it better to buy *falafel*, in Kfar Saba [Israel] or Qalqilya [West Bank]?

B: In Qalqilya.

A: Why?

B: Because you get the bottle for free.[50]

The bottle referenced here is that of the Molotov cocktail, one of the weapons of choice deployed by Palestinians during the first uprising. This joke evoked the history of Jewish Israeli eating in the Palestinian West Bank, a history familiar to Israeli readers. Indeed, the joke routes the outbreak of the Palestinian uprising through a history of Jewish leisure in the territories, illustrating a shift from the bottle as Israeli commodity to the bottle as Palestinian weapon. As such, it suggests the extent to which Israeli consumer practices had been altered by the course of political events.

For many Abu-Ghosh patrons, these histories of consumption constituted an important precedent for their visit. Many spoke of days spent wandering through the markets of Jerusalem's Old City and of frequent visits to Bethlehem and Ramallah for hummus and cheap consumer goods. One middle-aged Jewish patron from Tel Aviv, enjoying a solitary lunch on a quiet afternoon, described his postarmy years spent wandering through the West Bank, dropping acid and enjoying its restaurants. "But we couldn't go after the Intifada [broke out]," he remarked wistfully, echoing the sentiments of many. "You were afraid of getting knifed."

Culinary Histories

The Israeli culinary landscape was undergoing profound changes in the 1990s, many of which were at a considerable remove from the growth of Abu Ghosh as a restaurant sector. The changes took multiple forms. In accordance with the boom in the Israeli economy that followed the Oslo Accords and the growth of a new cadre of nouveau riche, this decade witnessed the flourishing of haute cuisine in Israel, a trend that ran counter to the historic Israeli disdain for fine dining and foreign fare.[51] Although its origins could be traced to the 1970s and 1980s, it was only during the 1990s that gourmet and internationally inspired food gained a substantive foothold in the Israeli marketplace. What some termed a "culinary revolution" was also made possible by the migration of young Israeli chefs to culinary institutes in Europe and North America and by the growing number of elite Israelis traveling to Europe and returning with tastes honed on its fare, a phenomenon that substantively began in the 1980s.[52] The Israeli culinary landscape was also being Americanized during this decade, with the arrival of franchises such as McDonald's, Starbucks, Burger King, Dunkin Donuts, and Pizza Hut. Although many exited the Israeli marketplace after the recession that followed the second Palestinian uprising, their presence in the 1990s challenged national notions of taste even as they disrupted the visual landscape of urban and rural centers.[53] Americanization was also credited for the fusion cooking that emerged in chic Israeli restaurants during this period, as internationally trained chefs combined Middle Eastern and European culinary arts and ingredients in highly unorthodox ways.[54] Nor were such changes occurring only in Israel's upper echelons. The massive immigration into Israel from the former Soviet Union also had a significant impact on the Israeli culinary scene. These years saw sizeable growth in the pork industry, which also catered to the growing population of foreign workers, and the emergence of Israel's first nonkosher supermarket chain (Tiv Ta'am), specializing in pork products.[55] Both were actively challenged by Israel's ultra-orthodox parties, in and out of court.[56]

Jewish Israelis were also enjoying Palestinian food in different ways during this decade, if on a smaller scale. Part of what changed was the geography of normative Israeli culinary desire—that is, the places that Israeli Jews went for such fare and the meanings they associated with these places. In part, this geographic shift was manifest in a new Jewish interest, albeit socially marginal, in rural Palestinian Arab places within Israel as culinary destinations, an interest that correlated with shifting state and popular Jewish perceptions of Israel's Palestinian population, and the forms of cultural tourism that such political shifts had generated. Palestinian restaurants in Jaffa and Haifa had long been favored destinations among Jewish Israeli eaters. So, too, were restaurants on the outskirts of rural Palestinian villages, notably those in the Galilee that were easily accessible from the road without requiring the consumer to enter the village's geographic center. But now, consumers began to visit Palestinian restaurants and informal eateries within the very heart of rural Galilee villages. Consumption of this kind took two forms, primarily. First, it occurred in the context of the rural festivals that were being organized

Figure 16.
Edibility on
display. Photo-
graph of Abu
Ghosh pastries
published in
Kol ha-Ir on
3 April 1995.
PHOTOGRAPH:
NOGA RAVIV.

within Israel. The first annual Olive Festival was launched in 1995, bringing hundreds of Jewish Israeli visitors to participate in the harvest, visit
historic presses, and learn about olive oil production—or so brochures
promised. In 1998, the Food Trail Festival enjoyed its first year, offering
tours organized around culinary themes through Palestinian and Jewish
villages alike, inviting guests to enjoy "the authentic taste of breakfast in
the Arab village of Kawkab" and "the *baqlawa* of Dayr Hannah."[57] Palestinian food was also being made available outside the festival circuit.
This period also witnessed the growth of an informal restaurant economy staged in the living rooms and courtyards of private Palestinian families who were eager to capitalize on the rise of ethnic tourism. By mid-
decade, discussion of these informal eateries was beginning to appear in
the mainstream media, and their popularity began to soar. The cuisine of
"the Hamoud family in Beit Jan" was now profiled in national food guides
alongside celebrated restaurants in Haifa, Tel Aviv, and Jerusalem.[58] Like

the emergence of ethnic tourism in the Palestinian Galilee, this attention to rural Palestinian food and culinary production marked a decisive shift in Jewish Israeli tourist logics.

Jewish Israeli consumers were also being invited into Palestinian kitchens in more figurative ways. The mainstream Israeli press offered the novice cook detailed instructions on the preparation of Arab, Druze, and sometimes explicitly "Palestinian" food.[59] Newspapers explored "The Druze Kitchen in Your Home," with a brief history of Druze culinary traditions and descriptions of "the secret of Arab *za'tar*," the fragrant mixture of hyssop and sesame seeds, while providing tips on how to recognize its freshness.[60] They provided recipes for *maklubeh*—the "Arab specialty" of chicken, lamb, and eggplant—and offered suggestions on pickling olives, noting that "Arab women generally soak [them] in rainwater."[61] Such recipes and instructional narratives often gestured toward regional traditions. Readers learned the best ways to grill *chamuli*, a cheese that "originated with the Bedouins of Arabia and Syria," and tips for using *tabil*, "a popular Tunisian spice mixture," in seasoning their "Middle Eastern meat and vegetable dishes."[62] The place of Abu Ghosh within this new culinary regime was most clearly illustrated by the 1996 publication of what was hailed as "the first Israeli-Arab cookbook" in Hebrew, comprising recipes from the kitchen of a celebrated Abu Ghosh chef and edited by the premier Israeli food critic, Nira Russo.[63] The text presumed a Jewish Israeli reader unfamiliar with the landscape of Arab culinary traditions, for whom even the most rudimentary histories of taste and modes of food preparation had to be explained.

This new culinary geography had other dimensions as well. Arab food was also being made available in elite restaurants in cosmopolitan centers. By the late 1990s, traditional Arab dishes were emerging alongside the haute cuisine of France in some of Tel Aviv's most trendy bistros under the sign of fusion cooking. "Shrimp soup, in the Provencal style," "a cold zabaglione . . . [with] Marsala wine," and "*mahlabi*, that classic Arab dessert," could be sampled as part of a single meal in fashionable Israeli eateries.[64] "To my great pleasure," wrote a prominent Jewish Israeli restaurant critic in 1998, "chef [Haim] Cohen continues to delight with his marriage of French, Italian, North African and local Mediterranean ingredients and cooking methods," noting that a typical meal opened with fettuccine primavera and closed with "the restaurant's interpretation of the North

African *kada'iff* pastry, served with hot figs and cardamom ice cream."[65] This hybrid culinary regime had multiple and sometimes contradictory ideological valences. It was often delineated by hegemonic ethnonational typologies, by which "Druze" was differentiated from "Arab" cooking. Yet the emphasis on fusion cooking also refused state interdictions against cultural mixing, blurring the lines between European and Middle Eastern ingredients and culinary histories.

These shifts in elite taste and consumption were intimately tied to political changes on both national and regional scales. As with the emergence of ethnic tourism in the Galilee, this culinary regime had been authorized, however implicitly, by the Oslo process. Regional diplomacy, in other words, had sanctioned certain kinds of gastronomic desires. In turn, the limits of such desires also had their root in political logics. For even as the Israeli press alerted readers to Tunisian and Syrian culinary histories, it largely ignored Palestinian cuisine and culinary traditions — or, more pointedly, those explicitly identified as such. And even as Jewish consumers began exploring Arab and Druze eateries in Israel's Galilee region during the mid-1990s, few were returning to once popular restaurants in East Jerusalem and Bethlehem. More than safety was at issue. The taste for these places had declined alongside their political marginalization.

The Abu Ghosh restaurant sector of the mid-1990s was enabled by these larger culinary trends. As such, its condition of edibility was haunted by a central contradiction. Although Jewish patrons came to Abu Ghosh for authentic Palestinian Arab food, having honed their taste in Palestinian territories, their patronage relied on a disavowal of the village's Palestinian or Arab identity. Thus, although most conceded that the food was Arab in character, they insisted that the village was not. As a description of Abu Ghosh, the terms Arab and Palestinian were vociferously refused. The national designator provided in their stead was flimsy at best. Although Abu Ghosh was identified by patrons as Israeli, and although its residents were implicitly required to perform their Israeli allegiance in restaurant spaces, few patrons would support full civic equity for its residents. Few were willing to advance a critique of Israel's uneven democracy. Few were invested in redressing its inequities.

For Jewish patrons, these contradictions had no substantial effects. For their Palestinian hosts, the gap between inclusion within a culinary regime and exclusion from the symbolic and juridical institutions of the nation-state often generated considerable melancholy. Few gave voice to this particular melancholy in restaurant spaces, as commercial success was at stake. But, at times, other melancholic narratives were enunciated in their stead.

Serving the Nation

In the fall of 1995, The Florida restaurant was closed by the Abu Ghosh local council on charges of improper building and failure to obtain necessary permits. On a warm Saturday in 1995, I sit with the restaurant's aging proprietor along the row of windows that flank his empty dining room, a room that once served over a hundred guests at a single seating. From this vantage on Abu Ghosh's eastern hillside, we look out over the southern slopes of Jerusalem and the neighboring kibbutz of Ma'ale Haḥamisha, built on land once owned by Abu Ghosh residents. As we watch from the window, a steady stream of lunchtime customers compete for parking in the narrow lot of his competitor. This neighboring restaurant is the village's oldest, serving Jewish and Palestinian clients in the Jerusalem area since the 1950s. During temperate months, it cannot accommodate consumer demand. Many clients are forced to wait outside or venture into the village center for a less celebrated alternative.

Yusif Ibrahim, proprietor of The Florida, was born in Abu Ghosh in 1931. In a Hebrew decorated with antiquated gentility, he describes his personal history in the tourism industry, laboring in some of Israel's most prestigious hotels. Ibrahim moved to the Tel Aviv Hilton in the 1950s, where he was employed as a busboy. He worked primarily as waitstaff in hotel restaurants, dutifully serving his country in every establishment.

"I've been a citizen of this state for forty years and I was always in hotels," he says, as we watch the growing crowds in the restaurant next door. "I started in room service at the King David Hotel. I was young and the managers loved me. When an important guest came to the hotel, they took him to me for service. President Weizman visited when I was working there, so I looked after him and paid him special attention."

His narrative circles repetitively around stories of loyal service to Israel's most prominent leaders, stories liberally decorated with proper names: "I met [Israeli Prime Minister] Ben Gurion in 1956 when I worked at the Sharon hotel. We were good friends. He would say, 'Where are you from? How are you? Are you married?' I would always sit and talk with him because he loved me. And I'd sit with his son Amos when he came to the hotel. We were like family, you understand?" He pauses to light a cigarette. "Moshe Sharett also came there for dinner when he was foreign minister."

Even his cadence is repetitive, betraying the narrative's multiple re-hearsals and reiterations. I ask for a clarification on dates, but Ibrahim finds such details unimportant.

"I served all the heads of state, wherever I worked: [Prime Ministers] Golda Meir and Levi Eshkol—everybody. I gave them good service, and they loved me for it. Back then, there was no difference between Arab and Jew.

"They weren't scared to be served by an Arab," he says, using a term of self-identification that most Abu Ghosh residents actively disavow, particularly the younger generation. "They loved me as their own son. I also served [Defense Minister] Moshe Dayan and [Prime Minister] Menachem Begin."

I ask Ibrahim about his family's experience of the 1948 war. He responds reluctantly, the details emerging slowly and selectively. His parents were working in East Jerusalem in the late 1940s where his father managed a restaurant, and both were caught in the city when fighting began. Fearful of returning to Abu Ghosh along the Jerusalem corridor where the battle was the most intense, they stayed in East Jerusalem through the course of the war. In 1949, when the eastern city became Jordanian territory, re-turn passage to Israel required permission from the Israeli government. Ibrahim sought reunification with his parents for six years without suc-cess.

"I was working in the Tel Aviv Hilton in 1955 when the interior minister came for lunch. He always sat at my table and we used to talk. So when he asked me how I was doing, I explained that I was very happy living in Israel [ba-arets] but sad about the absence of my parents. He said, 'Come to my office and I'll take care of it.' A few months later, my parents were allowed to return. That's how it happened."

Ibrahim retired from the hotel business in 1994 at the age of sixty-three to open this restaurant. Seven months later, he received notice from the local council that his business would be forcibly closed due to improper building permits. The Florida was flourishing before the closure, he says, even attracting guests from Arab countries. Ibrahim suspects the council had been bribed by local competitors who are envious of his emerging success.

"This is my reward? After years of service, my whole life, as a citizen of this state? I've always had a good name in Israel. Always. And this is what I get in return?"

He takes me to the corner of the restaurant near the door, where a handwritten letter has been framed and prominently displayed. It is inscribed to Ibrahim in Hebrew from Leah Rabin, the wife of the former prime minister Yitzhak Rabin, assassinated two weeks prior to our interview. Ibrahim narrates the story of the restaurant's closing through the figure of Leah Rabin and her postassassination status as a symbol of the nation-state.

"Mrs. Rabin came here and she told me she was very happy with the restaurant. Look at the letter. It says, 'You gave us very good food, and we'll come back again.' I told the head of the local council about this letter but he ignored it. I think he hates Rabin and his wife. I feel it."

Some two weeks after Rabin's assassination, his figure and proper name remain potent symbols in Abu Ghosh.[66] In the days immediately following the event, large photographs of the fallen leader were taped above cash registers, displayed in car windows, and hung from terraces (see figure 17). Restaurant spaces became places of public confession by Palestinian hosts before their Jewish guests, narrating their profound shock and sadness after news of "the disaster." The owner of a new establishment, rumored to have financed his business with winnings from a U.S. lottery, described the crowds of mourners who had streamed to Abu Ghosh for lunch after the funeral and his subsequent altercation with a Jewish Israeli businessman, himself a right-wing Jew, with whom he had financial dealings: "He called to say how sorry he was," he noted loudly, his words clearly audible to his patrons. "If he hadn't said those things, I would have discontinued our business partnership." To mourn from a restaurant was to mark it as a national site. To be witnessed publicly in one's mourning was to be hailed as national subject. As a proper name, Rabin was a mobile signifier, readily deployed to tell a story of injustice done to a loyal Israeli citizen.

Figure 17. Memorial poster. Reads: "Yitzhak Rabin 1922–1995. Fighter, Commander in Chief, Diplomat, Defense Minister, and Prime Minister."

"If a person wanted to give respect to Mrs. Rabin, he would reopen the restaurant. You know what happened to her husband. Doesn't it hurt her that they closed the restaurant? What will happen if she brings guests here? If they loved her, they would grant me a permit."

Between Restaurants and Nations

The borders between restaurants and nations blur in this account. The subject becomes legibly national—that is, Israeli—through labor in the restaurant sector. Ibrahim's loyalty as a waiter both reflects and instantiates his authenticity as a national subject. The terms of table service and national service are indistinct—indeed, isomorphic. And yet Ibrahim's autobiography is ambivalent. On the one hand, it affirms the hegemonic national narrative about Abu Ghosh's historic intimacy with the Jewish State. On the other, it testifies to the state's failures to reward these intimacies. He ends with a hybrid grievance about injustice suffered both in the restaurant business and the nation-state writ large: the injustice of unrecognized civic loyalty. This scene highlights what is, for many Abu Ghosh residents, the melancholic dimension of edibility and its founding contradiction in the era of Oslo: Arab commodities were recognized and afforded national value; Arab communities were not. Like many Abu Ghosh residents, Ibrahim decried a nation-state in which Arab and patriot were still perceived as antonyms.

This scene suggests something of the complicated nature of edibility in Abu Ghosh restaurants. I have argued that it depended on collaborative performances of national allegiance by Palestinian residents and Jewish guests in restaurant spaces. But, as the scene above suggests, the converse is also true. For Palestinian entrepreneurs in the restaurant sector, the ability to be recognized as Israeli in normative terms depended on the degree of Jewish consumer confidence in any given restaurant and its fare. That is, the terms of both symbolic and political belonging in the nation-state were intimately linked to the success of any given restaurant among Jewish clientele. In turn, the forced closure of Ibrahim's restaurant profoundly injured his national status. Again, the terms of restaurants and nations collapse. In the realm of restaurants, fiscal and national viability were intimately related.

As I have suggested, Ibrahim's melancholy was partially metonymic in nature, gesturing toward the complicated place of Palestinian Arabs within the Jewish state since the time of state formation. Because this history of inequity was radically at odds with the signs of allegiance that edibility required, it was infrequently narrated in restaurant spaces by Palestinian residents. Yet, in some exceptional moments, this more expansive melancholy was given voice.

The Condition of Inedibility

It's an unusually wet day in Abu Ghosh, and heavy rains have prevented the normal Saturday crowds. Drainage in the center of town is poor, and water rises quickly, splashing in low waves onto pedestrians from passing cars. A single middle-aged man sits alone at a table eating baqlawa and reading the Hebrew news to get out of the rain. In the kitchen behind the cash register, the proprietors, Samira and Ya'qub Jabr, prepare a tray of *ma'amul*, sweet pastries stuffed with a spicy date filling, flavored with rose water, and lightly dusted with confectioner's sugar.

Samira is a small woman in her late forties, her dark hair pulled back tightly from her face, her strong arms lifting the round trays onto the counter. I explain my project, as this is our first meeting, but it doesn't interest her. She has another story to tell.

"Tell them in America! I want all of America to know!" From behind the counter, she speaks in a Hebrew that is confident and surprisingly loud. Her story comes quickly, out of sequence, with greater urgency than precision. Ya'qub tries to quell her emotion, encouraging her in muted Arabic, but she ignores him.

"They swore on the Torah, on the holy book, and lied! They said my father hadn't worked for them! On the Torah, you understand?" The occasional entrance of patrons does not silence her. She raises her voice further, even in the face of business lost to impropriety.

Samira winds through a disjointed tale that rises and falls in pitch and narrative clarity. She speaks about her family's land, stolen by the state. She describes her grandfather's house that still stands in the neighboring Jewish settlement of Telz Stone on land that once belonged to Abu Ghosh and is now enclosed by a chain-link fence, designed to keep out their Palestinian neighbors. And she narrates the work her father "did for the Jews" in 1948. "He carried weapons for them on his donkey — at night, through fields! He could have been killed by wild animals!"

I can't follow her frenzied account and she doesn't stop to clarify its details. She describes the American rabbi who bought their former home ten years ago: "He is one of the richest men in America and he is living on our land! Come back later," she says to me. "I'll show you the house and you'll take pictures. I want everyone in America to know."

It's only after additional conversations with relatives that I begin to clarify the history of the Jabr family's considerable land holdings prior to state founding, their assistance to Zionist militias in the early 1940s, their flight from the village during the course of the 1948–49 War, the confiscation of their home by the state, and the family's eventual return to the residence as renters, paying a monthly fee to the government on condition that the house remain state property. In 1973, the Jewish community of Telestone was established on Abu Ghosh's historic lands, and although Jewish immigrants moved in around them, the Jabr family remained. The family moved to their current location when harassment proved too difficult to withstand. Rumors followed about an American rabbi who had taken up residence in their former property.

As a public narrative told in unapologetic tones in the foyer of a prominent village bakery, Samira's account was enormously unusual. Yet it could be situated within a broader narrative field that was occasionally referenced in my presence, a field of stories typically told outside the public spaces of restaurants where edibility had to be preserved. On the porch of his family home, a retired schoolteacher showed me a map of Abu Ghosh's vast land holding prior to 1948 and narrated the history of land taken by force. On the patio in front of his store, an Abu Ghosh shopkeeper described his efforts to start a local branch of the Communist Party, and how his attempts were frustrated by the Israeli security services, who threatened potential members with incarceration. In the private garden behind her family restaurant, a woman recalled the spontaneous mobilization of village schoolchildren during the first Palestinian uprising. Their stone throwing at neighboring settlements was quelled by teachers and parents, who punished their children soundly at home; the event did not recur. These histories were narrated cautiously, constrained by the possibility of state or civilian retribution for a political enunciation that did not conform to the allegiance model.

Samira's account defies a singular reading. Like its fluctuations in pitch and volume, it slides between political registers and histories. With muddled sequence and harried tone, Samira affirms the dominant Abu Ghosh narrative of allegiance as she describes her father's heroic labor on behalf of Zionist institutions in the face of multiple dangers. The central refrain in her narrative ("They swore on the Torah and lied") affirms the legitimacy of Jewish legal codes through an account of their defamation. Her rage coalesces around injustices committed in the name of the Jewish holy text whose precepts have been violated. Yet this is also an account of dispossession that mounts a powerful challenge to the discourses of national allegiance that circulate in restaurant spaces and on which edibility depends. In her account of lands and property lost, Samira inscribes her family into an explicitly Palestinian history of loss and Israeli state-sponsored violence. Speaking as a Palestinian, she dramatizes the histories of exclusion that haunt the Jewish state. Speaking as an Israeli citizen, she denounces the fiction of a multicultural nation-state in which symbolic and juridical belonging is allotted evenly across discrepant populations. Her insistent tale refuses the central fictions on which edibility in Abu Ghosh depended: notably, that of a village properly rewarded for its history of patriotism.

Such counternarratives were highly unusual in restaurant spaces. Yet they were perpetually present in the more private spaces of the kitchen and the mixing bowl, embedded in the very substance of the cuisine served and consumed in Abu Ghosh restaurants and bakeries, in their flavors and culinary histories. Their traces appear in the hummus recipes offered for my perusal at Abu Ghosh Ltd., whose cooks blended chickpeas and olive oil with spices gathered in the West Bank city of Shu'fat. They are evident in the culinary histories recounted by the proprietor of Abu Shukry's Restaurant, who prepares his hummus "the Lebanese way," in keeping with his family's traditions. Or peruse "the first Arab-Israeli cookbook" to see their marks. Despite the editor's insistence on the text's Israeli identity, the recipes situate Abu Ghosh within an expansive, transnational culinary geography. Kanafe, the sugar-soaked pastry filled with salty cheese and served in the Sweet Things Bakery, is described as a specialty of Nablus (West Bank). *Sambusak*, dumplings stuffed with savory meat and prepared in Abu Ghosh, are traced to Lebanon and falafel to Egypt. In the autobiographical narratives between recipes, the author recalls trips to East Jerusalem and the Gaza Strip with her mother to purchase delicacies for holiday meals. The kitchens and restaurants of Abu Ghosh are painted as hybrid places in these accounts, located at the nexus of pan-regional culinary itineraries. These narratives do the work of cartography: connecting Palestinian places inside Israel to those beyond its borders, and situating them within broader Arab networks. In so doing, they unsettle the fictitious divide between Abu Ghosh and its Palestinian Arab history. These culinary geographies depart from hegemonic logics of edibility to map Israel differently.

Of Cafés and Terror

[A] café is a port to which all gates of the imagination are open.
—Aron Appelfeld, *A Table for One*

In the spring of 2002, a Palestinian suicide bomber detonated his charge in Café Moment, a crowded West Jerusalem coffeehouse. The blast was deadly, killing eleven and injuring dozens. The site became a shrine, a place of secular homage. Mourners decked the demolished building with flowers and memorial candles as young girls recited psalms for the dead, their bodies draped in the Israeli flag.[1] The Israeli media joined this lamentation. "This is our café [*zeh ha-kafeh shelanu*]," began an article on the front page of a prominent newspaper. "We came here in the morning for an espresso and a croissant. We came in the evening for a Kilkenny [beer]. To grasp what is left of normalcy [and] our way of life." This account mourned the loss of life. It also grieved for cafés, lamenting an Israeli cultural institution whose future was thought to be in jeopardy.

This was a period of crisis in Israel, a crisis precipitated by the collapse of the Oslo process and the outbreak of the second Palestinian uprising. In the spring of 2002, Israelis were faced with a wave of Palestinian attacks on civilian targets within Israel's borders. Israelis had experienced attacks like these before.[2] Yet as the uprising grew more militarized, such attacks became more frequent and struck new targets.[3] Bombers were now setting their sights on middle-class commercial establishments in the heart of Israeli cities: a West Jerusalem pizzeria and pedestrian mall, a Netanya hotel, a Tel Aviv disco. Café bombings were also proliferating, including four during March 2002 alone.[4]

Media coverage of these events was highly selective.[5] Israeli newspapers and talk shows began to talk a lot about leisure and loss.[6] To dramatize the effects of Palestinian violence on everyday Israeli life, they told a story about Israeli consumption under attack. At the center of these narratives was the European-style café or coffeehouse, an urban institution targeted by Palestinian militants in relatively unprecedented ways. Yet the media investment in cafés greatly exceeded their status as targets. Stories about cafés proliferated disproportionately during this period, as did interviews with their patrons, proprietors, and waiters. Images of coffeehouses under fire were heavily freighted with symbolic meaning and deployed to both represent and manage the mounting threat of Palestinian violence inside Israel's borders. At times they functioned as proxies, as signs that stood in for the nation-state itself.

What follows is a reading of the café discourse within the dominant Israeli print media.[7] While previous chapters focused on Israeli tourist cultures in the midst of the Oslo process, this chapter is an attempt to understand its political aftermath. By 2002, the Israeli political landscape had undergone tremendous changes, as the rhetoric of coexistence characteristic of Oslo's peak gave way to the language of enmity, fear, and retribution. I argue that café narratives negotiated these shifts in mainstream Israeli political sensibilities. This study can be read as a sequel to chapter 1, which considered the ways that media narratives negotiated Oslo's regional possibilities. This chapter, by contrast, considers how media narratives contended with Oslo's unraveling. While chapter 1 charted the redrawing of Israeli national space in regional terms, this chapter considers the collapse of this geographical imagination in Oslo's wake. I have argued that we can understand Oslo as a rescaling process by which Israel was inserted into regional and global scales of commerce, culture, and labor in new ways. Yet Oslo's decline was also an occasion for rescaling, albeit in an inverted sense. Amid the political crisis of 2002, mainstream

Jewish society retreated to micronational scales, as people took refuge in private and local interiors in an effort to protect themselves from the threat of Palestinian violence, both real and imagined. Both as institutions and as signs, cafés were small scales par excellence. Through their figuration and in their spaces Israelis were producing a new geograpy of the nation-state befitting the current political moment. To read cafés as signs is not to ignore the trauma with which they have been associated in many Israeli lives. Rather, it is to consider how they were asked to bear its burden.

Oslo's Decline

Despite its political import, the Oslo process was relatively short-lived. While its decline had numerous origins, waning Palestinian support for the process was essential to its unraveling.[8] Although Oslo had provided the Palestinians with the symbolic trappings of statehood, it had failed to address the Palestinian aspiration for self-determination. Indeed, by many accounts, the Israeli military occupation grew ever more onerous during this decade. Even as Israelis enjoyed a massive expansion of the national economy and a greater sense of personal security, Israeli-imposed strictures on Palestinian movement increased markedly, resulting in growing economic hardship and political desperation in the Occupied Territories, even as Israeli construction of the settlement infrastructure continued. It was in the context of these gross political disparities that the Israelis and the Palestinians convened the Camp David summit in 2000. A wide gap remained between the parties, and negotiations quickly broke down. Israelis blamed the Palestinians for its collapse, praising then Israeli prime minister Ehud Barak for his political generosity at the negotiating table. Palestinians accused Israel of failing to meet their minimal political requirements. Even today, the gap between these accounts remains unresolved.

What followed Camp David were a series of political events that would dramatically alter the Israeli political landscape. The second Palestinian uprising began in September 2000, spurred by Ariel Sharon's visit to the Palestinian Temple Mount. Inside Israel, Palestinian citizens in the Galilee joined a strike in solidarity with the Palestinian uprising in the territories, and violent clashes with the Israeli army ensued. As the uprising grew more militarized and as Palestinian attacks on civilian targets within Israel's borders increased, popular Jewish Israeli politics shifted to the right, leading to Sharon's prime ministerial victory in 2001. Even self-described leftists, former proponents of the Oslo process, confessed a change of heart, endorsing the narrative of political disappointment with the Palestinian people and insisting that the besieged state must defend itself. By the winter of 2001, popular Jewish Israeli opinion had granted the Israeli government the authority to suppress the uprising at virtually any cost. The state acted on this authority in the spring of 2002, launching the largest military offensive since the 1967 War.[9] Over the course of the months that followed, the Israel Defense Forces blockaded Palestinian towns and villages with tanks; raided Palestinian NGOs, government ministries, and commercial establishments; razed civilian homes and orchards.[10] Palestinians were placed under curfew without exception for humanitarian emergencies.[11] Most Jewish Israelis supported these measures, citing an existential threat to the Jewish state.

Palestinian attacks on civilian targets inside Israel profoundly altered the rhythms of everyday life, particularly in the Jewish Israeli cities where attacks had been concentrated. Residents were forced to negotiate urban landscapes in new ways, rethinking daily spatial usage. They carefully weighed the question of when and whether to leave their house. They calculated shopping routes and venues studiously, avoiding dense traffic and threatening crowds. Many stopped riding buses, while those who continued did so with considerable caution, scrutinizing passengers with large bags and protruding coats, particularly the Arabs among them. Pedestrians favored back routes that enabled them to skirt major roadways and commercial areas where bombings had been more frequent. The attacks also inaugurated a new geography of leisure. Online dating services, accessible without leaving the house, began replacing bars as social venues. Now, urban dwellers favored the enclosed interiors of family living rooms over restaurants and cafés in downtown areas.[12] As families clustered in these private spaces, the consumption of comfort foods and alcoholic beverages rose, as did sales of furniture, large-screen televisions, ice cream makers, and espresso machines, sales attributed to the growth in private forms of recreation.[13] These private interiors also generated forms of social crisis. In the pages of the media, psychologists discussed the effects of posttraumatic stress syndrome and the growing Israeli interest in preparing last wills and testaments.[14] Israel's Palestinian population was also recalibrating its relationship to public space, but for different reasons and in different ways. Amid heightened racial profiling and suspicion within the Jewish population, they were increasingly searched by police and security guards, particularly on public buses and in shopping malls. Most were accustomed to speaking Arabic in muffled tones for fear of public suspicion. Now they were even more cautious about the ways they navigated Jewish urban spaces. Indeed, many avoided them altogether for fear of indiscriminate retribution.

Other Israeli itineraries were also being revised. Jewish Israeli tourism to Jordan virtually ceased during this period, as did popular fantasies of unimpeded travel through a borderless Middle East. The ethnic tourism market in the Palestinian Galilee was another casualty of the new political landscape, this despite its steady growth in the second half of the 1990s. Prior to Camp David, Sakhnin had hosted dozens of tourist buses on holiday weekends, boasting numerous new restaurants and guest facilities. But Jewish Israeli visits to Palestinian places inside Israel's borders dropped significantly after the outbreak of the second Palestinian uprising and the solidarity protests it spawned within the Palestinian Galilee. "We can't visit them while they throw stones," was a popular refrain.

Reading the Café

As the civilian death toll from Palestinian bombings mounted in the spring of 2002, the Israeli press began to turn its attention to cafés. Consider again the newspaper narrative with which this chapter began. On March 10, following the bombing of Café Moment, Israel's most literary newspaper broke from its standard reportage to deliver an intimate lament: "This is our café. We came here in the morning for an espresso and a croissant. We came here in the evening for a Kilkenny [beer]. To grasp what is left of normalcy, of our secular sanity. To grasp at what is left of our way of life." The text that followed graphically surveyed the attack, describing "the smell of burning," "the charred human flesh," the fragments of human bodies, and the screams of evacuated survivors. It also mounted a political critique. Although the Israeli left blamed the current crisis on the Israeli occupation, the author disagreed. This was a civilizational war:

Exactly one week ago, a peace demonstration was held outside. The War for the Peace of the Settlements, they chanted.[15] But when the police sappers walk amongst the dead youth, searching for another explosive device, it does not seem to be so. It seems very, very different. Maybe the War for Moment [Café]? Maybe the War for the chance of a Western society to survive in the Middle East? . . . We can no longer keep fooling ourselves. This is a war about the morning's coffee and croissant. About the beer in the evening. About our very lives.[16]

This lyrical eulogy, unusual for an Israeli newspaper committed to serious reporting, was highly resonant among Israeli publics, and was read aloud on numerous Israeli radio programs to considerable listener acclaim.[17] Yet it was only one instance of a story line that was rapidly growing ubiquitous. Images of cafés proliferated in the mainstream Israeli media as a way to narrate the Palestinian assault on Israeli cities. Newspapers and talk shows decried the loss of cafés to Palestinian terror. Journalists chronicled the "chilling quiet" that had befallen café districts in Tel Aviv and Jerusalem.[18] Some spoke in defiance about the ad hoc efforts of residents to "take back the cafés" in their neighborhoods and hailed victims of café bombings as exemplary Israeli citizens, as the "Everyman, [as] mainstream Israel."[19] The narrative took the form of popular bumper stickers: "[The crisis] is not about the settlements. It's about [Café] Moment."[20] Cafés were the subject of political cartoons, like one showing stoic patrons drinking coffee in an empty courtyard lined by security guards (see figures 18 and 19). On Israeli television, they were the object of satirical parodies designed to illustrate everyday Israeli life under this new regime of pervasive violence and fear. In one popular spoof, a Jewish couple in a café falls suddenly to the floor when the waiter opens their champagne. They had mistaken the cork's pop for a bomb.[21]

The café narrative was enormously mobile and flexible. It had an overtly politicized tenor in some renditions, as when used to narrate the decline of regional diplomacy: "[The] Oslo peace agreement meant that we should be able to have a cup of coffee in Baghdad. Instead it has turned out that we cannot even have a cup of coffee in Tel Aviv."[22] Indeed, so pervasive was the café trope that it was deployed by Prime Minister Sharon to defend his military offensive in the Palestinian territories. "The mur-

Figure 18. The assault on leisure. Spoof published in *Ha-aretz* on 16 May 2002. ARTIST: DANIELLA LONDON DEKEL.

Figure 19. Stoic consumption. Spoof published in *Ha-aretz* on 16 May 2002. ARTIST: AMOS BIDERMAN.

Figure 20. The inverted café narrative. DOONESBURY © 2002 G. B. Trudeau.

derous gangs," Sharon argued from the floor of the Israeli Parliament, have "one mission: to chase us out from here, from everywhere, from our home in Elon Moreh, from the supermarket in Jerusalem, from the café in Tel Aviv."[23] Even as it was used to bolster the case for military retribution, the café in this account was recruited into a redrawing of Israeli national space, one inclusive of Jewish settlements (e.g., Elon Moreh) and Tel Aviv coffeehouses alike. Nor was the story line confined to the Israeli media, but also traveled to the United States, where it circulated in similar ways, made possible by U.S. discourses of identification with Israel in the post–September 11 moment (e.g., "We are all Israelis now") and by Sharon's relationship to the "war on terror."[24] In the U.S. press, as in the Israeli media, photographs of solitary consumers in guarded cafés were installed to illustrate the Israeli political predicament.[25] The narrative made its way into the *Doonesbury* cartoon strip, but with an ironic inversion: the besieged café was in the occupied West Bank (see figures 20 and 21). This inversion underscored the distortion at work in the Israeli story line: it deployed the image of Israeli leisure under fire as a way to narrate the political present even as a massive Israeli incursion into the Occupied Territories was concurrently claiming numerous Palestinian lives. The café trope had grossly obfuscating effects, minimizing a scene of violence whose toll on everyday life was far more severe.

While the narrative had several dominant strands in the Israeli media, the theme of consumption as nationalist practice was chief among them. Because many urban cafés had temporarily closed due to declining sales among a consumer population fearful of city centers, those that remained open for table service were deemed privileged sites for the performance

Figure 21. Leisure under seige. Published in the *New York Times* on 8 April 2002.
PHOTO: RINA CASTELNUOVO. PERMISSION: *THE NEW YORK TIMES*/REDUX.

of patriotism. One's very presence as a consumer was configured as an act of national loyalty. Committed customers who had returned to their favorite coffee bars in the face of Palestinian terror were portrayed as heroes, as evidence of Israeli fortitude in the face of this violent assault. Interviews conducted with "everyday Israelis" after the Café Moment bombing enunciated this clearly: "Just about the most patriotic thing you can do now is go out and have a drink."[26] "If you want to understand [the state of Israel], come to Caffit [café] for breakfast," read an Israeli editorial from this period. "This is a people that aren't going away. They are not even going to stop drinking coffee . . ."[27] Many of these accounts borrowed from the U.S. narrative of courage through consumption that circulated after September 11, 2001, whereby the abnegation of normal expenditures was deemed a victory for terrorists: if we don't go out for drinks, "then they win."[28] Consumption itself was a form of political defiance.

Consumers were not the only subjects lionized by this discourse. Café employees were granted equal attention. The Israeli press was particularly attentive to the case of a young West Jerusalem waiter, dubbed "hero of the day" by one prominent newspaper, who detected a Palestinian man armed with explosives at the entrance of a crowded coffeehouse.[29] Many newspapers recounted the event in considerable detail:

> Harel, 23 years old, who had worked as a waiter . . . for a year and a half, explained that the Palestinian had aroused his suspicion. "I started to speak a little Arabic with him," Harel said. "He took out his blue identification card [marking him as a Jerusalem resident], he fell silent, and then asked for water. I pushed him out of the way and neutralized the wires on him [attached to an explosive device]. He didn't try to resist."[30]

As this quote suggests, a shift in the micropractices of national security was at work within the Israeli urban landscape. Employees in the service sector were increasingly asked to perform informal police work: both to interrogate suspicious subjects and physically apprehend those perceived as dangerous. Indeed, the fruits of this injunction to police were often rehearsed in the media, as in the following account from a security guard: "I can tell whether someone is suspicious in the blink of an eye. I can tell your precise social standing by your shoes. . . . Then I move to your clothes . . . [and] then to the face. By then I already know what to look for and what's in store."[31] This account is suggestive for what it disavows, insisting that criminality can be surmised primarily from style and only secondarily from racial diacritics ("the face"). Yet most testimonials from guards and patrons identified suspicion less euphemistically. Criminality typically coalesced around the "obviously Arab-looking person[s]" in Israeli cafés.[32]

While these policing practices were not new to the Israeli urban landscape, they had been infrequently performed on café thresholds. But a new regulatory geography was emerging. Cafés were being reimagined as theaters of war, as the press stated explicitly: "Not a soul was present at the large café . . . just the waiters who had become armed soldiers overnight."[33] "If there are thirty recreation venues in Jerusalem," noted another account, "and one explodes every week, then going out to recreate is really going to the front lines."[34] The leisure landscape was being reconfigured. The café was acquiring the status of a battleground and all its players were being conscripted into the war.

Yet coffeehouses were not the only institutions hit by Palestinian militants during this period. On the contrary, other institutions and spaces were being targeted with far greater frequency, resulting in much greater loss of life. Since the mid-1990s, public buses had been the most frequent and deadly targets of Palestinian suicide bombers.[35] Yet, unlike cafés, buses failed to achieve symbolic prominence within mainstream Israeli imaginations. That is, despite heightened Israeli concern about their vulnerability, buses did not circulate as signs whose meaning exceeded their functionality. Largely at issue was the highly discrepant socioeconomic status of these two institutions. Working-class and immigrant populations numbered heavily among bus users, particularly during times of political crisis, when those who could afford alternative transportation avoided bus usage. Urban cafés, by contrast, were sites of bourgeois congress. Both the prevalence and the symbolic import of the café story line depended on these social coordinates. Elite consumers could be installed as national proxies in ways that working-class populations could not.

Cafés and European Modernity

This was not the first time that cafés had been employed as national symbols. Indeed, the café narrative emerged from a long discursive tradition in which European-style cafés were marshaled as tropes of Zionist modernity. The development of Tel Aviv in the 1920s and 1930s, for example, was routed through this discourse. Hailed as "the first Hebrew city," Tel Aviv was fashioned as an explicitly European geography meant to contrast sharply with neighboring Palestinian Jaffa.[36] In "place of Jaffa's sand dunes," Zionist leaders envisioned a metropolis with "sidewalks of marble, with beautiful boulevards, with villas that contain all that one could find in European dwellings in the largest European city."[37] European-style cafés, modeled on those in Odessa and Vienna, were central to this vision.[38] By the late 1920s, Tel Aviv boasted as many cafés and restaurants per capita as those in European cities, offering patrons "European comfort" and sometimes ocean views.[39] Cafés were installed in large numbers along the city's main boulevards, where they served as venues for cultural performance, political discussion, and meeting places for prominent Jewish literary figures.[40] Outdoor tables became common in the 1930s and were soon a crucial component of café society and important players in the production of Zionist public space (see figure 22).[41]

Café culture expanded considerably in the 1930s following a wave of

Figure 22. Cafes and Zionist modernity. Depicts a sidewalk café in Tel Aviv, 1948.
PHOTOGRAPH: ROBERT CAPA. PERMISSION: MAGNUM PHOTOS.

middle-class German immigrants to Palestine. By the decade's end, Tel Aviv boasted nearly two hundred coffeehouses and restaurants.[42] Per capita coffee consumption also rose during this period, outpacing the popularity of tea among Eastern European Jews.[43] This wave of immigration altered café culture by introducing German-speaking waiters, "wonderful cream cakes," and International Style architecture that mimicked Western European models and configured cafés as important vehicles of immigrant nostalgia. ("When I came to Palestine," notes the protagonist in a short story by S. Y. Agnon, "I wanted to open a café in Tel Aviv like the one I used to have in Berlin.")[44] Increasing numbers offered musical entertainment and dance floors, generating frequent complaints about the noise from cabaret shows and jazz bands and municipal efforts to limit their hours on the Sabbath.[45] Cafés were prominent figures in the urban landscape by the decade's end, privileged symbols of its European cosmopolitanism.[46]

Yet café culture was not universally embraced in Jewish Palestine. Amid the emergence of a petit-bourgeois Jewish class in the 1930s and 1940s, these and other urban leisure institutions were decried as blights on the Jewish national project by adherents of Labor Zionism, particularly its youth movements. They leveled stern criticism on Palestine's bourgeois culture: its cinemas, dance clubs, and coffeehouses.[47] Many Labor movement youth preferred their coffee brewed "Bedouin-style," in keeping with the Arab idealization they practiced.[48] They argued that cafés and other bourgeois institutions hindered Jewish nation-making.

Café culture in Jerusalem was also growing during these decades, although on a much smaller scale. The garden suburb of Rehavia, future home of Café Moment, was a noted café district.[49] Founded in the 1920s and home to prominent Sephardi families, Rehavia grew to prominence during the German Jewish immigration of the 1930s. German culture dominated in subsequent decades, earning Rehavia its reputation as "the most modern neighborhood in Jerusalem," renowned for Bauhaus architecture, literary salons, and café culture.[50] Rehavia, in the words of one observer, was "a Prussian island in an Oriental sea."[51] In the decades after state formation, its cafés were important venues for bourgeois exchange, important loci of elite Ashkenazi culture that figured as privileged tropes in the story of Israel's European identity:

> During the 1950s and 1960s, Rehavia had a life of its own . . . German was the main language in Rehavia and in the cafés. Because of the language and because of the well-tended houses, Rehavia did not look as if it belonged in new Israeli life. It carried far more resemblance to a residential neighborhood in Dresden, Leipzig, or Berlin. At Café Rehavia and Café Hermon you could get a cup of coffee and a piece of strudel that tasted just like the ones served in those cities.[52]

The landscape of café culture in Rehavia would change considerably in subsequent decades. Following the wave of Jewish immigration from North Africa and the Middle East during the 1950s, many neighborhood coffeehouses were acquired by North African Jews and French café culture predominated. Beginning in the 1960s, the formally attired German and Austrian waiters serving cream cakes were replaced by informally clad youth. Italian coffee styles and culinary offerings would gain popularity in the 1970s, enabled by imported espresso machines and prepared coffees.[53] By the 1990s, both the literal and symbolic importance of café culture within the Rehavia literary scene had been substantially eroded.[54]

Other symbolic functions intervened as substitutes. The same cafés targeted by Palestinian militants were conscripted into the struggle between secular and religious Jewish communities, positioned as occasional targets of militant religious violence and icons of secular defiance. Although European-style coffeehouses remained a defining feature of the neighborhood at the turn of the century, they represented a cultural institution that was increasingly fragile, undercut by demographic and social shifts within the neighborhood and the nation-state as a whole.

National Landscapes

In the midst of the political crisis of 2002, Israeli space was changing. Palestinian attacks within Israel's borders generated new spatial practices and imaginations, and the café figured centrally within them. The city was the primary scale of respatialization. As I have suggested, Jewish residents of urban centers were increasingly avoiding downtown cafés, restaurants, and cinemas. Instead, they opted for leisure opportunities in their local neighborhoods or in outlying communities where attacks had been less frequent. In response, many downtown cafés began to curtail their offerings amid fears about declining sales, converting into takeout-only facilities. This conversion was met with considerable public concern: "While [picking up] my son [after school] . . . I [ran] into [a] neighbor, who told me that the Aroma Café . . . had moved all its tables and chairs so customers could no longer sit there. At first I didn't really understand what she was saying, and she had to repeat herself before I let the reality of that statement sink in: Aroma had become a take-out place."[55] This story was pervasive. The café conversion to takeout was covered by all major Israeli daily newspapers. More than curtailed consumption was at issue. Many urban residents feared a substantive shift in the landscape of civil society, a threat to the possibility of social intercourse within the city.[56] They feared an erosion of the public sphere, the loss of spaces in which disparate patrons became a community of citizens through the shared consumption of coffee and print.

Political geography was also being revised. This was particularly true in West Jerusalem in the aftermath of the Café Moment bombing in Rehavia. A fiction of spatial fixity had been disrupted. Prior to this moment, many café patrons had perceived the city's relationship to the conflict in spatially delimited terms. For many, the conflict had been geographically fixed in a set of relatively stable spaces: in Palestinian East Jerusalem, on the seam lines between the city's Jewish and Palestinian neighborhoods, and within the largely working-class sites where bombers had struck before (e.g., buses and open-air markets). The Café Moment bombing had forced a rethinking of this spatial fiction, albeit an incredulous and unwilling one, as many articles attested: "Rehavia had seemed to represent a safe place far from the conflict. There are no surrounding Arab neighborhoods, no history of conflict."[57] "They struck at us here in the heart of left-wingers, yuppies and secularists to show what they think: that everywhere, even Rehavia, is occupied land."[58] "It's here, right amongst us. In the middle of Rehavia. . . . The heart of old Jerusalem . . . a hint of sophisticated European joie de vivre."[59] What's clearly manifest in such accounts is the profound shock that attended this shift in geographical imaginaries. The bombing of Café Moment altered the fiction of a spatially incarcerated conflict, a geographically delimited occupation. Elite, European spaces within West Jerusalem were being violently re-marked as coordinates of conflict.

The café narrative also dramatized the changing status of the Israeli border. By 2002, the celebratory narrative of a borderless region that had circulated at Oslo's height was being replaced by impassioned demands for border defense and territorial fortification in the form of checkpoints, closures, and visa restrictions. It was during this period that public debate about the merits of a barrier separating Israel from its occupied Palestinian territories began in earnest.[60] The media investment in cafés emerged out of these spatial politics. Amid border panic and calls for territorial defense, many Israelis set their sites on spatial enclosures at smaller scales. Eschewing downtown ventures for fear of attack, Israeli consumers began to take refuge in neighborhood cafés, restaurants, and shopping malls, all of which were being protected by armed guards in unprecedented ways. These spaces offered forms of spatially demarcated security that the porous nation-state could not fully guarantee. The waiters and security personnel stationed outside cafés performed as both citizen-soldiers and border-guards within this new political regime. Their work on café thresholds can be read as fantastical acts, regulatory practices that compensated for failures on Israel's territorial border and seams. As such, cafés were spatial substitutes. They functioned as national enclosures writ small.

Yet they were enclosures of very particular kinds. As I have suggested, the coffeehouse memorialized by the Israeli press of this period was an explicitly European space and institution, a purveyor not merely of coffee but of espresso and croissants, a locus of Western bourgeois taste and society, "of sophisticated European joie de vivre."[61] Indeed, most of the establishments targeted by suicide bombers were precisely these kinds of places, Café Moment chief among them. Most fashioned their fare and décor on European coffeehouses; most were located in affluent neighborhoods with celebrated European cultural histories. As such, their figuration as national metonyms did important normative work. In the form of a lament about Palestinian terror, the café narrative was marshaled to preserve the terms of a dominant national fiction about a European nation-state out of place in the Arab Middle East. The press eulogy for Café Moment articulated this clearly: "Maybe it's a war for Café Moment? Maybe [it's a] war about the chance of a Western society to survive in the Middle East?" The political function of the café was thus multiple. As a place holder for the European nation-state, the café could also be marshaled to recast the conflict as a civilizational war. In this rendering, the Israeli occupation recedes from view.

These spatial imaginations were at a considerable distance from those of the Oslo era. The fantasy of a borderless region had unraveled. Israelis were now investing in a different set of scales: the national, the urban, the neighborhood, the private living room. In popular imaginations, security was inversely proportional to scale, whereby each successive jump downward provided greater protection. The Oslo process had promised to make Israeli Jews comfortable within the Arab Middle East. But now Israelis were uneasy in their very own cities—indeed, in the very neighborhoods in which they once sought political refuge. Cafés, as both protected enclosures and European islands, intervened to provide what the nation-state could not.

Empty Landscapes

One spatial trope reigned supreme. In the media of this moment, "emptiness" was virtually ubiquitous in both narrative and visual form (see

Figure 23. The empty café, Jerusalem. Published in *Ha-aretz* on 10 March 2002.
PHOTO: LIOR MIZRAHI/BAUBAU.

figure 23). Numerous discussions of the crisis began with a sweep of the depopulated urban landscape.[62] They spoke of half-empty cinemas and dwindling consumers in shopping malls, restaurants, and pubs.[63] They chronicled the ease of barhopping on a Saturday night, as a route that once took several hours could now be covered in fifteen minutes thanks to deserted locales.[64] Articles noted the "chilling quiet [that had] taken control of [Israeli cities]" and the large number of armed guards outside cafés and restaurants "watching empty places."[65] They spoke of bohemian neighborhoods where parking was usually at a premium, but during this political calamity, "only a few hardy souls [were] out wandering the streets."[66]

The truth of these accounts is not in question. Most cafés were indeed empty during this period of random and frequent violence, as were most leisure venues. Yet what merits attention is the sheer prevalence of this trope. Public media discourse invested heavily in images of desolation as a way to enunciate this moment of crisis.[67] In part, the trope was a substitution. That is, it took the place of other modalities of absence in which the Israeli media were less invested. One such absence was paramount. Palestinian Arabs, both residents of the Occupied Territories and citizens of Israel, were missing from Jewish cities. Fewer were using public transportation or entering Jewish neighborhoods and shopping districts in West Jerusalem. Residents of the Occupied Territories were prevented entry into Israel by checkpoints and visa restrictions. Israel's Palestinian citizens stayed away for fear of racial profiling by police and security guards. Such fears were clearly rooted in political realities. Anti-Arab rage was growing, articulated by the racist slogans outside downtown businesses: "We do not employ Arabs"; "Enemies should not be offered livelihood."[68] Missing Palestinians were largely overlooked in the mainstream media, obscured by images of Jewish absence.

The trope of emptiness was anything but new. Indeed, when harnessed to territory, the image is pervasive in early Zionist discourse, rehearsed in the writings of Theodore Herzl, Hayyim Bialik, Max Mandelstamm, and many others.[69] Tel Aviv's founding was often narrated through a related story line: the myth of a modern city born from sand.[70] As in the broader colonial archive on which this story drew, emptiness was a sign of pre-modernity, the mark of a territory outside time and history.[71] Read literally, such tropes were political fantasies.[72] Yet they have also functioned as political blueprints at various moments in Israeli history, ones enacted through the literal dispossession of Palestinians and the subsequent removal of their traces.[73]

Such blueprints were given new life in 2002, as the desire for Palestinian absence was articulated with new force. Among far-right politicians, Palestinian population transfer was reemerging as a viable political solution to the conflict, a means of contending with the so-called Palestinian problem. Such visions, despite their manifest violence, were not stigmatized. Rather, as national politics moved to the right, they were endorsed by a growing percentage of the Jewish Israeli public.[74] Some Israeli parliamentarians articulated this vision clearly, warning that if Palestinian violence escalated into a regional war, Palestinians from the Occupied Territories should anticipate another massive expulsion from their homes and lands.[75] Some argued to include Israel's Palestinian citizens in such expulsion as a means of forestalling the demographic threat within Israel's borders.

The trope of emptiness resonated with these political fantasies. Indeed, I suggest that the café narrative enunciated the terms of this political debate with a different vocabulary, replacing the language of politics with that of leisure. But the narrative took an additional step. Stories about empty leisure landscapes, with their images of once crowded cities rendered desolate, rehearsed the aftermath of population transfer. Yet a crucial transposition was at work. Jews and not Palestinian Arabs were missing from cafés, from the pubs, cinemas, and restaurants. While the *manifest* café narrative spoke of Jewish absence, the *latent* narrative envisioned a landscape that resonated closely with concurrent political blueprints of the Israeli right. One can construct the former in terms of a single sentence: "The Palestinians have emptied our cafés."[76] But the latent narrative told a different story. When formulated as a sentence, it engaged in a double transposition that altered the subject of locution and replaced the café with its symbolic referent, the Israeli nation-state: "We, the Israelis, have emptied their nation." Israeli geographical imaginaries were being refashioned in Oslo's wake. At moments, as in this spatial fantasy, they took profoundly dystopic forms. When empty cafés presaged empty nations, leisure narratives raised disquieting questions about Israel's future.

— · — · — · — · — · — · — **Oslo's Ghosts** — · — · — · — · — · — · — · — · — · — · — · —

In October 2004, a bomb exploded at the Hilton Hotel in Egypt's northern Sinai Peninsula where thousands of Israeli tourists had been spending their autumn holidays. The blast was deadly, killing thirty-four people, nearly half of them Israelis, and injuring over a hundred others. In the chaotic hours that followed, as Israeli rescue teams and ambulances rushed to the Egyptian border, a stream of Israelis began a hasty retreat across the border by car and on foot. They had come to Sinai despite travel warnings issued by the Israeli state several months earlier — warnings broad in scope, as they had been since the onset of the second Palestinian uprising in 2000, against Israeli travel in any neighboring Arab country.[1] Few Israeli Jews took these warnings seriously where Sinai was concerned; it was understood as an Arab exception. That is, amid the renewed politics of regional enmity that had followed the second uprising, Sinai's serene coastline appealed as a different kind of Middle Eastern place where Arab cultures and persons could be enjoyed in other ways, unmarked by the terms of the Arab-Israeli conflict. Sinai was perceived as an uncanny place, both within the Arab Middle East and thus affording tourists its cultural pleasures, yet outside the landscape of regional politics.[2] For Israelis, it was at once territorially proximate, and this was crucial to its appeal, yet situated at a conceptual distance from prevailing imagined geographies of the region.

The bombing shattered this fiction of geopolitical exceptionalism. In its wake, images of Israeli tourists saturated the Israeli and international media, with photographs of bloodied vacationers rushing toward the border dressed in their beachwear and carrying suitcases. Allegory was prevalent. Fleeing in haste with possessions in hand, some media cast them as "refugees."[3] Newspapers spoke of "a second exodus from Egypt."[4] For the Israeli Foreign Ministry, these leisure travelers were heralded as civilian diplomats in dangerous times, "reflect[ing] the strong and courageous will of those who seek peace in the Middle East."[5] Tourists in flight were represented as paradigmatic Israeli citizens, as mobile instances of the nation-state in its time of crisis.

The regional political landscape had changed considerably by the turn of the twenty-first century, as this event suggests, even if the figurative power of tourism had not. By 2000, after the eruption of the second uprising, Jewish Israeli society had largely renounced the politics of coexistence, returning to the conflict paradigm that had characterized Israel's relations with neighboring states prior to the onset of regional diplomacy in the 1990s. This political future had not been anticipated, neither by the Labor administration involved in Oslo's drafting nor by Jewish Israeli proponents of the diplomatic process—at least, not vocally so. They had argued that the political and economic effects of regional realignment could be charted with relative certainty.

But the Oslo process had never been wholly under the state's control, as the second uprising made dramatically manifest. That is, although Israel could dictate its terms, it could not determine its effects at either regional or national scales. While Israel could block the emergence of a sovereign and contiguous Palestinian state, it could not control changing Palestinian demographics in the region or the promise of a Palestinian majority between the Jordan River and the Mediterranean Sea in the subsequent half-century. Although the Israeli state could police the movement of foreign bodies into Israeli territory through militarized checkpoints and visa restrictions, it could not prevent the transnational circuits that Oslo had engendered nor thwart the forms of Arabization within the nation-state that might result from newly porous borders. The terms of what I have been calling national intelligibility were equally difficult to control. I have argued that the political transformations of this era had restructured prevailing ways of perceiving and understanding. These shifts, I have suggested, had a powerful impact on the very fabric of national definition. Israeliness was being reshaped and reseen within a new national protocol of recognition. But this new protocol produced multiple effects. At moments, it generated knowledges and subjects that exceeded the limits of dominant national imaginations. At moments, this new protocol generated a radical revision in the very idea of Israel.

For some Israeli Jews, these revisions were terrifying. For some, Oslo had unleashed a distinctly dystopic national future:

> We are going to gain in this "peace," but maybe, at the same time, lose everything: our country, our Jewish identity, and, in the end, the opportunity to live in what we once called the land of Israel . . . They expect millions of tourists [here] from the whole world. The foreigners will fill the streets of our cities in masses, until it is no longer clear who lives here and who is a tourist.[6]

This passage, which appeared in the Hebrew press in 1994, takes the figure of the tourist to illustrate Oslo's dark side. A profound fear is being enunciated: in the Oslo era, in the very heart of the Jewish metropolis, the line between tourist and citizen might blur. Persons from outside the nation-state might suddenly make themselves at home. These spectral figures threatened to render home itself unrecognizable.

In this passage, the threatening figure is anonymous, an unmarked "foreigner." But many Jewish Israelis could describe this threat with more specificity. Many feared the incoming migrant workers, the refugees, and especially the terrorists who might enter the state in tourist guise, enabled by newly porous borders and regional reconciliation. Arabs were the most threatening among them, particularly the Palestinian Arab refugees on tourist visas returning to repossess homes and lands, or so many Israelis imagined. *The foreigners will fill the streets of our cities in masses, until it is no longer clear who lives here and who is a tourist.* A dominant mythology is at work in this rendering, that of an Israeli nation-state that was secure and homogeneous prior to the Oslo process and the foreign incursion it catalyzed. In this rendering, Oslo had remade the nation-state as a place of terrifying difference.

Yet counter to this claim, Israel was already heterogeneous at the time of Oslo's arrival. That is, it was already an Arab place, Arab along both Muslim and Jewish lines, both Palestinian and Mizrahi. The anticipated tourist onslaught of the Oslo era, producing uncanny resemblances between incoming Arab travelers and Israeli citizens, threatened to expose the most foundational of Israeli fictions: that of a nation-state *neither in nor of* the Arab Middle East. Tourism thus articulated a panic about something becoming perceptible, about the appearance of unwanted forms of national intelligibility that had long been foreclosed as Israel's very condition of possibility. In the midst of this panic, historical fictions were being unseated. And in midst of this crisis, a different Israeli future was becoming visible.

Notes

Introduction

1. For discussion of the forms that Orientalism has taken in Israeli imaginations, see Eyal, *The Disenchantment of the Orient*; Y. Peleg, *Orientalism and the Hebrew Imagination*.

2. My discussion of national intelligibility draws heavily on Judith Butler's discussion of gendered norms of intelligibility. See *Gender Trouble* and *Giving an Account of Oneself*. Butler draws on Foucault's "grid of intelligibility" (*dispositif*) but revises his paradigm through attention to the "social dimensions of normativity that govern the scene of recognition": *Giving an Account of Oneself*, 22–26. Unlike Butler's use of "intelligibility," mine is particularly concerned with perception and the perceivable. Foundational work in this area includes Berger, *Ways of Seeing*; Crary, *Techniques of the Observer*; Jay, *Downcast Eyes*.

3. The theory of performativity has been elaborated in the work of Jacques Derrida and Judith Butler, building on the work of J. L. Austin in *How to Do Things with Words* (1962). Butler argues that while iterative practices sediment hegemonic institutions, they also occasion counterhegemonic redeployments and "the exposure of prevailing forms of authority and the exclusions by which they proceed": *Excitable Speech*, 158. On performativity, also see Derrida, "Signature, Event, Context."

4. The longer history of the Middle East Peace Process can be traced to the immediate aftermath of the 1967 War: Bar-Siman-Tov, *Israel and the Peace Process*; Quandt, *Peace Process*. The Oslo Declaration of Principles (DOP) set a time table for permanent status negotiations to commence no "later than the beginning of

the third year of the interim period, between the Government of Israel and the Palestinian people representatives": "*Israel-p.l.o. Agreements*." The secondary literature
on the Oslo Accords includes Aruri, *The Obstruction of Peace*; Beinin and Stein, *The
Struggle for Sovereignty*; Giacaman and Lønning, *After Oslo*; Hammami and Usher,
Palestine; Peleg, *The Middle East Peace Process*; Reinhart, *Israel/Palestine*; Said, *The End
of the Peace Process*; Usher, *Palestine in Crisis*. I discuss the Oslo process more exten-
sively in chapter 1.

5. For a general discussion of the political events of this period, see Beinin and Stein,
The Struggle for Sovereignty; Lazin and Mahler, *Israel in the Nineties*.

6. The primary Arab boycott against Israeli products was instituted in the late 1940s.
The secondary boycott, established in 1952, blacklisted firms that traded with Israel.
On October 1, 1994, the Gulf Cooperation Council—including Saudi Arabia, Bah-
rain, Kuwait, Oman, Qatar, and the United Arab Emirates—ended its blacklist of
Israeli goods and companies with Israeli ties. See Seliktar, "The Peace Dividend";
Shahak, *Open Secrets*, 99–124.

7. See chapter 1 for fuller discussion of these trends.

8. Peres, *The New Middle East*.

9. Seliktar, "The Peace Dividend"; Shafir and Peled, *Being Israeli*; Shafir and Peled, *The
New Israel*.

10. Chetrit, "Mizrahi Politics."

11. Courbage, "Reshuffling the Demographic Cards"; Kemp and Raijman, '*Ovdim Zarim*'
be-Yisrael.

12. For a critical review of post-Zionist scholarship of this and previous decades, albeit
one that ignores many trends in feminist and Mizrahi scholarship, see Silberstein, *The
Postzionism Debates*.

13. In the past decade, scholarship on Israel's Palestinian population has grown considerably. Recent and foundational work includes the following: Haidar, *On the Margins*; Jiryis, *The Arabs in Israel*; Kanaaneh, *Birthing the Nation*; Lustick, *Arabs in the
Jewish State*; Rabinowitz, *Overlooking Nazareth*; Rabinowitz and Abu Baker, *Coffins
on Our Shoulders*; Slyomovics, *The Object of Memory*; Zureik, *The Palestinians in Israel*;
Ghanem, *The Palestinian-Arab Minority in Israel*; Rouhana, *Palestinian Citizens*.

14. Sikui, *Duah Amutat Sikui: Shivyon ve-Shiluv ha-Ezrahim ha-Aravim be-Yisrael*.

15. This process was also enabled by the so-called Israelization of Israel's Palestinian
population in the aftermath of the first Palestinian uprising. See Rouhana, *Palestinian
Citizens*; Smooha, "The Israelization of Collective Identity."

16. Almog, *The Sabra*; Eyal, *The Disenchantment of the Orient*.

17. Eyal, *The Disenchantment of the Orient*.

18. See the anthropological literature on tourism for discussion of this ethnic template.
Recent scholarship includes Badone and Roseman, *Intersecting Journeys*; Brennan,
What's Love Got to Do with It?; Bruner, *Culture on Tour*; Ebron, *Performing Africa*; Ghod-
see, *The Red Riviera*; Ness, *Where Asia Smiles*; Padilla, *Caribbean Pleasure Industry*.

19. This is Said's term. See *Orientalism*, 53–54.

20. On the contingent nature of coexistence in the Australian postcolonial context, see Povinelli, *The Cunning of Recognition*.

21. On the politics of nomenclature in this context, see Rabinowitz, *"Nostalgyah Mizrahit."* Although these sectarian differences existed prior to the Zionist presence in Palestine, the Israeli state capitalized on them in an effort to fragment the Palestinian population within Israel's borders and diminish its oppositional potential: Lustick, *Arabs in the Jewish State*, 82–149. For a discussion of the state's relationship to its Druze minority and its efforts to foster animosity between Druze and Palestinian Muslims within Israel, see Firro, "Reshaping Druze Particularism in Israel"; Firro, *The Druze in the Jewish State*; Hajjar, *Courting Conflict*; Hajjar, "Israel's Intervention among the Druze"; Parsons, *The Druze between Palestine and Israel, 1947–49*.

22. For a recent discussion of such discrepancies, see Shafir and Peled, *Being Israeli*.

23. The growing popularity of Mizrahi popular music among elite Jewish Israeli audiences during this period was a countervailing trend. See Horowitz, "Dueling Nativities"; M. Regev and Seroussi, *Popular Music*, 191–235.

24. Aruri, *The Obstruction of Peace*; Beinin and Stein, *The Struggle for Sovereignty*; Hass, *Drinking the Sea at Gaza*; Reinhart, *Israel/Palestine*; Amnesty International, *Israel/ Occupied Territories and the Palestinian Authority*; Amnesty International, *Israel and the Occupied Territories*; B'tselem, *Human Rights in the Occupied Territories*; LAW, *Apartheid, Bantustans, Cantons*.

25. Long, *Imagining the Holy Land*; McAlister, *Epic Encounters*; Obenzinger, *American Palestine*; Shepherd, *Zealous Intruders*; Wharton, *Selling Jerusalem*.

26. On the relationship between the emergence of tourism in the nineteenth century and the development of transportation technology, see Buzard, *The Beaten Track*, 31–47. He notes that as this technology developed the bourgeois tradition of European travel in the Orient gave way to more popular forms of tourist excursion.

27. The Thomas Cook Company, cited in Katz, "The Israeli Teacher-Guide," 54. For a history of the Thomas Cook company in the Middle East, see Brendon, *Thomas Cook*; Pudney et al., *The Thomas Cook Story*; Shepherd, *Zealous Intruders*, 170–92.

28. D. Benvenisti and Benvenisti, *Panas ha-Kesem*; Klein, *The Second Million*, 189.

29. On the function and ideology of *ha-tiyul*, see Abu El-Haj, *Facts on the Ground*, 47, 57; Almog, *The Sabra*, 160–84; Katriel, "Touring the Land"; Katz, "The Israeli Teacher-Guide," 58; Shapira, *Land and Power*, 270–71. For a cinematic representation of hiking practices in the early Zionist context, see *Oded ha-Noded* [Oded the Wanderer], the first full-length feature film shot and produced within the Yishuv's Jewish community. See Shohat, *Israeli Cinema*, and Tryster, *Israel before Israel*, for discussion of the film.

30. The first travel guides aimed at Jewish travelers were published during the 1920s. This decade also witnessed the establishment of the Zionist Information Bureau for Tourists and a Palestine-based association of Jewish tour guides. It has been estimated that "over 70,000 total visitors came to [Palestine] from the West during 1924, and in the spring of 1925, 1,200 were present on a single day. Some 40,000, including

an estimated 4,000 Jews, saw Palestine in 1930, despite the ongoing Arab revolt and the deepening worldwide economic crisis": Berkowitz, *Western Jewry and the Zionist Project*, 125; Cohen-Hattab, "Zionism, Tourism, and the Battle for Palestine," 67, 73; Y. Katz, "Ha-Tsiyonut ve-Shivukah shel Erets-Yisrael," 88–89. For further discussion of the Zionist establishment's efforts to develop a tourism market in prestate Palestine aimed primarily at incoming Jewish tourists, see Cohen-Hattab and Katz, "The Attraction of Palestine"; Cohen-Hattab and Katz, "Mi-Terra Santa le-Tourism."

31. Klein, *The Second Million*, 85.

32. This literature proliferated during the 1990s. Important examples from this period include Behdad, *Belated Travelers*; Greenblatt, *Marvelous Possessions*; Grewal, *Home and Harem*; Pratt, *Imperial Eyes*; Spurr, *The Rhetoric of Empire*; Thomas, *Colonialism's Culture*.

33. The notion of colonial ambivalence is most associated with the work of Homi Bhabha. See *Location of Culture*.

34. This line of argument has become increasingly pronounced in recent scholarship: Abu El-Haj, *Facts on the Ground*; Lockman, *Comrades and Enemies*; Ram, *The Changing Agenda of Israeli Sociology*; Shafir and Peled, *Being Israeli*. It should nonetheless be stressed that Zionist settler-colonialism differed in some crucial ways from European colonial projects, perhaps most crucially in the absence of a single sovereign colonial sponsor. Further, as I have argued elsewhere, the postcolonial paradigm is a poor fit in the Israeli case because of the complexity of the Israeli political landscape: Stein, "Ballad of the Sad Cafe."

35. The postarmy itinerary grew in popularity, particularly among the Ashkenazi middle class, beginning in the 1980s. See Noy and Cohen, *Israeli Backpackers*; Avrahami, *The Israeli Backpackers*; Maoz, "Backpackers' Motivations"; Maoz, "The Conquerors and the Settlers"; Mevorach, "The Long Trip after Military Service"; Noy, "This Trip Really Changed Me"; Uriely, Yonay, and Simchai, "Backpacking Experiences." The Holocaust itinerary was introduced into the Israeli curriculum in the 1980s. See Feldman, "Marking the Boundaries of the Enclave," 85; Gruber, *Virtually Jewish*; Zertal, *Israel's Holocaust*. On the popularity of trips to former Palestinian villages among Palestinian citizens of Israel in the post-Oslo period, see Jamal, "The Ambiguities of Minority Patriotism," 457–60; Rekhess, "The Arabs of Israel after Oslo," 3–4, 31–32. Similar trips for Jewish Israelis were organized by *Zohrot*, a grassroots organization founded in 2002 that educates Jews about the Palestinian dispossession. For discussion of the Moroccan itinerary, see Levy, "Notes on the Jewish-Muslim Relationship"; Levy, "To Morocco and Back."

36. For discussion of the nineteenth-century context, see R. Khalidi, *Palestinian Identity*. On the Palestinian dispossession, see Morris, *The Birth of the Palestinian Refugee Problem*. On the military administration, see Lustick, *Arabs in the Jewish State*; Robinson, "Occupied Citizens." On Mizrahi immigration, see Hever, Shenhav, and Motzafi-Haller, *Mizrahim be-Yisrael*; Shenhav, *The Arab Jews*; Shohat, *Taboo Memories*. On restrictions on Palestinian movement, see Amnesty International, *Israel and the Occupied Territories*.

37. On the links between tourism and warfare, see Deotte et al., *Back to the Front*; Lloyd, *Battlefield Tourism*. On the culture of militarism in Israel see Ben-Ari, *Mastering Soldiers*; Lomsky-Feder and Ben-Ari, *The Military and Militarism in Israeli Society*.

38. Silberstein, *The Postzionism Debates*.

39. I discuss this history elsewhere: Stein and Swedenburg, "Popular Culture."

40. Ashkenazi Israelis retained this dominance even after becoming a Jewish minority within Israel following the mass immigration of Jews from North Africa, the Middle East, and the Levant (Mizrahim) during the 1950s. Mizrahim lost their numerical majority with the arrival of some seven hundred thousand Jews from the former Soviet Union in the first half of the 1990s. See Chetrit, "Mizrahi Politics in Israel," and Courbage, "Reshuffling the Demographic Cards," for analyses of changing ethnoracial demographics and power relations during the 1990s.

41. Lockman, *Comrades and Enemies*, 9. For an elaboration of the arguments made here, see Stein and Swedenburg, "Popular Culture."

42. Both Lockman and Shohat advance relational paradigms in their work. See Lockman, *Comrades and Enemies*, 8; Shohat, *Taboo Memories*, 207.

43. Abu Lughoud, "The Romance of Resistance"; H. Cohen, *Army of Shadows*.

44. "Itinerary" as metaphor appears, for example, in Gayatri Spivak's scholarship: "Can the Subaltern Speak?," 293. Derrida's work frequently relies on the language of travel. He has written of "a certain *wandering* in the tracing of difference," of différance as "*a detour*, a delay, a relay," and of "*the detour* of the sign" (emphasis added): "Différance," 7, 8, 9. In *The Postcard*, in an even more literal gesture toward the semiotics of tourism, the route of the signifier is figured as that of a postcard. For discussion of Derrida's grappling with the metaphorics of travel, see Malabou and Derrida, *Counterpath*.

45. De Certeau, *The Practice of Everyday Life*, 98–99.

46. Ibid., 129.

1. Regional Routes

1. Lior, "Higati la-Sela ha-Adom."

2. My analysis focuses on Israel's most widely consumed Hebrew-language daily newspapers, *Yediot Aharonot* and *Ma'ariv*, with daily circulations of 250,000 and 160,000, respectively, during the period in question. I also examine *Ha-aretz, Davar Rishon, Kol ha-Ir, Kol ha-Tsafon*, and *The Jerusalem Post* and *The Jerusalem Report*, Israel's primary English-language publications. On the politics of Israeli media during this and previous decades, see Caspi and Limor, *Ha-Metavkhim*; Caspi and Limor, *The In/Outsiders*; Wolfsfeld, *Media and Political Conflict*.

3. This chapter draws heavily on postcolonial studies of travel narrative, many of which have considered the trope of first contact. See, for example, Greenblatt, *Marvelous Possessions*; Hulme, *Colonial Encounters*; McClintock, *Imperial Leather*; Pratt, *Imperial Eyes*, 240.

4. Avraham, *Ha-Tikshoret be-Yisrael*.

5. By the early 1990s, political and economic conditions in the West Bank and Gaza

Strip were deteriorating. The PLO was crippled by the loss of revenue and military support from the former USSR and Gulf patrons following the Gulf War. The Intifada had fallen out of favor with the Western media, partially due to Arafat's alliance with Saddam Hussein. And, as poverty grew in the West Bank and Gaza Strip alongside dissatisfaction with Arafat's regime, the Islamic movement Hamas was becoming an increasingly popular alternative to the PLO: Aruri, *The Obstruction of Peace*.

6. Ibid., 213.

7. For academic discussion of the globalization of Israel during this decade, see Ben-Porat, *Global Liberalism, Local Populism*; Elizur, *Yisrael veha-Etgar ha-Globali*; Nitzan, *The Global Political Economy of Israel*; Rabinowitz, "Postnational Palestine/Israel?"; Ram, *The Globalization of Israel*; Shafir and Peled, *Being Israeli*; Shafir and Peled, eds., *The New Israel*; Stein and Swedenburg, eds., *Palestine, Israel, and the Politics of Popular Culture*.

8. Ryan, "Jordan in the Middle East Peace Process."

9. Bahgat, *Israel and the Persian Gulf*; Laskier, *Israel and the Maghreb*.

10. Seliktar, "The Peace Dividend," 225–26; Shahak, *Open Secrets*, 99–124.

11. Beinin, "The Oslo Process."

12. Shafir and Peled, eds., *The New Israel*, 231.

13. On the ways that this transnational economic circuit sidelined the Palestinian economy, see Samara, "Globalization."

14. Shafir and Peled, eds., *The New Israel*, 256, 259.

15. Many Israeli economists were more cautious in predicting Israel's place in a future regional economy, citing "xenophobic restrictions on foreign trade and investment" and the gross disparities between national economies: Seliktar, "The Peace Dividend," 228; Zilberfarb, "The Effects of the Peace Process."

16. In 1998 Israel's per capita GNP was six to ten times higher than that of neighboring states: Mundlak, "Labor in a Peaceful Middle East," 202.

17. On the role of liberalization, see Shafir and Peled, eds., *The New Israel*.

18. Farsakh, "Under Siege"; *Israeli Policy of Closure*; Roy, "De-Development Revisited"; Usher, "Closures"; Ziai, "Israel."

19. The number of work permits fell from approximately 120,000 daily in 1992 to 36,000 in 1996: Ben Efrat, "Close Minded."

20. Unemployment escalated from 11 percent in 1993 to 28 percent in 1996: Ibid.; Farsakh, "Under Siege."

21. Murphy, "Stacking the Deck"; Rabbani, "Palestinian Authority."

22. A. Gross, "Challenges to Compulsory Heterosexuality"; Sikui, *Duah 'Amutat Sikui Shivyon ve-Shiluv ha-Ezrahim ha-Aravim be-Yisrael*; Smooha, "The Israelization of Collective Identity."

23. The Mizrahi Haredi Party (Shas) enjoyed substantive gains during the national elections of 1999: Chetrit, "Mizrahi Politics in Israel"; Courbage, "Reshuffling the Demographic Cards."

24. Israel's Christian community grew tenfold from 1990 to 1996 to 183,000. Courbage notes, "With the massive arrival of Jews from the former Soviet Union beginning in 1991, the Law of Return was de facto extended to include the non-Jewish spouses of Jewish immigrants. As a result, the proportion of Jews among the immigrants fell from about 97 percent in 1990 to 75 percent in 1997": Courbage, "Reshuffling the Demographic Cards," 28. On foreign workers, see n. 96 below.

25. Ibid., 30; Amnon Sofer quoted in *Ha-aretz*, 28 June 2002.

26. The Jordanian private sector was equally optimistic about the effects of peace and began massive state-sponsored development of the national tourist infrastructure. Yet tourist numbers and revenues decreased rapidly in the late 1990s, fueling popular opposition to normalized relations with Israel: Clawson, *Tourism Cooperation in the Levant*; Hazbun, "Mapping the Landscape of the 'New Middle East.'"

27. Government of Israel, *Development Options for Cooperation*.

28. Sugarman, "Tourists with Reservations."

29. Ben Ari, "Peace Tourism Update"; Sugarman, "Make Tours, Not War."

30. Blackburn, "Reaching the Threshold." Most Israeli tourists visiting Jordan went only to Petra for the day: Hazbun, "Mapping the Landscape of the 'New Middle East.'"

31. Some forty thousand Israelis, many of Moroccan descent, visited Morocco in 1995, representing a substantial increase from the two thousand Israelis who had visited annually since the 1980s. See Levy, "To Morocco and Back." Some two hundred thousand Israelis visited Egypt and the Sinai in 1994, representing a 70 percent increase from the previous year: Hiel, "Tourism Revival."

32. Government of Israel, *Development Options for Cooperation*.

33. Ibid. A similar regional fantasy had been articulated by the Tourism Ministry in 1968 as Israeli policymakers began to conceptualize the touristic possibilities that had resulted from the 1967 occupation: Ministry of Tourism, *Divre Sar ha-Tayarut Moshe Kol* (1968). The subsequent year the fantasy was articulated thusly: "Israelis will visit Petra and Balbek, the pyramids of Egypt and the markets of Damascus; multitudes of Arab tourists will stream into Israel to visit their holy places and to see with their own eyes the foreign Israel, that they learned to hate from distorted propaganda. . . . This two-way foreign traffic will be our peace broker": Ministry of Tourism, *Divre Sar ha-Tayarut Moshe Kol* (1970).

34. For discussion of the economic, political, and social inequities generated by the Oslo process, see Aruri, *The Obstruction of Peace*; Beinin and Stein, *The Struggle for Sovereignty*.

35. Petra was first introduced to Western travelers in the nineteenth century by John Lewis Burckhardt's *Travels in Arabia*. A century of travelers followed Burckhardt's lead, including Orientalist scholars who traveled in disguise as Muslim pilgrims and Christian pilgrims who traversed the Holy Land in search of biblical geography. For discussion of the 1950s legacy of clandestine Israeli travel, and the national mythos that followed, see Rabinowitz, "Petra." This mythos was most famously captured in Arik Lavie's popular song "ha-Sela ha-Adom" (The Red Rock), which describes the

fatal journey to Petra of courageous young Israelis. Produced in the 1950s, the song was temporarily banned on Israeli radio "lest it encourage young men to cross the border and die outside the conventional framework of heroic death — military service": Ben-Zvi, "Zionist Lesbianism and Transexual Transgression," 3.

36. This desire was also the subject of derision. Dana International, a Mizrahi transsexual singer, produced "Nosa'at le-Petra" (Traveling to Petra) in 1994, a "sophisticated political-sexual parody of Arik Lavie's canonical song": Ben-Zvi, "Zionist Lesbianism," 3.

37. Lior, "Higati la-Sela ha-Adom."

38. In the history of colonial travel, discovery claims often relied on documentation. As Mary Pratt writes, "The 'discovery' itself, even within the ideology of discovery, has no existence of its own. It only gets 'made' for real after the traveler (or other survivor) returns home, and brings it into being through texts: a name on a map, a report to the Royal Geographical Society, the Foreign Office": Imperial Eyes, 240.

39. See Sontag for discussion of the authenticity effect of marked amateurism or anti-aestheticism in photography. Sontag, Regarding the Pain of Others, 26–27.

40. "Ha-Metayalim ha-Rishonim Ḥozrim mi-Yarden."

41. E. Iss, "Tayarim im Darkonim Yisre'elim Yotsim ha-Yom la-Rishonah le-Yarden." Representatives from the Tourism Ministry explained that prior to this date, Israeli tourists had crossed the border in violation of international agreements.

42. Levinshtein, "Masof Aravah Niftaḥ le-Ma'avar Kle Rekhev Pratiyim."

43. Abu-Tuma, "Iton be-Yarden"; Lior, "Higati la-Sela ha-Adom."

44. Israel Information Service, "$30 Million Raised"; Israel Information Service, "Direct Dialing."

45. Rodan, "Independence Day Fete in Amman Draws Throng"; Zaltzman, "Lahakot me-Yarden umi-Maroko Yirkedu be-Kharmiel"; Binder, "La-Rishonah 2: Sapar Yisre'eli Yishtatef be-Taḥarut be-Yarden."

46. D. Regev and Oren, "Zehava Ben Holekhet le-Aza"; Roli Rozen, "Temunot Ketsarot."

47. A. Lavi, "Natbag 2000."

48. Ivri, "Derishat Shalom mi-Beirut"; Kaspit, "Ha-Qatari"; Shalit, "Ha-Ya'ad ha-Ba"; "Teman: Matḥilah le-Hipataḥ la-Olam"; "Tunisyah: Neot Midbar ba-Saharah."

49. Ben, "Ha-Sar Tsor"; M. Lavi, "Sheloshim Devarim she-Lo Yadatem al Suryah"; Shalit, "Ha-Ya'ad ha-Ba"; Shehori, "Kamah Medinot Araviyot Yiftehu ba-Shavuot ha-Kerovim Netsigut Tayarutit be-Tel Aviv"; Sivan, "Be-Khol Dor va-Dor Kamim Aleinu." On the place of tourism in these interstate negotiations, see Shehori, "Misrad ha-Tayarut Megabesh Tokhnit le-Shituf Peulah Tayaruti im Suryah."

50. Shalit, "Ha-Ya'ad ha-Ba."

51. M. Lavi, "Sheloshim Devarim she-Lo Yadatem al Suryah."

52. Eshet, "Yihye Tov?"

53. Kaspit, "Ha-Qatari."

54. "Teman: Matḥilah le-Hipataḥ la-Olam"; "Tunisyah: Neot Midbar ba-Saharah." For a history of Israeli-Tunisian relations, see Laskier, Israel and the Maghreb, 187–218.

55. Shehori, "Kamah Medinot Araviyot Yiftehu ba-Shavuot ha-Kerovim Netsigut Taya-rutit be-Tel Aviv."

56. In his opening address to the Middle East Economic Summit in Amman, Jordan, in 1995, Israeli Prime Minister Yizhak Rabin reiterated this narrative of surprising prox-imity: "I arrived three hours ago from Jerusalem . . . A mere twenty-minute flight separates Amman from Jerusalem. A mere twenty minutes—and forty-eight years. Historians will ask one day if and why it was necessary to wait forty-eight years in order to travel those twenty minutes": Rabin, "Address to the Amman Economic Summit."

57. Y. Cohen, "20 Dinar le-Zug"; Schrag, "Closer Than You Think."

58. Iss, "Sha'ah va-Hetsi mi-Teveryah."

59. A political leaflet distributed by the Likud Party in 1995 calling for an end to the peace process illustrated such proximities in terms of their threat by dramatizing the neg-ligible distance between Israeli urban centers and West Bank locales.

60. For further discussion of the unevenness of the regional tourism market and the aspirations of the Palestinian private sector, see Stein, "Itineraries of Peace."

61. Most favored hikes through the Judean Desert and around the Dead Sea. For ex-ample, see Thon, *Hekafnu et Yam ha-Melah ba-Regel*. The trek up Masada acquired its popular status as a nationalist rite only in the 1940s. On the history of this rite, see Zerubavel, *Recovered Roots*, 121.

62. Thon, *Halakhnu la-Hermon ve-Higanu le-Damesek*; Ben-Zvi, *Masa'ot*; D. Benvenisti and Benvenisti, *Panas ha-Kesem*. Petra first became popular among Jewish travelers from Palestine in the 1920s and 1930s. As early as the spring of 1929, a group of some 150 pupils and teachers from the Herziliya Gymnasium of Tel Aviv, renowned for its nationalist commitment to the hike [*ha-tiyul*], traveled to Petra by motor convoy. One hundred members of the Wanderers' Association visited in 1933. A selection of Soskin's photographs from the former trip appears in Silver-Brody, *Documentors of the Dream*, 129–30. Also see Honig, "Sands of Time," and Shapira, *Land and Power*, 270.

63. D. Benvenisti and Benvenisti, *Panas ha-Kesem*.

64. During the British Mandate period, these routes often violated Mandate travel re-strictions: Ibid. Also see, Zerubavel, *Recovered Roots*, 121–22.

65. While Israeli travelers were also pursuing other clandestine itineraries, these routes never acquired equivalent mythic stature. Those that have been documented include trips to Latroun, the Litani River, and Mount Hermon (located in present-day Jor-dan, Lebanon, and Syria, respectively): Safran, "Ha-Sela ha-Adom."

66. Rabinowitz, "Petra"; Safran, "Ha-Sela ha-Adom."

67. Ibid.

68. See Segev, *1967*, for a brief discussion of the forms of Israeli travel that the occupation generated.

69. I discuss this phenomenon in more detail in chapter 4.

70. "200,000 at Western Wall in First Pilgrimage since Dispersion"; "350,000 Have Walked to the Western Wall."

71. Gaza City opened to Israeli civilians on 21 July 1967, and the Golan Heights on 25 August 1967, although Israelis appeared in the Golan in advance of this official opening. Appel, "Ke-35 Elef Yisre'elim Arkhu 'Shabat shel Keniyot' be-Aza"; Kessler, "Moreh Derekh la-Mevaker ba-Shetahim ha-Muhzakim"; Z. Lavie, "'Ha-Yisre'elim Ba'im'"; "Revavot Metayelim be-Ramat ha-Golan"; Talmi, "Tevilah be-El-Hama."

72. This phenomenon was described by Ghassen Kanafani in his 1969 novella *Return to Haifa* and was heavily documented by the Israeli media: Kanafani, *Palestine's Children*; "Call for Personal Good Will to Arabs"; M. Kohn and Safadi, "Talking to Palestinians"; Z. Lavie, "Ha-Mevukeshet ba-Ir ha-Atikah"; "Peace Is Possible"; "West Bank News."

73. Meirei, "Be-Eilat Mekavim 'La'asot Kesef' meha-Kevish he-Hadash le-Sharm-a-Sheikh."

74. The Israeli media reported that some ten thousand Israelis visited the Sinai during the national Passover holiday in 1972 and some fifty thousand in 1973. Tourist numbers declined briefly after the "bad mood" generated by the 1973 War, only to resume the subsequent year: Meirei, "Be-Eilat Mekavim 'La'asot Kesef' meha-Kevish he-Hadash le-Sharm-a-Sheikh"; Sedan, "Selaim 'le-Furkan Ketivah' Yekadmu et ha-Metayalim"; Talmi, "Ha-Im Yordim Dromah?" Organized hikes through the Sinai were often led by the Israeli Society for the Protection of Nature (SPNI). On the history of the SPNI, see Rabinowitz, "Tsiyonut O Erets be-Reshit: Rekvi'em Le-Tsuki David"; Tal, *Pollution in a Promised Land*. On the demographics of the Israeli hiking community, see Shtal, "Keitsad Hinkhu et ha-Ashkenazim le-Ehov Teva ve-Tiyulim."

75. Beinin, *The Dispersion of Egyptian Jewry*, 228; Kafir, "Normalizatsyah."

76. As Defense Minister Yitzhak Rabin noted, "Jews simply don't visit the territories as they used to. No one's wandering around the garages of Gaza any more these days." Cited in Tessler, "The Intifada and Political Discourse in Israel," 45. The exception was politically motivated travel among Israel's settler community for whom hikes through the Palestinian territories was still a means of laying claim to the territory.

77. One exception was the large number of Israeli Jews from a broad class and ethnic spectrum who patronized the Jericho casino following its construction in 1998.

78. A countertrend was the reissuing of travelogues written about, or during, the pre-state period whose relevance to Israeli readers was now heightened: D. Benvenisti and Benvenisti, *Panas ha-Kesem*; Thon, *Hekafnu et Yam ha-Melah ba-Regel*.

79. Schrag, "Closer Than You Think"; Y. Cohen, "20 Dinar le-Zug."

80. See Levy, "Notes on the Jewish-Muslim Relationships"; Levy, "To Morocco and Back."

81. Shapiro, "Israelis Flock to Jersash Festival"; Ya'ari, "The Jordanian Option."

82. Y. Cohen, "20 Dinar le-Zug."

83. Ibid.; Schrag, "Closer Than You Think."

84. Ministry of Tourism, *Tourism to Israel, 1995*, 14; Ministry of Tourism, *Tourism to Israel, 1997*, 19.

85. Stein, "Itineraries of Peace."

86. Rubin, "'Lo' le-Po'alim me-Aqaba."

87. Kaveh, "Milyon Tayarim Aravim Yevakru bi-Yerushalayim u-ve-Vet Leḥem im Heskem Oslo Bet."

88. In a 1995 report to the Israeli press, Galilee Tours admitted that its operators had been organizing tours for Muslim tourists, largely from East Asia, since the 1980s. Because formal diplomacy had not yet been established with their Muslim host countries, these tours were conducted in relative secrecy. In the post-Oslo period their Muslim clientele was increasingly Arab: Shapiro, "Across the Great Divide."

89. Plotzker, "Ha-Ḥalom Kevar Kan"; Sugarman, "Make Tours, Not War." Egyptians were also traveling into Israel during this decade, although in much more limited numbers. For a first-person account of such a voyage, see Salem, *A Drive to Israel*.

90. Shapiro, "Across the Great Divide."

91. Hareuveni, "Ha-Sar Bar'am Neged Tayarut Muslemit"; Ministry of Tourism, *Regional Tourism Cooperation Development Options*, i.

92. Hagit Ringel, interview by author, tape recording, Ministry of Tourism, Jerusalem, 27 September 1995.

93. Counter such statements, the first Israeli Ministry of Tourism survey on "Muslim Tourism to Israel" was published in 1994: Israeli Bureau of Statistics, *Tayarut Muslemit Le-Yisrael*.

94. My reading is informed by Malek Alloula's discussion of French colonial representation in *The Colonial Harem*.

95. Sapir, "'Arbev et ha-Tiaḥ, Jonny.'"

96. Ja'afari, "Foreign Arab Workers in Israel." According to state statistics, over twenty-five thousand Jordanian nationals visited Israel on tourist visas in 1994, and nearly fifty thousand in 1996. Many were thought to have illegally joined the Israeli workforce: Ministry of Tourism, *Tourism to Israel, 1994*, 14; Ministry of Tourism, *Tourism to Israel, 1997*, 19. In total, some eighty-nine thousand foreign laborers were working legally in Israel in 1995, and one hundred thousand more worked illegally on tourist visas: "Foreign Workers in Israel." For a discussion of the status of foreign workers within Israel, see Kemp and Raijman, "Tel Aviv Is Not Foreign to You"; Kemp et al., "Contesting the Limits of Political Participation"; Kemp, "Labour Migration and Racialisation"; Raijman, Schammah-Gesser, and Kemp, "International Migration"; Raijman, Semyonov, and Kemp, "Gender, Ethnicity, and Immigration."

97. H. Cohen, "Shalom 2"; Dar, "Yishuve ha-Aravim Meshamshim Makom Mistor le-Tayarim Bilti Ḥukiyim"; Sadeh, "6,000 Yardenim Ba'u le-Vikur ve-Nisharu ba-Shetaḥim."

98. Sadeh, "6,000 Yardenim Ba'u le-Vikur ve-Nisharu ba-Shetaḥim."

99. Silberstein, *The Postzionism Debates*.

100. Morris, *The Birth of the Palestinian Refugee Problem*.

101. H. Cohen, "Hekhanu et ha-Kh'ek."

2. Consumer Coexistence

1. In 1995, Sakhnin was granted the official status of a city, having been elevated from its prior position as a village. Yet most Jewish Israelis and state officials still referred to Sakhnin as a village, a consensual oversight that bolstered its rural appeal: "Sakhnin Becomes a City."

2. Almog, *The Sabra*; Eyal, *The Disenchantment of the Orient*.

3. For an analogous argument in the Australian case on which this analysis draws, see Povenelli, *The Cunning of Recognition*.

4. Jewish Israeli tourism to rural sites within the Jewish Galilee was also a new phenomenon that would expand greatly in popularity during this decade. I discuss this in chapter 3.

5. Jewish Israeli tourists have been visiting 'Isifiya and Dalyiat al-Karmil since at least 1958 in the context of independence day festivities. See Robinson, "Occupied Citizens," 289, n. 661. In 1968, the Israeli Ministry of Tourism commissioned its first official study of touristic development opportunities in Dalyiat al-Karmil: Industries Development Corporation Ltd., "Conceptual Plan."

6. Some of the first bed-and-breakfast facilities were established in the villages of Dayr Hannah and Kawkab.

7. Many of these initiatives were instigated by Ruti Avidor, a prominent local Jewish resident of the Jewish community of Yodfat: Rosen, "Al Rosh ha-Har."

8. A. Etinger, "Derishat Shalom mi-Sakhnin."

9. Ibid.

10. The Palestinian population of the Galilee was reduced by over 50 percent as a result of the war, chiefly in urban areas: Falah, "Israeli 'Judaization' Policy," 234. See chapter 4 for greater discussion of the war's effect on the Palestinian population.

11. Despite efforts to settle Jews into abandoned Palestinian territory in the war's wake and to forcibly remove Palestinian villages from border regions, no major efforts were undertaken to settle Jewish citizens in the Galilee during the first decade and a half after state formation: Falah, "Israeli 'Judaization' Policy"; Kimmerling, *Zionism and Territory*.

12. *Yediot Aharonot*, 28 August 1965, cited in Jiryis, *The Arabs in Israel*, 105.

13. *Yediot Aharonot*, 12 December 1963, cited in Kimmerling, *Zionism and Territory*, 141–42.

14. Kimmerling, *Zionism and Territory*, 142.

15. Falah, *Galilee and the Judaization Plan*; Geremy Foreman, "Settlement of Title in the Galilee"; Foreman and Kedar, "From Arab Land to 'Israel Lands'"; Jiryis, *The Arabs in Israel*; Yiftachel, *Planning a Mixed Region in Israel*. These scholars differ on the periodization of Judaization efforts. Falah traces its roots to the 1948–1949 War, Foreman to 1954, and Jiryis to 1959. Most agree that intensive Judaization began in the 1970s.

16. Kimmerling estimates that some 65 percent of the total land that remained in Arab hands between 1948 and 1963 was expropriated by the Israeli state: *Zionism and Territory*, 140. Estimates differ regarding the magnitude of land expropriation because, as

Lustick notes, no official figures are available: Ibid., 178. For another accounting of land lost to Judaization, see Jiryis, *The Arabs in Israel*, 292–96.

17. Ariel Sharon was then Israel's Minister of Agriculture. Cited in Lustick, *Arabs in the Jewish State*, 258.

18. Yiftachel, *Planning a Mixed Region in Israel*, 123–25.

19. Adalah, *Legal Violations*, 7.

20. Yiftachel, "Power Disparities"; Yiftachel, "State Policies."

21. On the politics of Misgav land use, see Yiftachel, "The Internal Frontier"; Yiftachel, *Planning a Mixed Region*. Yiftachel writes:

> Misgav was given a highly irregular geographical shape, in order to include most Jewish settlements, and exclude most Arab villages. This has reinforced patterns of functional and social segregation in the region, where nearly all services are provided on an ethnic basis. While in certain areas—such as education—this ethnic separation is desired by the Arabs, their exclusion from the Misgav has also denied them access to the many social services and recreational facilities now available to Jews in the region. The creation of the Misgav and the location of its boundaries have thus worked to *segregate* Arabs from Jews in the region as part of an overall effort to control the Arab population in a region perceived as an internal frontier. ("The Internal Frontier," 504)

22. Palestinians constituted 74 percent of the total population of the Galilee during the 1990s: Yiftachel, "The Internal Frontier," 499.

23. Lustick, *Arabs in the Jewish State*, 240; Rouhana, *Palestinian Citizens in an Ethnic Jewish State*, 68–69.

24. Ghanem, *The Palestinian-Arab Minority in Israel*; Rouhana, "The Intifada and the Palestinians of Israel"; Rouhana, *Palestinian Citizens in an Ethnic Jewish State*, 69.

25. Lustick, *Arabs in the Jewish State*, 255.

26. For a discussion of more recent Judaization practices, see Adiv, "Israel's Response to the October Uprising."

27. Sikui, *Equality and Integration of the Arab Citizens in the Misgav Region*.

28. Israeli Knesset member Azmi Bishara has referred to this process as the "Israelization" of the Palestinians. Scholarly debate about this process includes al-Haj, "Education towards Multiculturalism"; Bishara, "Israeli-Arabs"; Man'a, "Identity in Crisis"; Rouhana and Ghanem, "The Crisis of Minorities"; Smooha, "The Israelization of Collective Identity." For a review of these debates, see Rekhess, "The Arabs of Israel after Oslo."

29. Prior to this period, most Palestinian citizens of Israel who were employed in the Israeli tourist sector worked primarily in the blue-collar hotel sector. Ethnic tourism enabled some to imagine careers as tour guides, restaurateurs, and bed-and-breakfast hosts. As the decade progressed, many would pursue such careers through local and regional courses on the hospitality industry.

30. See chapter 3 for further discussion of such encouragement.

31. After the enormous success of the festival during its first two years, Misgav officials both increased its scale and muted its explicit ideological content. See Krauss, "Festival shel Sovlanut ve-Teva be-Gush Segev."

32. *Debke* is a traditional Palestinian folk dance.

33. On the history of the expulsion, see Morris, *The Birth of the Palestinian Refugee Problem*, 229–30.

34. According to surveys conducted by the Israeli Ministry of Tourism, 45 percent of Jewish consumers in the rural tourism market were of high "class standing," 28 percent were among Israel's wealthiest residents, and nearly 50 percent had graduate degrees: Ministry of Tourism, *Ha-Nofshim be-Eruah ha-Kafri*. Historically, Israel's "nature-loving" and hiking community has been dominated by middle-class Ashkenazi Jews. See Shtal, "Keitsad Hinkhu et ha-Ashkenazim le-Ehov Teva ve-Tiyulim."

35. See the introduction for a discussion of the politics of ethnic differentiation. Also see Lustick, *Arabs in the Jewish State*, 82–149.

36. Similar growth was under way in the villages of 'Isifiya and Dalyiat al-Karmil.

37. The number of Jewish Israeli guides leading groups through the so-called minority sector increased tremendously during this decade. Some of these guides had led groups of foreign tourists through Palestinian villages in prior years. By the mid-1990s, the Jewish Israeli tourist demand for such itineraries was outstripping the foreign demand. Michael Ben-Dror was one of the early guides to specialize in this sector and is the author of one of the first Hebrew-language guidebooks to focus on Palestinian communities in the Galilee: *Omanim, Merap'im ve-Ose Niflaot ba-Galil*.

38. Israeli press coverage of this market frequently employed the language of coexistence. See Krauss, "Festival Shel Sovlanut ve-Teva be-Gush Segev"; Rosenblum, "Keshe-Yavo Shalom al ha-Galil"; Rudge, "Baltimore Jews"; Teiman, "Musikah ha-Teva she-Tavi et ha-Shalom"; Weitzman, "Visiting Neighbors."

39. Lustick, *Arabs in the Jewish State*, 82–149.

40. Muslim religious institutions voiced their opposition to tourism in the early stages of market development (1992–94) with concerns about the ways that incoming Jewish tourists would impact conservative local culture. Yet in subsequent years such criticism was muted by the market's fiscal promise. Ongoing political disputes over land expropriation did obstruct the growth of some tourist initiatives, but organized opposition on these grounds was extremely limited.

41. For discussion of dominant Israeli geographical imaginations of this period and the previous decade, see Schnell, *Perceptions of Israeli Arabs*.

42. Ghanem and Ozacky-Lazar, "The Status of the Palestinians"; Rekhess, "The Arabs of Israel after Oslo."

43. On the history of state policy toward the Bedouin, see Falah, "How Israel Controls the Bedouin in Israel"; Falah, "The Development of Planned Bedouin Resettlement in Israel"; Kilot, "Bedouin Settlement Policy in Israel"; Medzini, "Bedouin Settlement in the Galilee"; Yiftachel, *Ethnocracy*, 188–210.

44. Levi, "Elef Boker u-Voker." The article's title is intended as a pun on *Elef Layla ve-Layla* (Arabian Nights).

45. A. Etinger, "Derishat Shalom mi-Sakhnin."

46. Morris, *The Birth of the Palestinian Refugee Problem*, 229.

47. Palti, "Shir Shalom."

48. For a discussion of the performance of this song by Aviv Gefen the night of Rabin's assassination, see M. Regev and Seroussi, *Popular Music*, 167–168. Following the assassination, the song was rewritten by the left-wing Ashkenazi party Meretz as a campaign jingle.

49. This was true of the majority of the Israel Museum's exhibits during the 1990s, even those that showcased Arabic artifacts. For discussion of the ways Israeli museums represented Arab culture during this decade, see Ben-Ze'ev and Ben-Ari, "Imposing Politics"; Goldstein, "Secular Sublime." On the cultural politics of Israeli museums, see Katriel, *Performing the Past*.

50. Sorek, "Memory and Identity."

51. As Lustick noted in 1980, "Because of the rhetorical inconvenience of this stress upon Judaization, Labor government spokesmen tended to substitute other phrases, notably Lichloos ha-Galil [*sic*] (to populate the Galilee) and Liftoach ha-Galil [*sic*] (to develop the Galilee). Nevertheless, the crucial concern remains making and keeping the Galilee Jewish": *Arabs in the Jewish State*, 333.

52. There is a considerable scholarship on the ways that Palestinian cultural histories, objects, and spaces have been remade as Israeli. See Abu El-Haj, *Facts on the Ground*; M. Benvenisti, *Sacred Landscape*; W. Khalidi, *All That Remains*; LeVine, *Overthrowing Geography*; Slyomovics, *The Object of Memory*.

3. Scalar Fantasies

1. Birnack Investments, *Dayr Hannah*.

2. Jiryis, *The Arabs in Israel*; Lustick, *Arabs in the Jewish State*; Robinson, "Occupied Citizens."

3. I am drawing on Bachelard's discussion of the ways that interior space functions as a repository of memory and history. See Bachelard, *The Poetics of Space*.

4. This chapter draws on the growing anthropological literature on everyday state practices. Recent work includes Hansen and Stepputat, *States of Imagination*; Scott, *Seeing Like a State*; Navaro-Yashin, *Faces of the State*; Sharma and Gupta, *The Anthropology of the State*. This chapter also draws on recent literature on the politics of space, architecture, and planning in Israel, including, Abu El-Haj, *Facts on the Ground*; M. Benvenisti, *Sacred Landscape*; LeVine, *Overthrowing Geography*; Mann, *A Place in History*; Monk, *An Aesthetic Occupation*; Segal and Weizman, *A Civilian Occupation*; Troen, *Imagining Zion*; Weizman, *Hollow Land*; Yiftachel, *Ethnocracy*; Zakim, *To Build and Be Built*.

5. Hareven and Ghanem, *Retrospect and Prospects*.

6. Abu El-Haj, *Facts on the Ground*; M. Benvenisti, *Sacred Landscape*; LeVine, *Overthrowing Geography*.

7. Morris, *The Birth of the Palestinian Refugee Problem*.

8. Azmi Bishara has argued that "with the foundation of the state of Israel in 1948 . . . Palestinian society lost the Palestinian city, having been reduced to a village society,

separate from but dependent for its subsistence upon a Jewish city that refuses to allow integration. Moreover, with the loss of agriculture as a basis for subsistence, village society became neither rural nor urban": "Israeli-Arabs," cited in Sorek, "Palestinian Nationalism Has Left the Field," 425.

9. Jiryis, *The Arabs in Israel*, 75–101; W. Khalidi, *All That Remains*.

10. On the decline of the Palestinian agrarian sector, see Falah, "Israeli 'Judaization' Policy"; Haidar, *On the Margins*.

11. Bishara, "Israeli-Arabs," cited in Sorek, "Palestinian Nationalism Has Left the Field," 425.

12. Gil Eyal has argued that the military government "effectively fixed the residence of Palestinians in the villages": *The Disenchantment of the Orient*, 156.

13. Robinson, "Occupied Citizens."

14. Eyal, *The Disenchantment of the Orient*, 157.

15. "Outline plans" delimit the parameters within which a community can legally build and expand: Khamaisi, *Planning and Housing*. Khamaisi argues that the central aim in the preparation of such plans has been the "fixing of Arab village boundaries within as small an area as possible" through increasing the land available for possible Jewish settlement expansion (88).

16. Ibid., 80.

17. Ibid., 96.

18. For a discussion of this history of exclusion, see ibid., 91, 98; Forester, Fischler, and Shmueli, "Rassem Khamaisi."

19. Falah, "Welfare Geography"; Falah, "Israeli 'Judaization' Policy"; Yiftachel, *Planning a Mixed Region*.

20. Falah, "Israeli 'Judaization' Policy."

21. The Jewish Agency, cited in Yiftachel, *Planning a Mixed Region*, 143.

22. Khamaisi, *Planning and Housing*, 71.

23. One can point to a few counterexamples of Palestinian residential patterns in predominantly Jewish Israeli cities, including in Nazareth Elite and Karmiel. See Rabinowitz, "The Frontiers of Urban Mix."

24. Eyal, *The Disenchantment of the Orient*, 169.

25. See chapter 2 for an elaboration.

26. On the politics of Palestinian allegiance to the Israeli state, see H. Cohen, *Army of Shadows*; Kanaaneh, *On the Edge of Security*.

27. The Israeli Ministry of Tourism first expressed interest in this market in the late 1980s, when the Israeli Government Tourist Cooperation commissioned a study on developmental prospects in the "Arab and Druze sectors." The publication of this study was delayed due to the outbreak of the first Palestinian uprising: Liram Architecture, Civil Engineering, and Environmental Design, *Tokhnit Av le-Fituah Tayarut ba-Migzar ha-Aravi*. The document was subsequently revised as *Seker Potentsiyal Tayarut ba-Migzar ha-Aravi*.

28. Marktest, *Seker Pituah Tayarut ba-Kefarim ha-Araviyim bi-Tsafon ha-Arets*. Development

plans for a small number of Palestinian villages were approved in 1994, including the villages of Abu Ghosh, Nazareth, and Kfar Kanna. For example, see Ministry of Tourism, *Tokhnit Programit le-Fituaḥ Ta'asiyat ha-Tayarut be-Abu Ghosh veha-Svivah*. For further discussion of Abu Ghosh's tourism sector, see chapter 5.

29. While budgetary gains under the Labor Party were significant, many of the state's discriminatory policies, particularly those related to land-use planning and education, remained in place: Hareven and Ghanem, eds., *Equality and Integration, Retrospect and Prospects*.

30. Ibid.; Prime Minister's Office, *Gidul Mashma'uti be-Takstive ha-Memshalah la-Migzar ha-Aravi*.

31. Hareven and Ghanem, eds., *Equality and Integration, Retrospect and Prospects*.

32. The state's budget for Nazareth rose from NIS 600,000 in 1992 to NIS 30 million in 1996: Middle East Report, "Palestinian Rights in Post-Oslo Israel."

33. In the mid-1990s, renovation and gentrification in 'Akka had begun to raise real estate values, forcing many lower income Palestinian families to move. As I was told by an employee of the Israeli Government Tourist Development Office in 'Akka, "We're not going to expel the Arabs like we did in Jaffa, but if they want to move, they can."

34. Development in Jisr al-Zarka was predicated on the village's history of political allegiance to the state. See Morris, "The Case of Abu Ghosh." On the state efforts to develop a local tourist market, see Hirschberg, "The Town That Got Left Behind."

35. Hagit Ringel, interview by author, tape recording, Ministry of Tourism, Jerusalem, 27 September 1995. Some Palestinian entrepreneurs in the Galilee did hope to attract tourists from the Arab World: Abbas, *Ḥadre Eruaḥ u-Kfar Nofesh be-Kefar Jat*.

36. Martins Hoffman Inc., *Seker be-Kerev ha-Migzar ha-Aravi be-Nose Tayarut Panim be-Yisrael*.

37. Ibid.

38. For discussion of rural tourism in Jewish towns in Israel, see A. Fleischer and Pizam, "Rural Tourism in Israel"; A. Fleischer and Felsenstein, "Support for Rural Tourism."

39. At the Annual Conference on Rural Tourism sponsored by the Israeli Ministry of Tourism on November 30, 1995, Arab villages were not mentioned. Also see Ministry of Tourism, *Yeḥidot ha-Eruaḥ ha-Kafri be-Yisrael*, 23.

40. The Jewish market grew considerably from the mid-1980s to the mid-1990s. A 1996 survey on market growth noted that "today the number of rooms stands at 4100 in 200 settlements [*yishuvim*] that work in rural tourism, compared with 566 rooms in 22 settlements in 1986": Development Study Center, *Ha-Nofshim be-Eruaḥ ha-Kafri*, 6.

41. For instances of an early Israeli planning document that narrates the Israeli countryside as a strictly Jewish domain, see Prion, *Development Trends*; Weitz, *The Envisioned Image of the Village*.

42. The "village core" is referred to by two Hebrew phrases that are used interchange-

ably in state documents: *galin ha-kefar* and *gar'in ha-kefar*. Translated literally, these terms refer to the "nucleus, kernel, or pit" of the village.

43. Gil Eyal has argued that through "the metaphor of the 'traditional core' [the] 'Arab village' is portrayed as an island of tradition amidst a roaring ocean of progress (i.e., the 'Western-modern Israeli society')": "The Discursive Origins of Israeli Separatism," 396, 99. Eyal cites the following excerpt from a 1976 text by an Israeli geographer as one example of such usage: "'Most Arab villages contain an old, traditional core. This densely populated core in the center of the village developed slowly through time and its structure adapted to the traditional needs and livihood of its inhabitants'": Eyal, *The Disenchantment of the Orient*, 169.

44. The Israeli Ministry of Tourism planned to develop village "cores" in Dayr Hannah, 'Arrabeh, Sakhnin, Horfeish, Yerka, Majd El Krum, and Beit Jan: Birnack Investments, *Majd El Krum*; Birnack Investments, *Programah le-Fituah Tayarut be-Beit Jan*; Fellner Development Ltd., *Seker Zmani be-Gar'in ha-Kefar Yerka*.

45. For example, see Birnack Investments, *Programah le-Fituah Tayarut be-Beit Jan*.

46. See chapter 2 for further discussion of the ways that the Ministry of Tourism positioned the European market in rural hospitality as a development exemplar.

47. See chapter 2 for discussion of the politics of authenticity.

48. Interiority was also emphasized within the Israeli academic discourse on the Arab village. See Eyal, *The Disenchantment of the Orient*, 168.

49. Fellner Development Ltd., *Seker Zemani be-Gar'in ha-Kefar Yerka*.

50. Rinot Ltd., *Dayr Hannah*.

51. Baran Designs, *Tokhnit Av le-Fituah Tayarut be-Ma'aliyah*.

52. Ibid.

53. This finding was supported by a 1994 survey on "internal tourism," which concluded that most Jewish-Israeli tourists vacationing in the rural Jewish sector sought vacation spots "surrounded by water and greenery, preferably with a view of snow, relatively isolated but also close to a city and recreation area . . . [with] organized hikes provided by the hotel at specific times . . . and hiking [possibilities] in the immediate area": Martins Hoffman Inc., *Seker Tayarut Panim be-Yisrael*. Additional surveys conducted in 1996 confirmed that the majority of the Jewish-Israeli client population was interested in nature, hiking, or water sports as opposed to cultural offerings: Development Study Center, *Ha-Nofshim ba-Eruah ha-Kafri*, 15.

54. Jeep tours through the Galilee's natural areas grew in popularity during this period: Rosenblum, "Jeeps, Cheese, Music."

55. The Jewish community of Hararit became a center of such services. See Inbari, "New Age"; University of Haifa, *Siah be-Nose Tikhnun Rekhes Hararit Yodfat*.

56. Development blueprints for an integrated tourist market in Misgav and Sakhnin recommended agricultural tourism for Misgav and ethnic tourism (*tayarut etnit*) for neighboring Arab areas: Mansfeld, *Tokhnit le-Fituah Tayarut ve-Nofesh, Ezor Misgav u-Vik'at Sakhnin*, 25.

57. See Segal and Weizman, *A Civilian Occupation*, 19, for discussion of the ways that "ele-

ments of planning and architecture have been conscripted as tactical tools in Israeli state strategy."

58. On Israeli Orientalism, see Eyal, *The Disenchantment of the Orient*; Y. Peleg, *Orientalism and the Hebrew Imagination*. For discussion of the romanticization of the Bedouin in the prestate period, see Almog, *The Sabra*, 185–208; Eyal, *The Disenchantment of the Orient*, 33–61.

59. See, for example, D. Benvenisti and Benvenisti, *Panas ha-Kesem*, 17, 19, 32–33, 79.

60. Ibid., 18.

61. Almog, *The Sabra*, 188; Eyal, *The Disenchantment of the Orient*, 92.

62. Said, *Orientalism*, 7.

63. For discussion of the ways that tourists conflate authenticity with interiority, or what he calls "back regions," see MacCannell, *The Tourist*. John Frow has noted that MacCannell's discussion of these spaces is infused with nostalgia for an unsullied authenticity. See Frow, "Tourism and the Semiotics of Nostalgia."

64. Fabian, *Time and the Other*.

65. Eyal makes a related argument on how "the combined effect of confiscation of landed property, tight control over the issuance of building permits, and zoning restrictions . . . produced a distinctive spatial structure, which . . . was identified by geographers as characteristic of the 'traditional' Arab village undergoing a slow modernization process": *The Disenchantment of the Orient*, 158.

66. This line of argument draws on the growing geographical literature on the production of scale. Recent work includes Brenner, "State Territorial Restructuring"; Delaney and Leitner, "The Political Construction of Scale"; Herod and Wright, *Geographies of Power*; Marston, "The Social Construction of Scale"; McCarthy, "Scale, Sovereignty, and Strategy"; Smith, "Contours of a Spatialized Politics."

67. Rosaldo, "Imperial Nostalgia."

68. Doumani, *Rediscovering Palestine*; W. Khalidi and Institute for Palestine Studies, *Before Their Diaspora*; Tamari, "Wasif Jawhariyyeh."

69. Neil Smith talks about an analogous process that he calls "jumping scales": "Contours of a Spatialized Politics," 66.

4. Culinary Patriotism

1. This chapter draws on an interdisciplinary scholarship on the cultural politics of food and eating. Recent work in this area includes Farquhar, *Appetites*; Mintz, *Tasting Food, Tasting Freedom*; Caldwell and Watson, *The Cultural Politics of Food and Eating*; Witt, *Black Hunger*; Yue, *The Mouth That Begs*. For a review of recent developments in the anthropology of food, see Sidney W. Mintz and Christine M. Du Bois, "The Anthropology of Food and Eating."

2. I am drawing on Lévi-Strauss, *Totemism*, particularly its discussion of "edible things."

3. Bourdieu, *Distinction*.

4. For further discussion, see Stein, "Ballad of the Sad Cafe."

5. I elaborate on this point in Stein and Swedenburg, "Popular Culture."

6. See Mahmood, *Politics of Piety*, for a related critique of Butler. This chapter draws on recent scholarly discussions of melancholia, including the following: Butler, *The Psychic Life of Power*; Eng and Kazanjian, eds., *Loss*; and Khanna, *Dark Continents*.

7. Abu Ghosh was also the site of a bi-annual festival of classical music that began in the 1960s, temporarily ceased operations in 1976, and was restarted in 1992. Elite Jews of European descent comprised the vast majority of festival visitors. The village's acclaim as a festival site also bolstered its restaurant sector.

8. This survey recommended infrastructural repair and development of cultural institutions, including an "Arab market," a "living museum" of "ancient Arab cultural life," and renovation of the historic village center (*gar'in ha-kfar*). This development protocol was soon abandoned. See Ministry of Tourism, *Tokhnit Programit le-Fituah Ta'asiyat be-Abu Ghosh veha-Sevivah*.

9. Eilon, "Ha-Mizrah he-Hadash Shel ha-'Ir." The phrase "the new old" (*ha-atikah ha-hadashah*), was a pun on "The New Middle East," suggesting ways that surging popularity in the restaurant sector was linked to concurrent political processes.

10. For primary accounts, see Chateaubriand, *Travels in Greece, Palestine, Egypt and Barbary during the Years 1806 and 1807*; Finn, *Stirring Times*; Fulton, *Palestine*; Kelman, *The Holy Land*; de Lamartine, *Voyage en Orient, 1832–1833*. For discussion of these travel histories and narratives, see Shepherd, *Zealous Intruders*.

11. There is disagreement among local residents as to the early history of this collaboration. Robinson, in "Occupied Citizens in a Liberal State," traces this history to 1919 (183). For a general history of Palestinian collaboration with the Zionists during the British Mandate period, see H. Cohen, *Army of Shadows*.

12. Morris, *The Birth of the Palestinian Refugee Problem*.

13. Morris, "The Case of Abu Ghosh." For a discussion of this history based on oral testimonies, see Robinson, "Occupied Citizens."

14. Most Palestinian refugees who attempted to return were criminalized as infiltrators. On the history of infiltration, see Morris, *Israel's Border Wars*.

15. Historians differ on the date of the eventual resettlement of neighboring villages. Morris contends it was 1965, while Walid Khalidi dates resettlement to 1962: W. Khalidi, *All That Remains*, 278; Morris, *The Birth of the Palestinian Refugee Problem*; Morris, "The Case of Abu Ghosh," 194–204.

16. Meletz and Sela, "Ha-Kefarim she-Lo Hayu" [The Villages That Never Were].

17. Kiryat Ye'arim Local Council, *Ye'arim*.

18. For a discussion of Palestinian soldiers in the Israeli army, see Kanaaneh, *On the Edge of Security*.

19. Local entrepreneurs did explore other tourist ventures during this period, including bed-and-breakfasts, guided tours, and history lectures. Without state backing, advertising and revenues were limited and such efforts ceased after several months.

20. On the history of *baqlawa* (also called *baklava*), see Perry, "The Taste for Layered Bread among the Nomadic Turks and the Central Asian Origins of Baklava." For a

general discussion of the cultural politics of food in the Middle East, see Zubaida and Tapper, eds., *Culinary Cultures of the Middle East.*

21. For discussion of the Palestinian vote in the Israeli national elections of 1992 and 1996, respectively, see al-Haj, "The Political Behavior of the Arabs"; Kaufman and Israeli, "The Odd Group Out." For discussion of state-sponsored celebrations of Israeli Independence Day within Israel's Palestinian communities in the decades after state formation, including Abu Ghosh, see Shammas, "At Half Mast"; Robinson, "Occupied Citizens in a Liberal State," 183–260. For a more general inquiry into festivals and patriotic memorials in Israel, see Handelman, *Nationalists and the Israeli State.*

22. Ben-Ze'ev, "Masoret, Mitos, ve-Zehut."

23. Swedenburg, "Seeing Double."

24. Almog, *The Sabra*; Eyal, *The Disenchantment of the Orient*; Y. Peleg, *Orientalism and the Hebrew Imagination.*

25. Almog, *The Sabra*, 12, 184; Bartal, *Cossack and Bedouin.* Memoirs from the period describe female settlers learning cooking practices from their Arab neighbors. See Raviv, "Recipe for a Nation," 59, 60. As Claudia Roden has suggested, the rejection of Ashkenazi food by early Jewish settlers was linked to efforts to refashion themselves as New Jews. See *The Book of Jewish Food*, 202–7.

26. Robinson, "Occupied Citizens in a Liberal State," 156. For a discussion of how, in Robinson's words, "the politics of food and hosting permeated relations between [military] governors and Bedouin communities," see Gitlis, *Ha-Moshel ha-Mekho'ar*, cited in Robinson, "Occupied Citizens in a Liberal State," 157.

27. Raviv, "Recipe for a Nation," 156, 159.

28. Ibid., 162.

29. During the 1960s "various Arab and Middle Eastern dishes were gradually nationalized and christened 'Israeli' due to their overwhelming popularity among native born Sabras (falafel and humus being two obvious examples)": Ibid., 243–44, and, Raviv, "Falafel." For a related discussion of how oranges have circulated in Israeli discourse as signs of Zionist modernity, therein erasing their histories within Palestinian economies, see Bardenstein, "Threads of Memory and Discourses of Rootedness."

30. For the related history of consumptive practices within the Palestinian community inside Israel, see Forte, "Shopping in Jenin"; Kanaaneh, *Birthing the Nation*, 81–103.

31. P. Kohn, "Old City Hotels Being Vacated."

32. Gillon, "Fraternization Banned."

33. "South West Bank Flooded with Tourists."

34. Hope, "Jerusalem Traffic."

35. Rieker, "Piknik be-Ḥavilat Ḥusein."

36. The term appeared in a photo caption in the *Jerusalem Post: Junior* 7 July 1967.

37. Z. Lavie, "Ha-Mevukeshet ba-Ir ha-Atikah"; Meron, "Andralamusyah ve-Shema Calcalit Hagadah."

38. Kenan, "Bikur be-Misadah be-Ḥevron."

39. "Keeping Posted."

40. Appel, "Ke-35 Elef Yisre'elim Arkhu 'Shabat Shel Keniyot' Be-Aza."

41. Meron, "Andralamusyah ve-Shema Kalkalit ha-Gadah."

42. Kessler, "Moreh Derekh la-Mevaker ba-Shetaḥim ha-Muḥzakim."

43. Meron, "Andralamusyah ve-Shema Kalkalit ha-Gadah."

44. Ibid.

45. Appel, "Ke-35 Elef Yisre'elim Arkhu 'Shabat Shel Keniyot' be-Aza."

46. Shamir, "Zohi Da'ati."

47. "Peace Is Possible."

48. On the history of the East Jerusalem tourist market before and after the 1967 occupation, see United Nations Conference on Trade and Development, *The Tourism Sector.*

49. The popularity of Palestinian restaurants in the newly occupied territories also changed the offerings of Israeli restaurants, as products from the territories began to make their way into Israeli establishments. See "Etsel Boulus be-Jafa."

50. Menusi, "Bediḥamin le-Shabat."

51. Personal correspondence with Daniel Rogov, 17 May 2006.

52. Sugerman, "Please Pass the Foie Gras"; personal correspondence with Rogov.

53. Maltz, "Fast Exit"; Azaryahu, "The Golden Arches of McDonald's"; Azaryahu, "Mcisrael?"; Ram, *The Globalization of Israel*; Ram, "Glocommodification." As a result of such trends, some Israelis feared the disappearance of the affordable Mizrahi eateries that had long populated Israeli cities: Dali, "Good Taste."

54. Personal correspondence with Daniel Rogov, 17 May 2007. For a comprehensive discussion of the Americanization of Israeli culture, see *Israel Studies* 5.1 (2000).

55. Personal correspondence with Daniel Rogov, 17 May 2007.

56. N. C. Gross, "Pigging Out."

57. Western Galilee Tourist Trust, "ha-Okhel ba-Galil ha-Ma'aravi."

58. The *Good Food Guide to Israel*, written by two prominent Ashkenazi food critics and published in 1998, was one of the most popular food guides of this period and was credited with the culinary rediscovery of the Galilee by Jewish Israeli consumers. The guide sold some eighty thousand copies during the first year of publication: Palti, "Obeying the Herd Instinct"; Riesenfeld and Farber, *Good Food Guide to Israel.*

59. For a literary analysis of cookbooks and culinary cultures in the Middle East context, see Fragner, "From the Caucasus to the Roof of the World"; Fragner, "Social Reality"; Heine, "The Revival of Traditional Cooking"; Perry, "The Taste for Layered Bread"; Zubaida and Tapper, *Culinary Cultures of the Middle East.*

60. Eilon, "Sodo Shel ha-Zatar ha-Aravi" [The Secret of Arab Zatar]; Levar, "Ha-Mitbaḥ ha-Druzi Etslekha ba-Bayit" [The Druze Kitchen in Your Home].

61. Rogov, "New Organic Products"; Rousso, "In Search of a Real Cookbook"; Rousso, "Kitchen Secrets."

62. Rogov, "Anise Way to Go"; Rogov, "Barbecuties."

63. The American food critic Joan Nathan praised this cookbook as a possible "bridge to peace": Nathan, "Israel's Silver Age," 32.

64. Rogov, "Rekindling the Faith."

65. Rogov, "Lunching at Leisure."

66. For discussion of Israeli representations of the Rabin assassination and the memorial culture that followed, see Azoulay, *Death's Showcase*; Erlich, *Reactions of Adolescents to Rabin's Assasination*; Peri, *The Assasination of Yitzhak Rabin*.

5. Of Cafés and Terror

1. On the nationalist politics of memorial in the Israeli context, see Handelman, *Nationalism and the Israeli State*; Zertal, *Israel's Holocaust*; Zerubavel, *Recovered Roots*.

2. On the history of these attacks, see Beinin and Stein, "Histories and Futures."

3. Walid Khalidi argues that café bombings were first introduced into the regional conflict by Zionist militants on March 17, 1936: *Palestine Reborn*, 151. Thanks to Joseph Massad for alerting me to this source.

4. These include the bombing of Café Moment (March 9, 2002), the attempted assault on Café Caffit in West Jerusalem (March 7, 2002), the attack on My Coffeshop in Tel Aviv (March 30, 2002), and bombing of a pedestrian mall in Netanya (March 30, 2002).

5. This chapter focuses on a variety of Israeli newspapers, including *Ha-aretz, Yedi'ot Aharonot, Ma'ariv* and *The Jerusalem Post*. See chapter 1 for discussion of these newspapers.

6. Robinson, "My Hairdresser Is a Sniper."

7. For discussion of the social function of cafés in the Middle East and Mediterranean context, see Hattox, *Coffee and Coffeehouses*; Örs, "Coffeehouses."

8. See Beinin and Stein, *The Struggle for Sovereignty*, chapters 1, 2, 6.

9. Ibid.; Reinhart, *Israel/Palestine*, 143–80.

10. Mouin Rabbani, cited in Reinhart, *Israel/Palestine*, 150.

11. Amnesty International, *Israel and the Occupied Territories*.

12. Lori, "The Age of Anxiety."

13. Ibid.

14. Ibid.

15. The slogan "War for the Peace of the Settlements" was a rallying cry of the Israeli left which attributed this period of conflict to settlement building and military occupation. The slogan punned on "War for the Peace of Galilee," the state's euphemism for its Lebanon war of 1982.

16. Shavit, "Milhemet Shalom Moment."

17. Goldenberg, "Bombing Shatters Illusions."

18. Galili, "Yerushalayim Hafkha le-Ir Shel 'Take Away.'"

19. "Taking Back the Cafés"; Goodman, "Blood, Sweat."

20. Others read: "It's not about the settlements. It's about Moment. It's about you and me": Harman, "For Israel's Peace Flanks." Another: "It's impossible to stop this moment": Weiss, "Et ha-Moment ha-Zeh i-Efshar le-Hafsik."

21. Freedman, "A Cork Pops."

22. Beaumont, "I Don't Want to Be Here."

23. Sharon delivered this speech before a special session of the Israeli Parliament on April 8, 2002: "Mideast Turmoil."

24. Sharon's official rhetoric often referenced this relationship, as when he described the Israeli offensive into the West Bank as part of the "international struggle of the free world against the forces of darkness who seek to destroy our liberty and way of life." Cited in Beinin, "The Israelization of American Foreign Policy Discourse," 125.

25. By the fall of 2002, visits to bombed cafés would be included as part of U.S. solidarity tourism to Israel. In subsequent years, such visits would be added to the official itineraries of the Birthright Israel program. See Rifkin, "Life Continues."

26. Lefkovits, "Hundreds Turn Café into Shrine."

27. Goodman, "Blood, Sweat."

28. One article read: "We can't stop living our normal lives. That's what they [the Palestinian bombers] want us to do. *If we change what we do, then they win*" (emphasis mine): Mason, "Personal Lessons in Coping."

29. Lefkovits, "Waiter Foils Jerusalem Café Bombing." This narrative would recur several months later, when a security guard in a Tel Aviv café foiled an attack. See Gutman, "Alert Tel Aviv Café Security Guard."

30. Weiss and Rofeh, "Ne'etsar Meḥabel Mitabed be-Reḥov Emek Refa'im bi-Yerushalayim."

31. Gutman, "Hired Guns."

32. For account of civilian profiling, see Kligman, "Am I a Racist?" This account ends with an unusual reflection on the practice: "But am I a racist?"

33. Galili, "Yerushalayim Hafkha le-Ir Shel 'Take Away.'"

34. Yoash, "Certain Half Deserted Streets."

35. Israeli buses were also targeted by Palestinian militants in 1950s and 1970s but were not favored targets during these decades.

36. LeVine, Overthrowing Geography, 21–51; Mann, A Place in History, 186–228.

37. Quoted in Troen, Imagining Zion, 91.

38. LeVine, Overthrowing Geography, 152–181.

39. The most famous café of this period was the seaside Casino café: Helman, "European Jews in the Levant Heat," 85; Mann, A Place in History, 93.

40. Regev has suggested that "many of the poets who wrote in the *pizmon* genre, including Natan Alterman, Leave Goldberg, Emanuel Harusi and Abraham Shlonsky, frequented "The Snow of Lebanon café." Alterman's literary legacy is also linked to Café Cassit: M. Regev and Seroussi, *Popular Music*, 80.

41. Helman, "European Jews in the Levant Heat," 85. Herzl's fictionalized account of the emergence of Zionism begins in "one of the most charming of Viennese cafés": Herzl, Old New Land, 3.

42. Troen, Imagining Zion, 142.

43. Helman, "European Jews in the Levant Heat," 77–78.

44. Ibid., 85.

45. Helman, "European Jews in the Levant Heat," 86. See also Helman, "Torah, Avodah, U-Vate Kafeh: Dat u-Farhesyah be-Tel Aviv ha-Mandatit."

46. Troen, *Imagining Zion*, 94. The iconic status of the café in Tel Aviv-Jaffa has spawned two performances which take the café as their organizing principle: *Ve-az Halakhnu le-Cassit* [And Off We Went to Café Cassit], by Hanna Marron and performed at the Herzilya Theater Ensemble in the winter of 2002, and *Let's Dance*, by the Arab-Hebrew Theater of Jaffa.

47. Almog, *The Sabra*, 12; Helman, "European Jews in the Levant Heat," 80. For discussion of how Israeli cafés as public spaces figured in the popular music culture, see M. Regev and Seroussi, *Popular Music and National Culture in Israel*, 80–81.

48. Almog, *The Sabra*, 210, 43.

49. Rehavia was founded as a garden suburb that emulated urban development projects under way in England and Germany. See Katz, "Ideology and Urban Development."

50. On the architectural history of Rehavia, see Kroyanker, Wahrman, and Makhon Yerushalayim le-Ḥeker Yisrael, *Adrikhalut bi-Yerushalayim*. On the bourgeois culture of the neighborhood, see Ramon, "Doktor Mul Doktor Gar," 50, 64, 66.

51. Kroyanker and Makhon Yerushalayim le-Ḥeker Yisrael, *Adrikhalut bi-Yerushalayim*, 280.

52. Appelfeld, Appelfeld, and Halter, *A Table for One*, 16.

53. Personal correspondence with Daniel Rogov, 17 May 2007.

54. The decline of literary café culture in West Jerusalem was epitomized by the closing of Café Atara, once frequented by Israeli authors such as S. Y. Agnon and featured in the writings of Amos Oz. It was converted into a Pizza Hut.

55. Mason, "Personal Lessons in Coping."

56. See Galili, "Yerushalayim Hafkha le-Ir Shel 'Take Away'"; Golan-Meiri, "Snifei 'Aroma' bi-Yerushalayim lo Ye'afsheru Lashevet be-Shiṭham"; Weiss, "Et ha-Moment ha-Zeh I-Efshar Lehafsik."

57. Gelfond, "And Now Rehavia."

58. Ibid.

59. Shavit, "Milḥemet Shalom Moment."

60. "The Siege of Jerusalem"; Shaviv, "Should a Security Fence Be Built?"

61. This construal obscured the history of Israeli cafés that were non-European in form, the Palestinian and Mizrahi institutions of both the present and the past, even as it obscured the central place of the coffeehouse within Arab public spheres in the Middle East. See note 7 above for discussion of these histories.

62. Galili, "Yerushalayim Hafkha le-Ir Shel 'Take Away'"; Golan, "Ha'ir Ha-Mifna et Gavah."

63. Newman, "Retaining Our Humanity"; Yoash, "Certain Half Deserted Streets."

64. Ben-Simon, "Tarbut Lailah Holekhet ve-Gova'at"; Khalbi, "Etslenu Hakhi Tov ba-Olam"; Vinod, "Ein le'an li-Veroaḥ."

65. Galili, "Yerushalayim Hafkha le-Ir Shel 'Take Away.'"

66. Hartog, "Taking Back the Cafés."

67. Y. Etinger and Pepper, "Mi-Yom le-Yom ha-Ir Nimḥeket"; Lefkovits, "Attacks Leave Capital's Restaurants, Cafés Empty"; Shahar, "Mi she-Lo Mukhraḥ."

68. Gordon, "Where Are the Peaceniks?"

69. For a recent discussion of this classic Zionist trope, see Piterberg, "Erasures." Also see Raz-Krakotzkin, "Galut bi-Tokh Ribonut: le-Vikoret 'Shelilat ha-Galut' ba-Tarbut ha-Yisre'elit"; Raz-Krakotzkin, "Galut bi-Tokh Ribonut: le-Vikoret 'Shelilat ha-Galut' ba-Tarbut ha-Yisre'elit, Ḥelek Sheni."

70. LeVine, *Overthrowing Geography*, 121–151.

71. Pratt, "Scratches on the Face of the Country."

72. Zachary Lockman has argued that the early Zionist slogan "a land without a people" should be read as a figurative account of a territory lacking the recognizable markers of a modern nation. *Comrades and Enemies*, 26–31.

73. W. Khalidi, *All That Remains*.

74. See Blecher, "Living on the Edge." Polls conducted by the Jaffee Center for Strategic Studies found that 46 percent of Israeli Jews surveyed supported the transfer of Palestinians from the West Bank and 31 percent supported Palestinian transfer from inside Israel: Barzilai, "Seker."

75. The far-right Israeli Knesset member Effi Eytan, who has openly supported Palestinian mass population transfer, made such statements in 2002. See Shavit, "Dear God, This Is Effi."

76. Spivak, "Can the Subaltern Speak?"

Postscript

1. Benn and Alon, "The Public Should Have Listened"; Melman, "The Task Force."

2. Bar, "The Other Within."

3. Erlanger, "Israelis Trudge Home."

4. Ibid.

5. Ibid.

6. R. Rozen, "Ha-Shalom ha-Shahor ha-Zeh."

Bibliography

Abbas, Yigal. *Ḥadre Eruaḥ u-Kefar Nofesh be-Kefar Jat* (Guest Houses and Vacation Village in Jat Village). Jat: n.p., 1995.

Abu El-Haj, Nadia. *Facts on the Ground: Archeological Practice and Territorial Self-Fashioning in Israeli Society*. Berkeley: University of California Press, 2001.

Abu Lughoud, Lila. "The Romance of Resistance." *American Ethnologist* 17 (1990): 41–55.

Abu-Tuma, Khalid. "Iton be-Yarden: ha-Tayarim ha-Yisre'elim Kamtsanim ve-Okhlim Rak Falafel" (Newspaper in Jordan: The Israeli Tourists Are Stingy and Only Eat Falafel). *Jerusalem* 8 September 1995.

Adalah. *Legal Violations of Arab Minority Rights in Israel*. Shfaram: Adalah (The Legal Center for Arab Minority Rights in Israel), 1998.

Adiv, Assaf. "Israel's Response to the October Uprising: 'Judaizing' Galilee!" *Challenge* May–June 2001.

After Oslo: The Shape of Palestine to Come. Washington, D.C.: Middle East Research and Information Project, 1994.

Alexandrowicz, Ra'anan, et al. *The Inner Tour: A Journey through Israel in 7 Chapters*. Zeitgeist Video, S.1., 2004.

al-Haj, Majid. "Education towards Multiculturalism in Light of the Peace Process." In *Rav-Tarbutiyut be-Medinah Demokratit ve-Yehudit: Sefer Zikaron le-Ariel Rozen-Tsevi* (Multiculturalism in a Democratic and Jewish State), ed. Menachem Mautner, Abraham Sagi, and Ronen Shamir. Tel-Aviv: Dayan Center, 1998: 703–14.

———. "The Political Behavior of the Arabs in Israel in the 1992 Elections: Integration vs. Segregation." In *The Elections in Israel: 1992*, ed. Asher Arian and Michal Shamir. Albany: State University of New York Press, 1995: 141–60.

Alloula, Malek. *The Colonial Harem*. Minneapolis: University of Minnesota Press, 1986.

Almog, Oz. *The Sabra: The Creation of the New Jew*. Berkeley: University of California Press, 2000.

Amnesty International. *Israel and the Occupied Territories: Surviving under Siege. The Impact of Movement Restrictions on the Right to Work*. London: International Secretariat, 2003.

Amnesty International and Amnesty International USA. *Israel/Occupied Territories and the Palestinian Authority: Five Years after the Oslo Agreement. Human Rights Sacrificed for "Security."* New York: Amnesty International USA, 1998.

Appel, David. "Ke-35 Elef Yisre'elim Arkhu 'Shabat Shel Keniyot' be-Aza" (Some 35 Thousand Israelis Spent a "Shopping Shabbat" in Gaza). *Yediot Aḥaronot* 23 July 1967: 19.

Appelfeld, Aron, Meir Appelfeld, and Aloma Halter. *A Table for One: Under the Light of Jerusalem*. New Milford, Conn.: Toby, 2005.

Arbel, Rachel, and Chaya Galai. *Blue and White in Color: Visual Images of Zionism, 1897–1947*. Tel Aviv: Beth Hatefutsoth, The Nahum Goldmann Museum of the Jewish Diaspora, 1996.

Aruri, Naseer H. *The Obstruction of Peace: The United States, Israel, and the Palestinians*. Monroe, Maine: Common Courage Press, 1995.

Avraham, Eli. *Ha-Tikshoret be-Yisrael: Sikuran shel Ayarot ha-Pituaḥ* (The Media in Israel: Coverage of the Development Towns). Tel Aviv: Breirot Publishers, 1993.

Avrahami, Eliyahu. "The Israeli Backpackers: A Study in the Contexts of Tourism and Postmodern Condition." Unpublished manuscript, 2002.

Azaryahu, Maoz. "The Golden Arches of McDonald's: On the 'Americanization' of Israel." *Israel Studies* 5.1 (2000): 41–64.

Azoulay, Ariella. *Death's Showcase: The Power of Image in Contemporary Democracy*. Cambridge, Mass.: MIT Press, 2001.

Bachelard, Gaston. *The Poetics of Space*. Boston: Beacon Press, 1969.

Badone, Ellen, and Sharon R. Roseman, eds. *Intersecting Journeys: The Anthropology of Pilgrimage and Tourism*. Urbana: University of Illinois Press, 2004.

Bahgat, Gawdat. *Israel and the Persian Gulf: Retrospect and Prospect*. Gainesville: University Press of Florida, 2006.

Bar, Neta. "The Other Within: Jewish Israeli Tourism in Sinai." Unpublished manuscript, 2006.

Baran Designs. *Tokhnit Av le-Fituaḥ Tayarut be-Ma'aliyah* (Master Plan for Tourism Development in Ma'aliya). Haifa: Baran Designs Ltd., 1994.

Bardenstein, Carol. "Threads of Memory and Discourses of Rootedness: Trees, Oranges, and Prickly Pear Cactus in Israel/Palestine." *Edebyiat* 8 (1998): 1–36.

Bar-Siman-Tov, Yaacov. *Israel and the Peace Process, 1977–1982: In Search of Legitimacy for Peace*. Albany: State University of New York Press, 1994.

Bartal, Israel, ed. *Cossack and Bedouin: A New National Imagery*. Jerusalem: Yad Ben-Tzvi, 1997.

Barzilai, Amnon. "Seker: 46% meha-Yehudim be'ad Transfer ba-Shetaḥim" (Survey: 46% of Jews Favor Transfer from the Territories). *Ha-aretz*, 10 June 2003.

Beaumont, Peter. "I Don't Want to Be Here . . . But What Would You Do?" *Observer* 7 April 2002.

Behdad, Ali. *Belated Travelers: Orientalism in the Age of Colonial Dissolution*. Durham: Duke University Press, 1994.

Beinin, Joel. *The Dispersion of Egyptian Jewry: Culture, Politics, and the Formation of a Modern Diaspora*. Berkeley: University of California Press, 1998.

———. "The Israelization of American Foreign Policy Discourse." *Social Text* 21.2 (2003): 125–39.

———. "The Oslo Process and the Limits of a Pax-Americana." In *The Struggle for Sovereignty: Palestine and Israel, 1993–2005*, ed. Joel Beinin and Rebecca L. Stein. Stanford: Stanford University Press, 2006: 21–37.

———. *Was the Red Flag Flying There? Marxist Politics and the Arab-Israeli Conflict in Egypt and Israel, 1948–1965*. Berkeley: University of California Press, 1990.

Beinin, Joel, and Rebecca L. Stein. "Histories and Futures of a Failed Peace." In *The Struggle for Sovereignty: Palestine and Israel, 1993–2005*, ed. Joel Beinin and Rebecca L. Stein. Stanford: Stanford University Press, 2006: 1–20.

Beinin, Joel, and Rebecca L. Stein, eds. *The Struggle for Sovereignty: Palestine and Israel, 1993–2005*. Stanford: Stanford University Press, 2006.

Ben, Aluf. "Ha-Sar Tsor: Petiḥat Damesek le-Tayarim Yisre'elim Einah Sibah le-Vater al Sidure Bitaḥon" (Minister Tsor: The Opening of Damascus to Israeli Tourists Is No Reason to Relinquish Security Arrangements). *Ha-aretz* 20 December 1995.

Ben Ari, Mordecai. "Peace Tourism Update." Jerusalem: Israeli Ministry of Tourism, 1996.

Ben-Ari, Eyal. *Mastering Soldiers: Conflict, Emotions, and the Enemy in an Israeli Military Unit*. New York: Berghahn Books, 1998.

Ben-Dror, Mikhael. *Omanim, Merapim, ve-Ose Nifla'ot ba-Galil* (Artists, Healers and Miracle Workers in the Galilee). Jerusalem: Ariel, 1993.

Ben-Efrat, Yacov. "Close Minded: Changing the Nature of Control." *Challenge* May–June 1993: 6–7.

Benn, Aluf, and Gideon Alon. "The Public Should Have Listened, Says Intelligence Chiefs." *Ha-aretz*, 10 October 2004.

Ben-Porat, Guy. *Global Liberalism, Local Populism: Peace and Conflict in Israel/Palestine and Northern Ireland*. Syracuse, N.Y.: Syracuse University Press, 2006.

Ben-Simon, Shira. "Tarbut Lailah Holekhet ve-Gova'at" (Night Life Is Dying). *Ma'ariv* 4 April 2002.

Benvenisti, David, and Meron Benvenisti. *Panas ha-Kesem: Masa'ot be-Erets-Yisrael shel Pa'am* (The Magic Lantern: Travels in Erets Yisrael of the Past). Jerusalem: Keter, 1994.

Benvenisti, Meron. *Sacred Landscape: The Buried History of the Holy Land since 1948*. Berkeley: University of California Press, 2000.

Ben-Ze'ev, Efrat. "Masoret, Mitos, ve-Zehut: Girsaot la-Historiyah be-al Peh shel ha-Kefar Abu Ghosh" (Tradition, Myth, and Identity: Versions of the Oral History of Abu Ghosh). M.A. thesis, Hebrew University, n.d.

Ben-Ze'ev, Efrat, and Eyal Ben-Ari. "Imposing Politics: Failed Attempts at Creating a Museum of 'Co-Existence' in Jerusalem." *Anthropology Today* 12.6 (1996): 7–13.

Ben-Zvi, Itzhak. *Masa'ot* (Travels). Jerusalem: Israeli Publishing Institute, 1960.

Ben-Zvi, Yael. "Zionist Lesbianism and Transsexual Transgression: Two Representations of Queer Israel." *Middle East Report* 28.1 (1998): 26–28.

Berger, John. *Ways of Seeing*. London: British Broadcasting Corporation, 1972.

Berkowitz, Michael. *Western Jewry and the Zionist Project, 1914–1933*. Cambridge: Cambridge University Press, 2002.

Bhabha, Homi. *Location of Culture*. London: Routledge, 1994.

Binder, Uri. "La-Rishonah 2: Sapar Yisre'eli Yishtatef be-Taharut be-Yarden." (For the First Time: Israeli Hairdresser Enters Jordanian Competition). *Ma'ariv*, 13 March 1995.

Birnack Investments. *Dayr Hannah: Programah le-Fituah Tayarut* (Dayr Hannah: Plan for Tourist Development). Jerusalem: Kobi Birnack Investments, 1995.

———. *Majd El Krum: Programah le-Fituah Tayarut* (Majd El Krum: Plan for Tourist Development). Jerusalem: Kobi Birnack Investments, 1995.

———. *Programah le-Fituah Tayarut be-Beit Jan* (Plan for the Development of Tourism in Beit Jan). Jerusalem: Kobi Birnack Investments, 1994.

Bishara, Azmi. "Israeli-Arabs: Reading a Fragmented Political Discourse." *al-Ahram*, 11 February 1998.

Blackburn, Nicky. "Reaching the Threshold." *Link: Israel's International Business Magazine*, Fall 1995: 21.

Blecher, Rob. "Living on the Edge: The Threat of Transfer in Israel and Palestine." In *The Struggle for Sovereignty: Palestine and Israel, 1993–2005*, ed. Joel Beinin and Rebecca L. Stein. Stanford: Stanford University Press, 2006: 191–200.

Bourdieu, Pierre. *Distinction: A Social Critique of the Judgment of Taste*. Cambridge, Mass.: Harvard University Press, 1984.

Brendon, Piers. *Thomas Cook: 150 Years of Popular Tourism*. London: Secker and Warburg, 1991.

Brennan, Denise. *What's Love Got to Do with It? Transnational Desires and Sex Tourism in the Dominican Republic*. Durham: Duke University Press, 2004.

Brenner, Neil. "State Territorial Restructuring and the Production of Spatial Scale: Urban and Regional Planning in the Federal Republic of Germany, 1960–1990." *Political Geography* 16.4 (1997): 273–306.

Bruner, Edward M. *Culture on Tour: Ethnographies of Travel*. Chicago: University of Chicago Press, 2005.

B'tselem: The Israeli Information Center for Human Rights in the Occupied Territories and The Palestinian Human Rights Monitoring Group. *Human Rights in the Occupied Territories since the Oslo Accords*. Jerusalem: B'tselem, 1996.

Burckhardt, John Lewis. *Travels in Arabia, Comprehending an Account of Those Territories in Hadjaz Which the Mohammedans Regard as Sacred.* London: H. Colburn, 1829.

Butler, Judith. *Bodies That Matter: On the Discursive Limits of Sex.* New York: Routledge, 1993.

———. *Excitable Speech: A Politics of the Performative.* New York: Routledge, 1997.

———. *Gender Trouble: Feminism and the Subversion of Identity.* New York: Routledge, 1990.

———. *Giving an Account of Oneself.* New York: Fordham University Press, 2005.

———. *The Psychic Life of Power.* Stanford: Stanford University Press, 1997.

Buzard, James. *The Beaten Track: European Tourism, Literature, and the Ways to "Culture" 1800–1918.* Oxford: Claredon Press, 1993.

"Call for Personal Good Will to Arabs." *Jerusalem Post* 30 June 1967.

Capturing the Holy Land: M. J. Diness and the Beginnings of Photography in Jerusalem. Cambridge, Mass.: Harvard Semitic Museum, 1993.

Caspi, Dan, and Yehiel Limor. *Ha-Metavkhim: Emtsa'e ha-Tikshoret be-Yisrael, 1948–1990.* (The Mediators: The Press in Israel, 1948–1990). Tel Aviv: Am Oved Publishers, 1992.

———. *The In/Outsiders: Mass Media in Israel.* Cresskill, N.J.: Hampton Press, 1999.

Chateaubriand, Françoise René. *Travels in Greece, Palestine, Egypt and Barbary during the Years 1806 and 1807.* Philadelphia: Moses Thomas, 1813.

Chetrit, Sami Shalom. "Mizrahi Politics in Israel: Between Integration and Alternative." *Journal of Palestine Studies* 29.4 (2000): 51–65.

Clawson, Patrick. *Tourism Cooperation in the Levant.* Washington D.C.: Washington Institute, 1994.

Cohen, Geulah. *Women of Violence: Memoirs of a Young Terrorist, 1943–1948.* New York: Holt, Rinehart, and Winston, 1966.

Cohen, Hillel. *Army of Shadows: Palestinian Collaboration with Zionism, 1917–1948.* Berkeley: University of California Press, 2007.

———. "Hekhanu et ha-Kh'ek" (We Prepared the Check). *Kol ha-Ir* 16 February 1996.

———. "Pesak Halakhah: Mutar le-Hitpalel be-Har ha-Bayit" (Religious Verdict: Permission to Pray at the Temple Mount). *Kol ha-Ir* 2 February 1996.

———. "Shalom 2: Palestinim Ezrahei Yarden Ba'im ke-Tayarim ve-Nisharim be-Yisrael" (Peace 2: Palestinian Citizens of Jordan Come as Tourists and Stay in Israel). *Kol ha-Ir* 27 October 1995.

Cohen, Yossi. "20 Dinar le-Zug, Kolel Mizug Avir" (Twenty Dinars Per Couple, Including Air Conditioning). *Kol ha-Ir* 22 July 1994: 65–69.

Cohen-Hattab, Kobi. "Zionism, Tourism, and the Battle for Palestine: Tourism as a Political-Propaganda Tool." *Israel Studies* 9.1 (2004): 61–85.

Cohen-Hattab, Kobi, and Yossi Katz. "The Attraction of Palestine: Tourism in the Years 1850–1948." *Journal of Historical Geography* 27.2 (2001): 178–95.

———. "Mi-Terra Santa le Tourism: Ha-Mehkar ha-Geografi-histori shel ha-Tayarut u-Mekomo be-Heker Erets-Yisrael" (From Terra-Santa to Tourism: The Historical

Geography of Tourism and Its Place in the Study of Erets Yisrael). *Katedra* 91 (1999): 113–36.

Courbage, Youssef. "Reshuffling the Demographic Cards in Israel/Palestine." *Journal of Palestine Studies* 28.4 (1999): 21–39.

Crary, Jonathan. *Techniques of the Observer: On Vision and Modernity in the Nineteenth Century.* Cambridge, Mass.: MIT Press, 1990.

Dali, Doron. "Good Taste." *Jerusalem Report* 3 April 1997: 57.

Dar, Yuli. "Yishuve ha-Aravim Meshamshim Makom Mistor le-Tayarim Bilti Ḥukiyim" (Arab Towns Used as a Hiding Place for Illegal Tourists). *Kol ha-Tsafon* 26 January 1996.

de Certeau, Michel. *The Practice of Everyday Life.* Berkeley: University of California Press, 1988.

Delaney, David, and Helga Leitner. "The Political Construction of Scale." *Political Geography* 16.2 (1997): 93–97.

Deotte, Jean-Louis, et al. *Back to the Front: Tourisms of War.* Princeton: Princeton Architectural Press, 1994.

Derrida, Jacques. "Différance." In *Margins of Philosophy.* Chicago: University of Chicago Press, 1982: 3–27.

———. *The Post Card: From Socrates to Freud and Beyond.* Chicago: University of Chicago Press, 1987.

———. "Signature, Event, Context." In *Limited Inc.* Evanston: Northwestern University Press, 1988: 1–23.

Development Study Center. *Ha-Nofshim ba-Eruaḥ ha-Kafri: Seker Ma'akav* (Recreation in Rural Tourism: Follow-up Survey). Jerusalem: Ministry of Tourism, 1996.

Doumani, Beshara. *Rediscovering Palestine: Merchants and Peasants in Jabal Nablus, 1700–1900.* Berkeley: University of California Press, 1995.

Ebron, Paulla A. *Performing Africa.* Princeton: Princeton University Press, 2002.

Eilon, Yuri. "Ha-Mizraḥ he-Ḥadash shel ha-Ir" (The City's New East). *Kol ha-Ir* 1 March 1996.

———. "Sodo Shel ha-Zatar ha-Aravi" (The Secret of Arab Zatar), *Kol ha-Ir* 16 February 1996.

Elizur, Yuval. *Yisrael ve-ha-Etgar ha-Globali* (Israel and the Global Challenge). Yerushalayim: Karmel, 2005.

Eng, David L., and David Kazanjian, eds. *Loss: The Politics of Mourning.* Berkeley: University of California Press, 2003.

Erlanger, Steven. "Israelis Trudge Home, in Shock after Bombing." *New York Times* 9 October 2004.

Erlich, Shmuel. "Reactions of Adolescents to Rabin's Assassination: A Case of Patricide?" *Annals of American Society for Adolescent Psychiatry* 22 (1998): 189–205.

Eshet, Gideon. "Yihye Tov?" (Will It Be Good?). *Yediot Aḥaronot* 28 October 1994.

Etinger, Ami. "Derishat Shalom mi-Sakhnin" (Best Wishes from Sakhnin). *Ma'ariv* 23 August 1994.

Etinger, Yair, and Anshel Pepper. "Mi-Yom le-Yom ha-Ir Nimḥeket, Amru ha-Toshavim" (From Day to Day, the Residents Say, the City Is Being Erased). *Ha-aretz* 22 March 2002.

"Etsel Boulus Be-Jafa" (With Boulus in Jaffa). *Ma'ariv* 23 June 1971.

Eyal, Gil. "The Discursive Origins of Israeli Separatism: The Case of the Arab Village." *Theory and Society* 25 (1996): 389–429.

———. *The Disenchantment of the Orient: Expertise in Arab Affairs and the Israeli State*. Stanford: Stanford University Press, 2006.

Fabian, Johannes. *Time and the Other: How Anthropology Makes Its Object*. New York: Columbia University Press, 1983.

Falah, Ghazi. "The Development of Planned Bedouin Resettlement in Israel, 1964–82: Evaluation and Characteristics." *Geoforum* 14 (1983): 311–23.

———. *Galilee and the Judaization Plan*. Beirut: Institute for Palestine Studies, 1993.

———. "How Israel Controls the Bedouin in Israel." *Journal of Palestine Studies* 14 (1985): 35–51.

———. "Israeli 'Judaization' Policy in Galilee and Its Impact on Local Arab Urbanization." *Political Geography Quarterly* 8.3 (1989): 229–53.

———. "The 1948 Israeli-Palestinian War and Its Aftermath: The Transformation and De-Signification of Palestine's Cultural Landscape." *Annals of the Association of American Geographers* 86.2 (1996): 256–85.

———. "Welfare Geography of a Peripheralized National Minority: The Case of Israel's Arab Population." *Urban Geography* 20.5 (1999): 417–37.

Farquhar, Judith. *Appetites: Food and Sex in Post-Socialist China*. Durham: Duke University Press, 2002.

Farsakh, Leila. "Under Siege: Closure, Separation, and the Palestinian Economy." *Middle East Report* 30.217 (2000): 22–24.

Feldman, Jackie. "Marking the Boundaries of the Enclave: Defining the Israeli Collective through the Poland 'Experience.'" *Israel Studies* 7 (2002): 84.

Fellner Development Ltd. *Seker Zemani be-Gar'in ha-Kefar Yerka* (Temporary Survey in the Village Center of Yerka). Haifa: Fellner Development Ltd., 1994.

Finn, James. *Stirring Times, or Records from Jerusalem Consular Chronicles of 1853 to 1856*. London: C. Kegan Paul, 1878.

Firro, Kais M. *The Druze in the Jewish State*. Leiden: Brill, 1999.

———. "Reshaping Druze Particularism in Israel." *Journal of Palestine Studies* 30.2 (2001): 40–53.

Fleischer, Aliza, and Daniel Felsenstein. "Support for Rural Tourism: Does It Make a Difference?" *Annals of Tourism Research* 27.4 (2000): 1007–24.

Fleischer, Aliza, and A. Pizam. "Rural Tourism in Israel." *Tourism Management* 18.6 (1997): 367–72.

Fleischer, Aliza, and Steve Buccola. "War, Terror, and the Tourism Market in Israel." *Applied Economics* 34.11 (2002): 1335–43.

"Foreign Workers in Israel." *Migration News* 4.8 (1997).

Foreman, Geremy. "Settlement of Title in the Galilee: Dawson's Founding Principals." *Israel Studies* 7.3 (2002): 61–83.

Foreman, Geremy, and Alexandre Sandy Kedar. "From Arab Land to 'Israel Lands': The Legal Dispossession of the Palestinians Displaced by Israel in the Wake of 1948." *Society and Space* 22.6 (2004): 809–30.

Forester, John, Raphael Fischler, and Deborah Shmueli. "Rassem Khamaisi: Planning in an Arab Municipality." In *Israeli Planners and Designers: Profiles of Community Builders*, ed. John Forester, Raphael Fischler, and Deborah Shmueli. Albany: State University of New York Press, 2001: 205–22.

Forte, Tania. "Shopping in Jenin: Women, Homes and Political Persons in the Galilee." *City and Society* 13.2 (2001): 211–43.

Fragner, Bert. "From the Caucasus to the Roof of the World: A Culinary Adventure." In *Culinary Cultures of the Middle East*, ed. Sami Zubaida and Richard Tapper. London: I. B. Taurus, 1994: 49–62.

———. "Social Reality and Culinary Fiction: The Perspective of Cookbooks from Iran and Central Asia." In *Culinary Cultures of the Middle East*, ed. Sami Zubaida and Richard Tapper. London: I. B. Tauris, 1994: 63–72.

Freedman, Samuel G. "A Cork Pops, People Duck, and Israel Laughs." *New York Times* 30 June 2002.

Frow, John. "Tourism and the Semiotics of Nostalgia." *October* 57 (1991): 123–51.

Fulton, John. *Palestine: The Holy Land*. Philadelphia: Henry T. Coates, 1900.

Fussell, Paul. *Abroad: British Literary Traveling between the Wars*. New York: Oxford University Press, 1980.

Galili, Lili. "Yerushalayim Hafkha le-Ir shel 'Take Away'" (Jerusalem Becomes a City of "Take Away"). *Ha-aretz* 11 March 2002.

Gelfond, Lauren. "And Now Rehavia." *Jerusalem Post* 9 April 2002.

Ghanem, As'ad. *The Palestinian-Arab Minority in Israel, 1948–2000*. Albany: State University of New York Press, 2001.

Ghanem, As'ad, and Sarah Ozacky-Lazar. "The Status of the Palestinians in Israel in an Era of Peace: Part of the Problem but Not Part of the Solution." In *The Israeli Palestinians: An Arab Minority in the Jewish State*, ed. Alexander Bligh. London: Taylor and Francis, 2003: 263–89.

Ghodsee, Kristen Rogheh. *The Red Riviera: Gender, Tourism, and Postsocialism on the Black Sea*. Durham: Duke University Press, 2005.

Giacaman, George, and Dag Jørund Lønning. *After Oslo: New Realities, Old Problems*. London: Pluto Press, 1998.

Gillon, Paul. "Fraternization Banned—except with Old Friends." *Jerusalem Post* 11 June 1967.

Gitlis, Barukh. *Ha-Moshel ha-Mekho'ar: ha-Emet 'Al ha-Mishal ha-Tesvai* (The Ugly Governor: The Truth about the Military Government). Jerusalem: Ugdan, 1967.

Golan, Avirama. "Ha-Ir ha-Mifna et Gavah" (The City Turns Its Back). *Ha-aretz* 10 March 2001.

Golan-Meiri, Shirli. "Snifei 'Aroma' bi-Yerushalayim Lo Ye'afsheru la-Shevet be-Shitham"

(Aroma Branches in Jerusalem Forbid Sitting in Their Spaces). *Yediot Aḥaronot* 11 March 2005.

Goldenberg, Suzanne. "Bombing Shatters Illusions in an Oasis of Civility." *Guardian* 11 March 2002.

Goldstein, Kaylin. "Secular Sublime: Edward Said at the Israel Museum." *Public Culture* 17.1 (2005): 27–54.

Goodman, Hirsch. "Blood, Sweat, and Cappuccino." *Jerusalem Post* 8 April 2002.

Gordon, Neve. "Where Are the Peaceniks?" *Nation* 29 April 2002: 4–5.

Government of Israel. *Development Options for Cooperation: The Middle East/East Mediterranean Region*. Jerusalem: Government Publishing House, 1995.

Greenblatt, Steven. *Marvelous Possessions: The Wonder of the New World*. Chicago: University of Chicago Press, 1991.

Grewal, Inderpal. *Home and Harem: Nation, Gender, Empire, and the Cultures of Travel*. Durham: Duke University Press, 1996.

Gross, Aeyal. "Challenges to Compulsory Heterosexuality: Recognition and Non-Recognition of Same-Sex Couples in Israeli Law." In *Legal Recognition of Same-Sex Partnerships: A Study of National, European and International Law*, ed. Robert Wintemute and Mads Andenas. Oxford: Hart Publishing, 2001: 391–414.

Gross, Netty C. "Pigging Out." *Jerusalem Report* 31 January 2000: 16.

Gruber, Ruth Ellen. *Virtually Jewish: Reinventing Jewish Culture in Europe*. Berkeley: University of California Press, 2002.

Gutman, Matthew. "Alert Tel Aviv Café Security Guard Foils Suicide Bomb Attack." *Jerusalem Post* 13 October 2002.

———. "Hired Guns, Delivered to Your Door." *Jerusalem Post* 15 March 2002.

Haidar, Aziz. *On the Margins: The Arab Population in the Israeli Economy*. New York: St. Martin's Press, 1995.

Haine, W. Scott. "'Café Friend': Friendship and Fraternity in Parisian Working-Class Cafés, 1850–1914." *Journal of Contemporary History* 27.4 (1992): 607–26.

———. *The World of the Paris Café: Sociability among the French Working Class*. Johns Hopkins University Studies in Historical and Political Science, No. 2. Baltimore: Johns Hopkins University Press, 1996.

Hajjar, Lisa. *Courting Conflict: The Israeli Military Court System in the West Bank and Gaza*. Berkeley: University of California Press, 2005.

———. "Israel's Intervention among the Druze." *Middle East Report* 26 (1996): 2–6.

"Ha-Metayalim ha-Rishonim Ḥozrim mi-Yarden" (The First Travelers Returned from Jordan). *Yediot Aḥaronot* 12 August 1994.

Hammami, Rema, and Graham Usher. *Palestine: Diplomacies of Defeat*. Race and Class 37, No. 2. London: Institute of Race Relations, 1995.

Handelman, Don. *Nationalism and the Israeli State: Bureaucratic Logic in Public Events*. Oxford: Berg, 2004.

Hansen, Thomas Blom, and Finn Stepputat. *States of Imagination: Ethnographic Explorations of the Postcolonial State*. Durham: Duke University Press, 2001.

Hareuveni, Eyal. "Ha-Sar Bar'am Neged Tayarut Muslemit" (Minister Baram Is Against Muslim Tourists). *Kol ha-Ir* 1 September 1995.

Hareven, Alouph, and As'ad Ghanem, eds. *Equality and Integration, Retrospect and Prospects: 1992–1996.* Jerusalem: Sikui, 1996.

Hareven, Alouph, and As'ad Ghanem, eds. *Retrospect and Prospects, Equality and Integration: 1996–1997.* Jerusalem: Sikui, 1997.

Harman, Danna. "For Israel's Peace Flanks, Dwindling Ranks." *Christian Science Monitor* 25 April 2002.

Hartog, Kelly. "Taking Back the Cafés." *Jerusalem Post* 29 March 2002.

Hass, Amira. *Drinking the Sea at Gaza: Days and Nights in a Land under Siege.* New York: Henry Holt, 1996.

Hattox, Ralph S. *Coffee and Coffeehouses: The Origins of a Social Beverage in the Medieval Near East.* Seattle: University of Washington Press, 1985.

Hazbun, Waleed. "Mapping the Landscape of the 'New Middle East': The Politics of Tourism Development and the Peace Process in Jordan." In *Jordan in Transition*, ed. George Joffé. London: Hurst, 2002: 330–45.

Heine, Peter. "The Revival of Traditional Cooking in Modern Arabic Cookbooks." In *Culinary Cultures of the Middle East*, ed. Sami Zubaida and Richard Tapper. London: I. B. Tauris, 1994: 143–52.

Helman, Anat. "European Jews in the Levant Heat: Climate and Culture in 1920s and 1930s Tel Aviv." *Journal of Israeli History* 22.1 (2003): 71–90.

———. "Torah, Avodah, u-Vate Kafeh: Dat u-Farhesiyah be-Tel Aviv ha-Mandatit" (Torah, Work and Cafés: Religion and the Public Sphere in Tel Aviv under the British Mandate). *Katedra* 105 (2002): 85–110.

Herod, Andrew, and Melissa W. Wright. *Geographies of Power: Placing Scale.* Malden, Mass.: Blackwell, 2002.

Herzl, Theodore. *Old New Land.* New York: Herzl Press (1896), 1987.

Hever, Hannan, Yehouda A. Shenhav, and Pnina Motzafi-Haller. *Mizrahim Be-Yisrael* (Mizrahim in Israel). Jerusalem: Van Leer Institute, 2002.

Hiel, Betsy. "Tourism Revival in the Land of the Pharaohs." *Arab World Online* 2 June 1995.

Hirschberg, Peter. "The Town That Got Left Behind." *Jerusalem Report* 20 October 1994: 22.

Honig, Sarah. "Sands of Time." *Jerusalem Post* 17 February 1989.

Hope, Ronnie. "Jerusalem Traffic: Hardening of the Arteries." *Jerusalem Post: Weekend Magazine* 7 July 1967: 3.

Horowitz, Amy. "Dueling Nativities: Zehava Ben Sings Umm Kulthum." In *Palestine, Israel, and the Politics of Popular Culture*, ed. Rebecca L. Stein and Ted Swedenburg. Durham: Duke University Press, 2005: 202–30.

Hulme, Peter. *Colonial Encounters: Europe and the Native Caribbean, 1492–1797.* London: Routledge, 1986.

Inbari, Assaf. "New Age: The Fall of the Secular State." *Ha-aretz* 10 September 1999.

Industries Development Corporation, Ltd. "Conceptual Plan for a Commercial and Tourist Center in Dalyiat El Carmel." Israel: Israeli Ministry of Tourism, 1968.

Israeli Bureau of Statistics. *Tayarut Muslemit le-Yisrael* (Muslim Tourism to Israel). Jerusalem: Israeli Bureau of Statistics, December 1994.

Israel Information Service. "Direct Dialing between Israel and Jordan." 26 February 1995.

———. "$30 Million Raised to Establish Joint Israeli-Jordanian College." 9 May 1995.

Israeli Policy of Closure: Legal, Political and Humanitarian Evaluation. Gaza City: Palestinian Centre for Human Rights, 1995.

"Israel-P.L.O. Agreements." *Journal of Palestine Studies* 23.4 (1994): 102–18.

Iss, Edna. "Tayarim im Darkonim Yisre'elim Yotsim ha-Yom la-Rishonah le-Yarden" (Tourists with Israeli Passports Depart Today for Jordan for the First Time). *Yediot Aḥaronot* 18 December 1995.

Ivri, Ya'akov. "Derishat Shalom mi-Beirut" (Best Wishes from Beirut). *Musaf Ha-aretz* 22 December 1995.

Ja'afari, Kamal. "Foreign Arab Workers in Israel." *Challenge* January–February 1996: 14–15.

Jamal, Amal. "The Ambiguities of Minority Patriotism: Love for Homeland among Palestinian Citizens of Israel." *Nationalism and Ethnic Politics* 10.3 (Autumn 2004): 433–71.

Jay, Martin. *Downcast Eyes: The Denigration of Vision in Twentieth-Century French Thought.* Berkeley: University of California Press, 1993.

Jiryis, Sabri. *The Arabs in Israel.* New York: Monthly Review Press, 1976.

Jones, Rachel Leah, dir. *500 Dunams on the Moon.* RLJ Productions. 2002.

Kafir, Ilan. "Normalizatsiyah: Shavua Rishon" (Normalization: The First Week). *Yediot Aḥaronot* 1 February 1980.

Kanaaneh, Rhoda. *Birthing the Nation: Strategies of Palestinian Women in Israel.* Berkeley: University of California Press, 2002.

———. "Boys or Men? Duped or 'Made'? Palestinian Soldiers in the Israeli Military." *American Ethnologist* 32.2 (2005): 260–75.

———. *On the Edge of Security: Palestinian Soldiers in the Israeli Military.* Stanford: Stanford University Press, forthcoming.

Kanafani, Ghassan. *Palestine's Children.* 1961. Washington D.C.: Three Continents Press, 1984.

Kaplan, Caren. *Questions of Travel: Postmodern Discoveries of Displacement.* Durham: Duke University Press, 1996.

Kaspit, Ben. "Ha-Katari: Yedidenu he-Ḥadash mi-Mizraḥ" (The Qatari: Our New Friend from the East). *Ma'ariv* 5 April 1996.

Katriel, Tamar. *Performing the Past: A Study of Israeli Settlement Museums.* Mahwah, N.J.: Lawrence Erlbaum, 1997.

———. "Touring the Land: Trips and Hiking as Secular Pilgrimages in Israeli Culture." *Jewish Ethnology and Folklore Review* 17.1–2 (1995): 6–13.

Katz, Shaul. "The Israeli Teacher-Guide: The Emergence and Perpetuation of a Role." *Annals of Tourism Research* 12 (1985): 49–72.

Katz, Yossi. "Ideology and Urban Development: Zionism and the Origins of Tel Aviv, 1906–1914." *Journal of Historical Geography* 12.4 (1986): 402–24.

———. "Ha-Tsiyonut ve-Shivukah shel Erets-Yisrael: Madrikhei ha-Tayarut ha-Tsiyunit be-Tekufat ha-Mandat ha-Beriti" (Zionism and the Marketing of the Land of Israel: Zionist Tour Guides in the British Mandate Period). *Katedra* 97 (2000): 85–116.

Kaufman, Ilana, and Rachel Israeli. "The Odd Group Out: The Arab-Palestinian Vote in the 1996 Elections." In *The Elections in Israel: 1996*, ed. Asher Arian and Michal Shamir. Albany: State University of New York Press, 1999: 85–116.

Kaveh, Avshalom. "Milyon Tayarim Aravim Yevakru bi-Yerushalayim u-Veit Leḥem im Heskem Oslo Bet" (A Million Arab Tourists Will Visit Jerusalem and Bethlehem after the Oslo II Agreement). *Davar Rishon* 23 January 1996.

"Keeping Posted." *Jerusalem Post* 3 July 1967.

Kelman, John. *The Holy Land*. London: Adam and Charles Black, 1912.

Kemp, Adrianna. "Labour Migration and Racialisation: Labour Market Mechanisms and Labour Migration Control Policies in Israel." *Social Identities* 10.2 (2004): 267–92.

Kemp, Adriana, et al. "Contesting the Limits of Political Participation: Latinos and Black African Migrant Workers in Israel." *Ethnic and Racial Studies* 23.1 (2000): 94–119.

Kemp, Adriana, and Rebeca Raijman. *'Ovdim Zarim' be-Yisrael* ("Foreign Workers" in Israel). Tel Aviv: Merkaz Advah, 2003.

———. "Tel Aviv Is Not Foreign to You: Urban Incorporation Policy on Labor Migrants in Israel." *International Migration Review* 38.1 (2004): 26–51.

Kenan, Amos. "Bikur be-Misadah be-Ḥevron" (Visit to a Hebron Restaurant). *Yediot Aḥaronot* 22 June 1967.

Kessler, Zvi. "Moreh Derekh la-Mevaker ba-Shetaḥim ha-Muhzakim" (Tour Guide for the Reinforced Territories). *Yediot Aḥaronot* 18 July 1967.

Khalbi, Mouin. "Etslenu ha-Khi Tov ba-Olam" (Here, the Best in the World). *Ma'ariv* 10 April 2002.

Khalidi, Rashid. *Palestinian Identity: The Construction of Modern National Consciousness*. New York: Columbia University Press, 1997.

Khalidi, Walid. *All That Remains: The Palestinian Villages Occupied and Depopulated by Israel in 1948*. Washington, D.C.: Institute for Palestine Studies, 1992.

———. *Palestine Reborn*. London: I. B. Taurus, 1992.

Khalidi, Walid, and Institute for Palestine Studies. *Before Their Diaspora: A Photographic History of the Palestinians, 1876–1948*. Washington, D.C.: Institute for Palestine Studies, 2004.

Khamaisi, Ghassem. *Planning and Housing among the Arabs in Israel*. Tel Aviv: International Center for Peace in the Middle East, 1990.

Khanna, Ranjana. *Dark Continents: Psychoanalysis and Colonialism*. Durham: Duke University Press, 2003.

Khazzom, Aziza. "The Great Chain of Orientalism: Jewish Identity, Stigma Management, and Ethnic Exclusion in Israel." *American Sociological Review* 68 (2003): 481–510.

Kimmerling, Baruch. *Zionism and Territory: The Socio-Territorial Dimensions of Zionist Politics*. Berkeley: Institute of International Studies, University of California, 1983.

Kiryat Ye'arim Local Council. *Ye'arim*. Telz Stone: Kiryat Ya'arim Local Council, 1999.

Klein, Chaim H., ed. *The Second Million: Israel Tourist Industry, Past and Present*. Jerusalem: Amir Publishing, 1973.

Kligman, Nachum. "Am I a Racist?" *Ha-aretz* 22 August 2002.

Kliot, Nurit. "Bedouin Settlement Policy in Israel: Another Perspective." *Geoforum* 16 (1985): 428–39.

Kohn, Moshe, and Anan Safadi. "Talking to Palestinians." *Jerusalem Post: Weekend Magazine* 18 August 1967: 4.

Kohn, Paul. "Old City Hotels Being Vacated." *Jerusalem Post* 26 June 1967.

Krauss, Orli. "Festival Shel Sovlanut ve-Teva be-Gush Segev" (Festival of Tolerance and Nature in Segev Block). *Dividend* 29 July 1994: 10.

Kroyanker, David, and Makhon Yerushalayim le-Ḥeker Yisrael. *Adrikhalut bi-Yerushalayim: Ha-Beniyah bi-Tekufat ha-Mandat ha-Beriti* (Architecture in Jerusalem: Construction in the British Mandate Period). Jerusalem: Keter and Makhon Yerushalayim le-Ḥeker Yisrael, 1989.

Kroyanker, David, Dror Wahrman, and Makhon Yerushalayim le-Ḥeker Yisrael. *Adrikhalut bi-Yerushalayim: Shekhunot u-Vinyene Tsibur Yehudiyim mi-Ḥuts la-Ḥomot 1860–1914* (Architecture in Jerusalem: The Jewish Quarters and Public Buildings outside the Old City Walls, 1860–1914). Yerushalayim: Keter and Makhon Yerushalayim le-Ḥeker Yisrael, 1987.

———. *Adrikhalut bi-Yerushalayim: Tekufot ve-Signonot* (Jerusalem Architecture: Periods and Styles). Jerusalem: Makhon Yerushalayim le-Ḥeker Yisrael and Domino, 1983.

Lamartine, Alphonse Marie Louis de. *Oeuvres Complètes De Lamartine: Voyage En Orient, 1832–1833*. Paris: C. Grosselin, 1845.

Laskier, Michael M. *Israel and the Maghreb: From Statehood to Oslo*. Gainesville: University Press of Florida, 2004.

Lavi, Aviv. "Natbag 2000" (Airport 2000). *Kol ha-Ir* 29 December 1995.

Lavi, Moshik. "Sheloshim Devarim she-Lo Yadatem al Suriyah" (Thirty Things That You Didn't Know about Syria). *Yediot Aḥaronot* 1 December 1995.

Lavie, Zvi. "Ha-Mevukeshet ba-Ir ha-Atikah: Totseret Sin ha-Amitit" (Desirables in the Old City: Authentic Chinese Products). *Ma'ariv* 2 July 1967: 3.

———. "Ha-Yisre'elim Ba'im . . . Ha-Yisre'elim Ba'im . . ." (The Israelis Are Coming . . . The Israelis Are Coming). *Ma'ariv* 25 June 1967.

Lavsky, Hagit. "German Zionists and the Emergence of Brit Shalom." In *Essential Papers on Zionism*, ed. Jehuda Reinharz and Anita Shapira. New York: New York University Press, 1996: 648–70.

LAW. *Apartheid, Bantustans, Cantons: The ABC of the Oslo Accords*. Jerusalem: LAW, 1998.

Lazin, Frederick A., and Gregory S. Mahler. *Israel in the Nineties: Development and Conflict*. Gainesville: University Press of Florida, 1996.

Lefkovits, Etgar. "Attacks Leave Capital's Restaurants, Cafés Empty." *Jerusalem Post* 12 March 2002.

———. "Hundreds Turn Cafe into Shrine." *Jerusalem Post* 11 March 2002.

———. "Waiter Foils Jerusalem Cafe Bombing." *Jerusalem Post* 8 March 2002.

Levar, Sharit. "Hamitbaḥ ha-Druzi Etslekha ba-Bayit" (The Druze Kitchen in Your Home). *Davar Sheni* 17 December 1995.

Levi, Orni. "Elef Boker u-Voker" (A Thousand and One Mornings). *Kol ha-Ir* 5 March 1996.

LeVine, Mark. *Overthrowing Geography: Jaffa, Tel Aviv, and the Struggle for Palestine, 1880–1948.* Berkeley: University of California Press, 2005.

Levinshtein, Revital. "Masof Aravah Niftaḥ Le-Ma'avar Kle Rekhev Pratiyim" (Arava Border Crossing Opens to Private Vehicles). *Ha-aretz* 8 April 1996.

Lévi-Strauss, Claude. *Totemism.* Boston: Beacon Hill, 1962.

Levy, Andre. "Notes on the Jewish-Muslim Relationships: Revisiting the Vanished Moroccan Jewish Community." *Cultural Anthropology* 18.3 (2003): 365–97.

———. "To Morocco and Back: Tourism and Pilgrimage among Moroccan-Born Israelis." In *Grasping Land: Space and Place in Contemporary Israeli Discourse and Experience*, ed. Eyal Ben-Ari and Yoram Bilu. Albany: State University of New York Press, 1997: 25–46.

Lifshitz, Oded. "Lo Hayinu ha-Yeḥidim" (We Weren't the Only Ones). *Al ha-Mishmar* 7 September 1990.

Lior, Gad. "Higati la-Sela ha-Adom" (I Got to the Red Rock). *Yediot Aḥaronot* 18 July 1994.

Liram Architecture, Civil Engineering, and Environmental Design. *Seker Potentsiyal Tayarut ba-Migzar ha-Aravi* (Survey on Potential Tourism in the Arab Sector). Jerusalem: Ministry of Tourism, 1993.

———. *Tochnit Av le-Fituaḥ Tayarut ba-Migzar ha-Aravi* (Master Plan for Tourism Development in the Arab Sector). Jerusalem: Ministry of Tourism, 1992.

Lissak, Moshe. "Ha-Mahapekhah ha-Demografit Ḥevratit bi-Shenot ha-Ḥamishim: Klitat ha-Aliyaḥ ha-Gedolah" (The Social-Demographic Revolution in the 1950s: The Great Immigration Wave). In *Atsma'ut: 50 ha-Shanim ha-Rishonot* (Independence: The First 50 Years), ed. Anita Shapira. Jerusalem: Zalman Shazar Center, 1998: 13–56.

Lloyd, David. *Battlefield Tourism: Pilgrimage and the Commemoration of the Great War in Britain, Australia, and Canada, 1919–1939.* Oxford: Berg, 1998.

Lockman, Zachery. *Comrades and Enemies: Arab and Jewish Workers in Palestine, 1906–1948.* Berkeley: University of California Press, 1996.

Lomsky-Feder, Edna, and Eyal Ben-Ari. *The Military and Militarism in Israeli Society.* Albany: State University of New York Press, 1999.

Long, Burke. *Imagining the Holy Land: Maps, Models, and Fantasy Travels.* Bloomington: Indiana University Press, 2003.

Lori, Aviva. "The Age of Anxiety." *Ha-aretz Magazine* 16 May 2002: 10–13, 26.

Lustick, Ian. *Arabs in the Jewish State: Israel's Control of a National Minority.* Austin: University of Texas Press, 1980.

MacCannell, Dean. *The Tourist: A New Theory of the Leisure Class*. New York: Schocken Books, 1976.

Mahmood, Saba. *Politics of Piety: The Islamic Revival and the Feminist Subject*. Princeton: Princeton University Press, 2005.

Malabou, Catherine, and Jacques Derrida. *Counterpath: Traveling with Jacques Derrida*. Stanford: Stanford University Press, 2004.

Maltz, Judy. "Fast Exit." *Jerusalem Report* 10 March 2003: 41.

Man'a, Adel. "Identity in Crisis: The Arabs in Israel vis-à-vis the Israel-PLO Agreement." In *Ha-Politikah ha-Aravit be-Yisrael: 'Al Parashat Derakhim* (Arab Politics in Israel at a Crossroad), ed. Eli Rekhess and Tamar Yegnes. Tel-Aviv: Dayan Center, 1995: 81–86.

Mann, Barbara E. *A Place in History: Modernism, Tel Aviv, and the Creation of Jewish Urban Space*. Stanford: Stanford University Press, 2006.

Mansfeld, Yoel. "The Middle-East Conflict and Tourism to Israel, 1967–90." *Middle Eastern Studies* 30.3 (1994): 646–67.

———. *Tokhnit le-Fituah Tayarut ve-Nofesh, Ezor Misgav u-Vik'at Sakhnin* (Development Plans for Tourism and Lesisure, Misgav and Sakhnin Valley Area). Haifa: Czamanski Consultants, 1996.

Maoz, Darya. "Backpackers' Motivations: The Role of Culture and Nationality." *Annals of Tourism Research* 34.1 (2007): 122–40.

———. "The Conquerors and the Settlers: Two Groups of Young Israeli Backpackers in India." In *The Global Nomad: Backpacker Travel in Theory and Practice*, ed. Greg Richards and Julie Wilson. Clevedon, England: Channel View Publications, 2004: 109–22.

Marktest. *Seker Pituah Tayarut ba-Kefarim ha-Araviyim bi-Tsafon ha-Arets* (Survey on Tourist Development in the Arab Villages in the North of Israel). Tel Aviv: Ministry of Tourism, 1996.

Marston, Sally A. "The Social Construction of Scale." *Progress in Human Geography* 24.2 (2000): 219–42.

Martins Hoffman Inc. *Seker be-Kerev ha-Migzar ha-Aravi be-Nose Tayarut Panim be-Yisrael* (Survey in the Arab Sector on the Subject of Internal Tourism in Israel). Tel Aviv: Israeli Ministry of Tourism, 1996.

———. *Seker Tayarut Panim be-Yisrael* (Survey on Internal Tourism in Israel). Tel Aviv: Israeli Ministry of Tourism, 1994.

Masalha, Nur. "Critique of Benny Morris." In *The Israel/Palestine Question*, ed. Ilan Pappé. London: Routledge, 1999: 211–20.

Mason, Ruth. "Personal Lessons in Coping." *Jerusalem Post* 20 March 2002.

McCarthy, J. "Scale, Sovereignty, and Strategy in Environmental Governance." *Antipode* 37.4 (2005): 731–53.

McClintock, Anne. *Imperial Leather: Race, Gender, and Sexuality in the Colonial Context*. New York: Routledge, 1995.

McDowall, David. *Palestine and Israel: The Uprising and Beyond*. Berkeley: University of California Press, 1989.

Medzini, Arnon. "Bedouin Settlement in the Galilee." In *The Lands of Galilee*, ed. Avshalom Shmueli, Nurit Kliot, and Arnon Sofer. Haifa: Haifa University and Ministry of Defense, 1983: 549–64.

Meirei, Baruch. "Be-Eilat Mekavim 'La'asot Kesef' meha-Kevish he-Ḥadash le-Sharm-a-Sheikh" (In Eilat, Hopes to "Make Money" from the New Road to Sharm El-Sheikh). *Ma'ariv* 9 September 1971.

Meletz, Ehud, and Michal Sela. "Ha-Kefarim she-Lo Hayu" (The Villages that Never Were). *Kol ha-Ir* 31 August 1984.

Melman, Yossi. "The Task Force Barked a Warning and Israelis Blithely Streamed South." *Ha-aretz* 12 October 2004.

Menusi, Didi. "Bediḥamin le-Shabat" (Jokes for Shabbat). *Yediot Aḥaronot* 1 April 1988.

Meron, Haim. "Andralamusyah ve-Shema Kalkalit ha-Gadah" (The West Bank Economy in Disorder and Ruin). *Yediot Aḥaronot* 14 July 1967.

Mevorach, Oded. "The Long Trip after Military Service: Characteristics of the Travelers, the Effects of the Trip and Its Meaning." Ph.D. diss. Hebrew University, 1997.

"Middle East Turmoil." *New York Times* 9 April 2002.

Ministry of Tourism. *Divre Sar ha-Tayarut Moshe Kol* (Notes from Tourism Minister Moshe Kol). Jerusalem: Government Publishing House, 1968.

———. *Divre Sar ha-Tayarut Moshe Kol* (Notes from Tourism Minister Moshe Kol). Jerusalem: Government Publishing House, 1970.

———. *Divre Sar ha-Tayarut Moshe Kol* (Notes from Tourism Minister Moshe Kol). Jerusalem: Government Publishing House, 1971.

———. *Ha-Nofshim ba-Eruaḥ ha-Kafri* (Vacationers in the Rural Sector). Jerusalem: Government Publishing House, 1996.

———. *Regional Tourism Cooperation Development Options*. Jerusalem: Government Publishing House, 1995.

———. *Siu'a Misrad ha-Tayarut le-Fituaḥ Kefarim Druzim be-Kh'erkesim* (Ministry of Tourism Aid to Druze and Circassi Villages). Jerusalem: Government Publishing House, 1995.

———. *Tayarut le-Yisrael 1996: Duaḥ Statisti* (Tourism to Israel 1996: Statistical Report). Jerusalem: Government Publishing House, 1997.

———. *Tokhnit Programit le-Fituaḥ Ta'asiyat ha-Tayarut be-Abu Ghosh veha-Svivah* (Programmatic Plan for the Development of the Tourism Industry in Abu Ghosh and the Environs). Jerusalem: Government Publishing House, 1994.

———. *Tourism to Israel, 1994: Statistical Report*. Jerusalem: Government Publishing House, 1995.

———. *Tourism to Israel, 1995: Statistical Report*. Jerusalem: Government Publishing House, 1996.

———. *Tourism to Israel, 1997: Statistical Report*. Jerusalem: Government Publishing House, 1998.

———. *Yeḥidot ha-Eruaḥ ha-Kafri be-Yisrael* (Units of Rural Tourism in Israel) Jerusalem: Government Publishing House, 1994.

Mintz, Sidney. *Tasting Food, Tasting Freedom: Excursions into Eating, Culture, and the Past*. Boston: Beacon Press, 1996.

Mintz, Sidney W., and Christine M. Du Bois. "The Anthropology of Food and Eating." *Annual Review of Anthropology* 31 (2002): 99–119.

"Misadah Al Ramah" (Restaurant on the Heights). *Ma'ariv* 18 August 1971.

Monk, Daniel Bertrand. *An Aesthetic Occupation: The Immediacy of Architecture and the Palestine Conflict.* Durham: Duke University Press, 2002.

Morris, Benny. *The Birth of the Palestinian Refugee Problem, 1947–1949.* Cambridge: Cambridge University Press, 1987.

———. "The Case of Abu Ghosh and Beit Naqquba, Al Fureidis and Khirbet Jirs Az Zarka in 1948—or Why Four Villages Remained." In *1948 and After: Israel and the Palestinians.* Oxford: Clarendon Press, 1990: 191–218.

———. *Israel's Border Wars, 1949–1956.* Oxford: Clarendon Press, 1993.

Mundlak, Guy. "Labor in a Peaceful Middle East: Regional Prosperity or Social Dumping?" In *The Middle East Peace Process: Interdisciplinary Perpectives,* ed. Ilan Peleg. Albany: State University of New York Press, 1998: 199–228.

Murphy, Emma. "Stacking the Deck: The Economics of the Israeli-PLO Accords." *Middle East Report* 25.3–4 (1995): 35–38.

Nathan, Joan. "Israel's Silver Age." *Food and Wine* (December 1997): 26–32.

Navaro-Yashin, Yael. *Faces of the State: Secularism and Public Life in Turkey.* Princeton: Princeton University Press, 2002.

Ness, Sally Ann. *Where Asia Smiles: An Ethnography of Philippine Tourism.* Ed. Sally Ann Ness. Philadelphia: University of Pennsylvania Press, 2003.

Newman, David. "Retaining Our Humanity." *Jerusalem Post* 13 March 2002.

Nitzan, Jonathan Bichler Shimshon. *The Global Political Economy of Israel.* London: Pluto Press, 2002.

Noy, Chaim. "This Trip Really Changed Me: Backpackers' Narratives of Self-Change." *Annals of Tourism Research* 32.1 (2004): 78–102.

Noy, Chaim, and Erik Cohen. *Israeli Backpackers: From Tourism to Rite of Passage.* Albany: State University of New York Press, 2005.

Obenzinger, Hilton. *American Palestine: Melville, Twain, and the Holy Land Mania.* Princeton: Princeton University Press, 1999.

Örs, İlay. "Coffeehouses, Cosmpolitanism, and Pluralizing Modernities in Istanbul." *Journal of Mediterranean Studies* 12.1 (2002): 119–45.

Padilla, Mark. *Caribbean Pleasure Industry: Tourism, Sexuality, and AIDS in the Dominican Republic.* Chicago: University of Chicago Press, 2007.

"Palestinian Rights in Post-Oslo Israel." *Middle East Report* 26.4 (1996): 23–26.

Palti, Michal. "Obeying the Herd Instinct in 'the Real Galilee.'" *Ha-aretz,* 6 April 1999.

———. "Shir Shalom, Shir le-Milḥamah" (Song of Peace, Song of War). *Ha-aretz* 15 April 2002.

Pappe, Ilan. "The New History of the 1948 War." *Teoryah u-Vikoret* 3 (1993): 99–114.

Parsons, Laila. *The Druze between Palestine and Israel, 1947–49.* New York: St. Martin's Press and St. Antony's College, Oxford, 2000.

"Peace Is Possible." *Jerusalem Post* 30 June 1967.

Peleg, Ilan, ed. *The Middle East Peace Process: Interdisciplinary Perspectives*. Albany: State University of New York Press, 1998.

Peleg, Yaron. *Orientalism and the Hebrew Imagination*. Ithaca, N.Y.: Cornell University Press, 2005.

Peres, Shimon. *The New Middle East*. New York: Henry Holt, 1993.

Peri, Yoram, ed. *The Assasination of Yitzhak Rabin*. Stanford: Stanford University Press, 2000.

Perry, Charles. "The Taste for Layered Bread among the Nomadic Turks and the Central Asian Origins of Baklava." In *Culinary Cultures of the Middle East*, ed. Sami Zubaida and Richard Tapper. London: I. B. Taurus, 1994: 87–92.

Piterberg, Gabi. "Erasures." *New Left Review* 10 (2001): 31–46.

Plotzker, Savar. "Ha-Halom Kevar Kan" (The Dream Is Already Here). *Yediot Aharonot* 25 July 1994.

Povinelli, Elizabeth A. *The Cunning of Recognition: Indigenous Alterities and the Making of Australian Multiculturalism*. Durham: Duke University Press, 2002.

Pratt, Mary Louise. *Imperial Eyes: Travel Writing and Transculturation*. London: Routledge, 1992.

———. "Scratches on the Face of the Country: Or, What Mr. Barrows Saw in the Land of the Bushman." In *Race, Writing, and Difference*, ed. Henry Louis Gates Jr. Chicago: University of Chicago Press, 1985: 138–62.

Prime Minister's Office. *Gidul Mashma'uti be-Taktsive ha-Memshalah la-Migzar ha-Aravi* (Significant Growth in Government Funding for the Arab Sector). Jerusalem: Government Publishing House, 1996.

Prion, Israel. *Ha-Hitpathut ha-Megamatit shel ha-Shituf ha-Ben-Kafri be-Yisrael* (Development Trends of Spatial Cooperation in Israel). Rehovot: Ha-Merkaz le-Heker ha-Hityashvut, 1968.

Pudney, John, et al. *The Thomas Cook Story*. London: M. Joseph, 1953.

Quandt, William B. *Peace Process: American Diplomacy and the Arab-Israeli Process Since 1967*. Berkeley: University of California Press, 1993.

Rabbani, Mouin. "Palestinian Authority, Israeli Rule: From Transitional to Permanent Arrangement." *Middle East Report*. 201 (1996): 2–6, 22.

Rabin, Yitzhak. "Address to the Amman Economic Summit." October 29, 1995. At http://www.mfa.gov.il. Accessed May 1998.

Rabinowitz, Dan. "The Frontiers of Urban Mix: Palestinians, Israelis, and Settlement Space." In *Ethnic Frontiers and Peripheries: Landscapes of Inequality in Israel*, ed. Oren Yiftachel and Avinoam Meir. Boulder, Colo.: Westerview Press, 1998: 69–87.

———. "Nostalgyah Mizrahit: Ekh Hafkhu ha-Falastinim le-'Arviye Yisrael'" (Oriental Nostalgia: How the Palestinians Became 'Israel's Arabs'). *Teoriyah u-Vikoret* 4 (1993): 141–52.

———. *Overlooking Nazareth: The Ethnography of Exclusion in the Galilee*. Cambridge: Cambridge University Press, 1997.

———. "Petra: Ha-Epos veha-Patos" (Petra: The Epic and the Pathos). *Sevivot* 21 (1989):

————. "Postnational Palestine/Israel? Globalization, Diaspora, Transnationalism, and the Israeli-Palestinian Conflict." *Critical Inquiry* 26.4 (2000): 757–72.

————. "Tsiyonut O Erets be-Reshit: Rekvi'em le-Tsuki David" (Zionism or the Land of Genesis: Requiem for Suki David). *Sevivot* (1989): 195–215.

Rabinowitz, Dan, and Khawla Abu Baker. *Coffins on Our Shoulders: The Experience of the Palestinian Citizens of Israel.* Berkeley: University of California Press, 2005.

Raijman, Rebecca, Moshe Semyonov, and Adriana Kemp. "Gender, Ethnicity, and Immigration: Double Disadvantage and Triple Disadvantage among Recent Immigrant Women in the Israeli Labor Market." *Gender and Society* 11.1 (1997): 108–25.

Raijman, Rebecca, Silvina Schammah-Gesser, and Adriana Kemp. "International Migration, Domestic Work, and Care Work: Undocumented Latina Migrants in Israel." *Gender and Society* 17.5 (2003): 727–49.

Ram, Uri. *The Changing Agenda of Israeli Sociology: Theory, Ideology, and Identity.* Albany: State University of New York Press, 1995.

————. *The Globalization of Israel: Mcworld in Tel Aviv, Jihad in Jerusalem.* London: Routledge, 2007.

————. "Glocommodification: How the Global Consumes the Local. McDonald's in Israel." *Current Sociology* 52.1 (2004): 11–31.

Ramon, Amnon. *"Doktor Mul Doktor Gar": Shekhunat Rehavyah bi-Yerushalayim: Historyah, Havai, Maslule Siyur* (Rehavia Neighborhood in Jerusalem). Yerushalayim: Hotsabiat Yad Yitshak Ben Tsevi, 1998.

Raviv, Yael. "Falafel: A National Icon." *Gastronomica* 3.3 (2003): 20–25.

————. "Recipe for a Nation: Cuisine, Jewish Nationalism, and the Israeli State." Ph.D. diss. New York University, 2002.

Raz-Krakotzkin, Amnon. "Galut bi-Tokh Ribonut: Le-Vikoret 'Shelilat ha-Galut' ba-Tarbut ha-Yisre'elit" (Exile within Sovereignty: Toward a Critique of the "Negation of Exile" in Israeli Culture). *Teoryah u-Vikoret* 4 (1993): 23–55.

————. "Galut bi-Tokh Ribonut: Le-Vikoret 'Shelilat ha-Galut' ba-Tarbut ha-Yisre'elit, Helek Sheni" (Exile within Sovereignty: Toward a Critique of the "Negation of Exile" in Israeli Culture, Part 2). *Teoryah u-Vikoret* 5 (1994): 113–32.

Regev, David, and Amos Oren. "Zehava Ben Holekhet le-Aza" (Zehava Ben Goes to Gaza). *Yediot Aharonot* 3 September 1995.

Regev, Motti, and Edwin Seroussi. *Popular Music and National Culture in Israel.* Berkeley: University of California Press, 2004.

Reinhart, Tanya. *Israel/Palestine: How to End the War of 1948.* New York: Seven Stories Press, 2002.

Rekhess, Elie. "The Arabs of Israel after Oslo: Localization of the National Struggle." *Israel Studies* 7.3 (2002): 1–44.

"Revavot Metayelim be-Ramat ha-Golan" (Tens of Thousands Hike the Golan Heights). *Yediot Aharonot* 9 July 1967.

Rieker, Gidon. "Piknik be-Havilat Husein" (Picnic in the Hussein Villa). *Yediot Aharonot* 21 June 1967.

Riesenfeld, Ofra, and Hanokh Farber. *Good Food Guide to Israel*. Tel Aviv: Map Ltd., 1998.

Rifkin, Ira. "Life Continues, Amazingly, in a War Zone." *Jerusalem Post* 1 October 2002.

Rinot Ltd. *Dayr Hannah: Programah le-Fituaḥ Tayarut* (Dayr Hannah: Plan for the Development of Tourism). Haifa: Rinot Ltd., 1995.

Robinson, Shira. "My Hairdresser Is a Sniper." In *The Struggle for Sovereignty: Palestine and Israel, 1993–2005*, ed. Joel Beinin and Rebecca L. Stein. Stanford: Stanford University Press, 2006: 237–40.

———. "Occupied Citizens in a Liberal State: Palestinians under Military Rule and the Colonial Formation of Israeli Society, 1948–1966." Ph.D. diss. Stanford University, 2005.

Rodan, Steve. "Independence Day Fete in Amman Draws Throng." *Jerusalem Post* 5 May 1995.

Roden, Claudia. *The Book of Jewish Food: An Odyssey from Samarkand to New York*. New York: Knopf, 1997.

Rogov, Daniel. "Anise Way to Go." *Ha-aretz* 30 April 1999.

———. "Barbecuties." *Ha-aretz* 2 May 1999.

———. "Lunching at Leisure." *Ha-aretz Magazine* 27 November 1998.

———. "New Organic Products Delight." *Ha-aretz* 1 March 1998.

———. "Rekindling the Faith." *Ha-aretz Magazine* 5 February 1999.

Rosaldo, Renato. "Imperial Nostalgia." *Representations* 26 (1989): 107–22.

Rosenblum, Irit. "Keshe-Yavo Shalom al ha-Galil" (When Peace Comes to the Galilee). *Ha-aretz* 28 January 1996.

———. "Jeeps, Cheese, Music and Mediation in the Meadows." *Ha-aretz* 28 May 1998.

Rouhana, Nadim. "The Intifada and the Palestinians of Israel: Resurrecting the Green Line." *Journal of Palestine Studies* 19.3 (1990): 58–75.

———. *Palestinian Citizens in an Ethnic Jewish State: Identities in Conflict*. New Haven: Yale University Press, 1997.

Rouhana, Nadim, and As'ad Ghanem. "The Crisis of Minorities in Ethnic States: The Case of Palestinian Citizens in Israel." *International Journal of Middle East Studies* 30.3 (1998): 321–46.

Rousso, Nira. "In Search of a Real Cookbook." *Ha-aretz Magazine* 11 December 1998.

———. "Kitchen Secrets." *Ha-aretz* 26 March 1999.

Roy, Sara. "De-Development Revisited: Palestinian Economy and Society Since Oslo." *Journal of Palestine Studies* 28.3 (1999): 64–82.

Rozen, Rami. "Ha-Shalom ha-Shaḥor ha-Zeh" (This Black Peace). *Musaf Ha-aretz* 9 September 1994.

Rozen, Roli. "Temunot Ketsarot, Yerushalayim" (Short Pictures, Jerusalem). *Kol ha-Ir* 1 December 1995.

Rozen, Tali. "Al Rosh ha-Har" (On the Top of the Mountain). *Yediot Aḥaronot* 3 April 1996.

Rubin, Betsalel. "'Lo' le-Fo'alim me-Aqaba" ('No' to Workers from Aqaba). *Erev Erev* 29 December 1994.

Rudge, David. "Baltimore Jews Boost Coexistence in Galilee." *Jerusalem Post* 17 October 1996.

Ryan, Curtis. "Jordan in the Middle East Peace Process: From War to Peace with Israel." In *The Middle East Peace Process: Interdisciplinary Perspectives*, ed. Ilan Peleg. Albany: State University of New York Press, 1998: 161–78.

Sadeh, Dani. "6,000 Yardenim Bau le-Vikur ve-Nisharu ba-Shetaḥim" (6,000 Jordanians Came to Visit and Stayed in the Territories). *Yediot Aḥaronot* 3 September 1995.

Safran, Nasia. "ha-Sela Ha-Adom: Mabat le-Aḥor" (The Red Rock: A Glance Back). *Keshet* (Spring 1973): 5–22.

Said, Edward. *The End of the Peace Process: Oslo and After*. New York: Pantheon Books, 2000.

———. *Orientalism*. New York: Vintage Books, 1978.

Sakakini, Hela. *Jerusalem and I: A Personal Record*. Amman, Jordan: Economic Press Co., 1987.

"Sakhnin Becomes a City." *Jerusalem Post* 6 March 1995.

Salem, Ali. *A Drive to Israel: An Egyptian Meets His Neighbors*. Tel Aviv: Dayan Center, 1994.

Samara, Adel. "Globalization, the Palestinian Economy, and the 'Peace Process.'" *Journal of Palestine Studies* 29.2 (2000): 20–34.

Sapir, Shuli. "'Arbev et ha-Tiaḥ, Jonny'" ('Mix the Plaster, Jonny'). *Davar Rishon* 26 March 1996.

Schnell, Izhak. *Perceptions of Israeli Arabs: Territoriality and Identity*. London: Aveburty, 1994.

Schrag, Carl. "Closer Than You Think." *Jerusalem Post Magazine* 29 July 1994: 10–12.

Scott, James C. *Seeing Like a State: How Certain Schemes to Improve the Human Condition Have Failed*. New Haven: Yale University Press, 1998.

Sedan, Gil. "Sela'im 'le-Furkan Ketivah' Yekadmu et ha-Metayalim" (Writing on the Rocks Precedes Tourists to Sinai). *Yediot Aḥaronot* 15 April 1973.

Segal, Rafi, and Eyal Weizman. *A Civilian Occupation: The Politics of Israeli Architecture*. New York: Verso, 2003.

Segev, Tom. *1967: Israel, the War, and the Year That Transformed the Middle East*. New York: Metropolitan Books, 2007.

Seliktar, Ofira. "The Peace Dividend: The Economy of Israel and the Peace Process." In *The Middle East Peace Process: Interdisciplinary Perspectives*, ed. Ilan Peleg. Albany: State University of New York Press, 1998: 223–35.

Shafir, Gershon, and Yoav Peled. *Being Israeli: The Dynamics of Multiple Citizenship*. Cambridge: Cambridge University Press, 2002.

Shafir, Gershon, and Yoav Peled, eds. *The New Israel: Peacemaking and Liberalization*. Boulder, Colo.: Westview Press, 2000.

———. "Peace and Profits: The Globalization of Israeli Business and the Peace Process." In *The New Israel: Peacemaking and Liberalization*, ed. Gershon Shafir and Yoaz Peled. Boulder, Colo.: Westview Press, 2000: 243–64.

Shahak, Israel. *Open Secrets: Israeli Nuclear and Foreign Policies*. London: Pluto Press, 1997.

Shaḥar, Ilan. "Mi she-Lo Mukhraḥ, Lo Magia le-Mizraḥ ha-Ir" (Whoever Doesn't Have to, Doesn't Go Downtown). *Ha-aretz* 22 March 2002.

Shalit, David. "Ha-Ya'ad ha-Ba: Damesek" (The Next Destination: Damascus). *Musaf Ha-aretz* 25 November 1994.

Shamir, Aaron. "Zohi Da'ati: Ketsat Ga'avah!" (My Opinion: A Little Pride!). *Yediot Aḥaronot* 7 July 1967.

Shammas, Anton. "At Half Mast—Myths, Symbols, and Rituals of the Emerging State: A Personal Testimony of an 'Israeli Arab.'" In *New Perspectives on Israeli History: The Early Years of the State*, ed. Lawrence Silberstein. New York: New York University Press, 1991: 216–26.

Shapira, Anita. *Land and Power: The Zionist Resort to Force, 1881–1948*. New York: Oxford University Press, 1992.

Shapiro, Haim. "Across the Great Divide." *Jerusalem Post Magazine* 13 October 1995: 20–21.

———. "Israelis Flock to Jersash Festival." *Jerusalem Post* 12 July 1995.

Sharma, Aradhana, and Akhil Gupta. *The Anthropology of the State: A Reader*. Malden, Mass.: Blackwell, 2006.

Shavit, Ari. "Dear God, This Is Effi." *Ha-aretz* 23 March 2002.

———. "Milḥemet Shalom Moment" (The War for a Moment's Peace). *Ha-aretz* 10 March 2002.

Shaviv, Miriam. "Should a Security Fence Be Built between Israel and the West Bank?" *Jerusalem Report* 25 February 2002: 56.

Sheḥori, Alon. "Kamah Medinot Araviyot Yiftehu ba-Shavuot ha-Kerovim Netsigut Tayarutit be-Tel Aviv" (Several Arab Countries Will Open Tourist Offices in Tel Aviv in Upcoming Weeks). *Israel Tourist Guide* 1 February 1996: 1.

———. "Misrad ha-Tayarut Megabesh Tokhnit le-Shituf Pe'ulah Tayaruti im Suriyah" (The Ministry of Tourism Crystallizes a Plan to Participate in Touristic Activities with Syria). *Israel Tourist Guide* 14 September 1995.

Shenhav, Yehouda A. *The Arab Jews: A Postcolonial Reading of Nationalism, Religion, and Ethnicity*. Stanford: Stanford University Press, 2006.

Shepherd, Naomi. *Zealous Intruders: The Western Rediscovery of Palestine*. London: Harper Collins, 1987.

Shlaim, Avi. "The Debate about 1948." In *The Israel/Palestine Question*, ed. Ilan Pappé. London: Routledge, 1999: 171–92.

———. "The Oslo Accord." *Journal of Palestine Studies* 23.3 (1994): 24–40.

Shohat, Ella. *Israeli Cinema: East/West and the Politics of Representation*. Austin: University of Texas Press, 1987.

———. *Taboo Memories, Diasporic Voices*. Durham: Duke University Press, 2006.

Shtal, Avraham. "Ketsad Ḥinkhu et ha-Ashkenazim le-Ehov Teva ve-Tiyulim" (How the Ashkenazim Were Taught to Love Nature and Hikes). *Studies in Education* 31 (1981): 61–76.

"The Siege of Jerusalem." *Jerusalem Post* 1 February 2002.

Sikui. *Duaḥ Amutat Sikui: Shivyon ve-Shiluv ha-Ezraḥim ha-Aravim be-Yisrael* (Report on Equality and Integration of the Arab Citizens in Israel). Jerusalem: Sikui, 1996.

———. *Equality and Integration of the Arab Citizens in the Misgav Region.* Jerusalem: Sikui, 2001.

Silberstein, Laurence J. *The Postzionism Debates: Knowledge and Power in Israeli Culture.* New York: Routledge, 1999.

Silver-Brody, Vivienne. *Documentors of the Dream: Pioneer Jewish Photographers in the Land of Israel, 1890–1933.* Jerusalem: Magnes Press, Hebrew University, 1998.

Sivan, Imanuel. "Be-Khol Dor va-Dor Kamim Aleinu" (In Every Generation They Rise upon Us). *Ha-aretz* 23 March 1996.

Slyomovics, Susan. *The Object of Memory: Arab and Jew Narrate the Palestinian Village.* Philadelphia: University of Pennsylvania Press, 1998.

Smith, Neil. "Contours of a Spatialized Politics: Homeless Vehicles and the Production of Geographic Scale." *Social Text* 30.3 (1992): 54–81.

Smooha, Sammy. "The Israelization of Collective Identity and the Political Orientation of the Palestinian Citizens of Israel: A Reexamination." In *Ha-Politikah ha-Aravit be-Yisrael: 'Al Parashat Derakhim* (Arab Politics in Israel at a Crossroad), ed. Elie Rekhess and Tamar Yegnes. Tel Aviv: Dayan Center, 1998: 41–53.

Sontag, Susan. *Regarding the Pain of Others.* New York: Farrar, Straus and Giroux, 2003.

Sorek, Tamir. "Memory and Identity: The Land Day Monument." *ISIM Newsletter* 10 (2002): 17.

———. "Palestinian Nationalism Has Left the Field: A Shortened History of Arab Soccer in Israel." *International Journal of Middle East Studies* 35.3 (2003): 417–37.

"South West Bank Flooded with Tourists." *Jerusalem Post* 27 June 1967.

Spivak, Gayatri Chakravorty. "Can the Subaltern Speak?" In *Marxism and the Interpretation of Culture*, ed. Cary Nelson and Lawrence Grossberg. Chicago: University of Illinois Press, 1988: 271–313.

Spurr, David. *The Rhetoric of Empire: Colonial Discourse in Journalism, Travel Writing, and Imperial Administration.* Post-Contemporary Interventions. Durham: Duke University Press, 1993.

Stein, Rebecca. "Ballad of the Sad Cafe: Israeli Leisure, Palestinian Terror, and the Post/Colonial Question." In *Postcolonial Studies and Beyond*, ed. Ania Loomba, Suvir Kaul, and Matti Bunzl. Durham: Duke University Press, 2005: 317–36.

———. "Itineraries of Peace: Remapping Israeli and Palestinian Tourism." *Middle East Report* 25.5 (1995): 16–19.

———. "National Itineraries, Itinerant Nation: Israeli Tourism and Palestinian Cultural Production." *Social Text* 56.16 (1998): 91–124.

Stein, Rebecca L., and Ted Swedenburg, eds. *Palestine, Israel, and the Politics of Popular Culture.* Durham: Duke University Press, 2005.

Stein, Rebecca L., and Ted Swedenburg. "Popular Culture, Transnationality, and Radical History." In *Palestine, Israel, and the Politics of Popular Culture*, ed. Rebecca L. Stein and Ted Swedenburg. Durham: Duke University Press, 2005: 1–23.

Sugarman, Margo Lipschitz. "Make Tours, Not War." *Jerusalem Report* 25 August 1994: 34–36.

———. "Please Pass the Foie Gras. Todah." *Jerusalem Report* 14 September 1998: 42.

———. "Tourists with Reservations." *Jerusalem Report* 31 October 1996: 47–48.

Swedenburg, Ted. "Seeing Double: Palestinian/American Histories of the Kufiya." *Michigan Quaterly Review* 31.4 (1992): 557–77.

"Taking Back the Cafés." *Jerusalem Post* 29 March 2002.

Tal, Alon. *Pollution in a Promised Land: An Environmental History of Israel.* Berkeley: University of California Press, 2002.

Talmi, Menachem. "Ha-Im Yordim Deromah?" (Will They Go South?). *Ma'ariv* 5 April 1974.

———. "Tevilah be-El-Ḥama" (Baptism at El-Ḥama). *Ma'ariv* 23 June 1967.

Tamari, Salim. "Wasif Jawhariyyeh, Popular Music, and Early Modernity in Jerusalem." In *Palestine, Israel, and the Politics of Popular Culture,* ed. Rebecca L. Stein and Ted Swedenburg. Durham: Duke University Press, 2005: 27–50.

"Teman: Matḥilah le-Hipataḥ la-Olam" (Yemen: Starting to Open to the World). *Ma'ariv* 5 April 1996.

Teiman, Miki. "Musikat ha-Teva she-Tavi et ha-Shalom" (Nature Music Will Bring Peace). *Ma'ariv* 28 March 1996.

Tessler, Mark. "The Intifada and Political Discourse in Israel." *Journal of Palestine Studies* 19.2 (1990): 43–61.

Thomas, Nicholas. *Colonialism's Culture: Anthropology, Travel and Government.* Princeton: Princeton University Press, 1994.

Thon, Rafi. *Halakhnu la-Ḥermon ve-Higanu le-Damesek* (We Walked to Hermon and Got to Damascus). Tel Aviv: ha-Kibbutz ha-Meuḥad, 1979.

———. *Hekafnu et Yam ha-Melaḥ ba-Regel* (We Circled the Dead Sea on Foot). Tel Aviv: ha-Kibbutz ha-Meuḥad, 1977.

"350,000 Have Walked to the Western Wall." *Jerusalem Post* 18 June 1967.

Troen, S. Ilan. *Imagining Zion: Dreams, Designs, and Realities in a Century of Jewish Settlement.* New Haven: Yale University Press, 2003.

Tryster, Hillel, and Steven Spielberg Jewish Film Archive. *Israel before Israel: Silent Cinema in the Holy Land.* Jerusalem: Steven Spielberg Jewish Film, 1995.

"Tunisyah: Neot Midbar ba-Saharah" (Tunisia: Oasis in the Sahara). *Ma'ariv* 5 April 1996.

"200,000 at Western Wall in First Pilgrimage Since Dispersion." *Jerusalem Post* 15 June 1967.

United Nations Conference on Trade and Development. *The Tourism Sector and Related Services in the Palestinian Territory under Israeli Occupation.* Geneva, Switzerland: United Nations Conference on Trade and Development, 1991.

University of Haifa. *Siaḥ be-Nose Tikhnun Rekhes Hararit Yodfat* (Discussion on the Subject of Development in Hararit/Yodfat). Haifa: University of Haifa Press, 1998.

Uriely, Natan, Yuval Yonay, and Dalit Simchai. "Backpacking Experiences: A Type and Form Analysis." *Annals of Tourism Research* 29.2 (2002): 520–38.

Usher, Graham. "Closures, Cantons and the Palestinian Covenant." *Middle East Report* 199 (1996): 33–37.

———. *Palestine in Crisis: The Struggle for Peace and Political Independence after Oslo*. London: Pluto Press, 1995.

Vinod, Noam. "En Le'an li-Veroaḥ" (Nowhere to Escape). *Ma'ariv* 4 April 2002.

Watson, James L., and Melissa L. Caldwell. *The Cultural Politics of Food and Eating: A Reader*. Oxford: Blackwell Publishing, 2004.

Weiss, Efrat. "Et ha-Moment ha-Zeh I-Efshar le-Hafsik" (It's Impossible to Stop This Momentum). *Yediot Aḥaronot*, 10 March 2002.

Weiss, Efrat, and Sharon Rofeh. "Ne'etsar Meḥabel Mitabed be-Reḥov Emek Refa'im bi-Yerushalayim" (Suicide Bomber Arrested on Emek Refaim Street in Jerusalem). *Yediot Aḥaronot*, 7 March 2002.

Weitz, Ranan. *The Envisioned Image of the Village in Israel*. Jerusalem: Land Settlement Department, 1963.

Weitzman, Lydia. "Visiting Neighbors." *Jerusalem Post* 20 December 1996.

Weizman, Eyal. *Hollow Land: Israel's Architecture of Occupation*. London: Verso, 2007.

———. "The Politics of Verticality." *Open Democracy* 2002. At http://www.open democracy.net.

"West Bank News." *Jerusalem Post* 11 July 1967: 6.

Western Galilee Tourist Trust. "Derekh ha-Okhel ba-Galil ha-Ma'arvi" (Western Galilee Food Trail). Haifa: Department for the Promotion of Domestic Tourism, 1998.

Wharton, Annabel. *Selling Jerusalem: Relics, Replicas, Theme Parks*. Chicago: Chicago University Press, 2006.

Witt, Doris. *Black Hunger: Soul Food and America*. Minneapolis: University of Minnesota Press, 2004.

Wolfsfeld, Gadi. *Media and Political Conflict: News from the Middle East*. New York: Cambridge University Press, 1997.

Ya'ari, Ehud. "The Jordanian Option." *Jerusalem Report* 9 February 1995: 28–30.

Yiftachel, Oren. *Ethnocracy: Land and Identity Politics in Israel/Palestine*. Philadelphia: University of Pennsylvania Press, 2006.

———. "The Internal Frontier: Territorial Control and Ethnic Relations in Israel." *Regional Studies* 30.5 (1996): 493–508.

———. "Israeli Society and Jewish-Palestinian Reconciliation: 'Ethnocracy' and Its Territorial Contradictions." *Middle East Journal* 51.4 (1997): 505–19.

———. *Planning a Mixed Region in Israel: The Political Geography of Arab-Jewish Relations in the Galilee*. Aldershot, England: Avebury, 1992.

———. "Power Disparities in the Planning of a Mixed Region: Arabs and Jews in the Galilee, Israel." *Urban Studies* 30.1 (1993): 157–82.

———. "State Policies, Land Control, and an Ethnic-Minority: The Arabs in the Galilee Region, Israel." *Environment and Planning D — Society and Space* 9.3 (1991): 329–62.

Yiftachel, Oren, and M. D. Segal. "Jews and Druze in Israel: State Control and Ethnic Resistance." *Ethnic and Racial Studies* 21.3 (1998): 476–506.

Yoash, Foldesh. "Certain Half Deserted Streets." *Ha-aretz*, 17 March 2002.

Yue, Gang. *The Mouth That Begs: Hunger, Cannibalism, and the Politics of Eating in Modern China*. Durham: Duke University Press, 1999.

Zakim, Eric Stephen. *To Build and Be Built: Landscape, Literature, and the Construction of Zionist Identity*. Philadelphia: University of Pennsylvania Press, 2006.

Zaltzman, Avivah, "La-Hakot me-Yarden umi-Maroko Yirkedu be-Kharmiel." (Dancers from Jordan and Morocco Will Dance in Karmiel). *Davar* 5 June 1995.

Zertal, Idith. *Israel's Holocaust and the Politics of Nationhood*. Cambridge: Cambridge University Press, 2005.

Zerubavel, Yael. *Recovered Roots: Collective Memory and the Making of Israeli National Tradition*. Chicago: University of Chicago Press, 1995.

Ziai, Fatemeh. "Israel: Israel's Closure of the West Bank and Gaza Strip." *Human Rights Watch/Middle East* 8.3 (1996).

Zilberfarb, Ben-Zion. "The Effects of the Peace Process on the Israeli Economy." *Israel Affairs* 1.1 (1994): 84–95.

Zubaida, Sami, and Richard Tapper, eds. *Culinary Cultures of the Middle East*. London: I. B. Taurus, 1994.

Zureik, Elia. *The Palestinians in Israel: A Study in Internal Colonization*. London: Routledge and Kegan Paul, 1979.

Index

Abu Ghosh: ethnic identity of, 108–9, 119; Israel state relations with, 97–99, 101–2, 107–8, 119, 125–26; land expropriation in, 102, 125, 126; municipal services in, 110, 124; as old and new (ha-atikah ha-ḥadashah), 100; patriotism performed in, 120–23, 126–27; perceived tranquility of, 103, 104, 105; police harassment of residents of, 108; reaction to Rabin assassination in, 122; relations with other Palestinians, 102, 103, 108. See also Palestinians in Israel; Patriotism

Abu Ghosh restaurants: cookbook, 118; edibility in, 111, 117, 119, 124; history of, 100; Israeli national artifacts in, 97; Jewish Israeli clientele of, 100, 102–3, 104–5, 109–10. See also Edibility; Food

'Akka, 79

Allegiance: counternarratives of, 126–27; Israeli elections and, 107, 173n21; Israeli national artifacts, as evidence of, 64, 107; market potential of, 91; performance of, 98–99, 105–8, 110; to state, 78, 79, 169n34

Alternative medicine, 89–90

Anxieties, Jewish Israeli: about incoming Arab tourists, 40–42; about incoming foreigners, 151–52; about Israel's relations with Arab world, 32–33; of Jewish Israeli tourists, 102–3, 114–15; about Palestinian demographics, 51; performances of allegiance and, 110; after second Palestinian Uprising, 132; about visits to the Palestinian Galilee, 45, 51, 56, 57

'Arabbeh, 1–4, 50, 52, 53, 78

Arab boycott. See Boycott of Israeli goods

Arabic language, 37–38, 106, 133

Arab identity: disavowal of, 107–8, 119; hospitality and, 36, 45, 71, 77, 88; Jewish Israelis on, 108–9; language and, 37–38, 106; Palestinian identity compared with, 108–9; religious identity and, 109; revaluation of, after Oslo process, 9

Arab Jews. See Mizraḥim

Arab Middle East: boycott of Israeli goods by, 4, 22, 154n6; Israel as European nation-state in, 144; Israeli first-time narratives and, 19, 31–32; Israeli tourist fantasies about, 8, 26–27, 74, 133, 143, 159n33; Morocco, 6, 22, 24, 38, 156n35, 159n31; Muslim Arabs, 8–9, 40, 109,

Arab Middle East (*continued*)
163n88; North Africa, 4, 6, 22, 24, 31,
38, 119, 156n35, 159n31; Oman, 4, 22;
Qatar, 4, 22; Saudi Arabia, 32; Syria, 6,
31, 38; trade relations with, 4, 154n6;
Tunisia, 22, 32. *See also* Egypt; Jor-
danian-Israeli relations

Arab tourism, incoming, 19–20, 39–42, 79,
159n33, 163n88, 169n34

Arafat, Yasser, 20, 158n5

Army, Israeli. *See* IDF (Israel Defense
Forces)

'Arrabeh, 1–4, 50, 52, 53, 78

Ashkenazim, 6, 19, 37–38, 157n40

Assassination of Yitzhak Rabin, 63, 64,
122–23

Authenticity (*otenti*), perceived: of Bedouin identity, 91–92; of everyday culture, 17–18, 59–62, 86–87, 134; of food,
13, 97, 100, 110–11, 117, 173n29; hospitality and, 36, 45, 71, 77, 88; interiority
as, 86, 87–88, 89–93, 93–94; *ha-kafri*
(the rural) and, 79–80, 169–70n40; of
neglected landscapes, 82–83; oranges
and, 173n29; Orientalism and, 1, 12, 36,
40, 61–62, 88, 91, 92, 110–11; Palestinian
politics and, 59; performance of, in
tourist sites, 59–62, 68–69; of personal
narratives, 60–61, 64–65; of pre-1948
Arab goods, 112; public mourning and,
36, 63–64, 111, 115, 122, 130, 132; of rural
aesthetics, 103; of tourist experience,
55–57, 85

Avidor, Ruti, 164n7

Barak, Ehud, 131

Bed-and-breakfast facilities: construction
of, 50, 55; conversations with Palestinian hosts of, 60–61; European culture and, 83–84; interior spaces in, 45,
88; Israeli national artifacts displayed
in, 64; state regulation of, 88

Bedouins in Israel: food preparation by,

110–11; forced relocation of, 59, 91;
hospitality of, 36; Negev, 61, 68; Orientalism and, 1, 12, 36, 40, 61–62, 88,
91, 92, 110–11; perceived authenticity
of, 91–92; romanticization of, 92;
state discourse about, 9; tents and,
91–93; tourism and, 55, 61, 78, 90. *See
also* Citizenship, Israeli; Palestinian
Galilee; Palestinians in Israel

Benvenisti, David, 11f1, 35f9, 47, 47f11,
48f12

Bethlehem, 36, 112, 114, 119

Bishara, Azmi, 168n8

Bombings: of buses, 56, 132, 139; of cafés,
129–30, 175nn3, 4; of Hilton Hotel
(Egypt), 149–50

Borders: flight of Hilton Hotel bombing
victims over, 150; Israeli fantasies of
having none, 25–28m, 26–27, 74, 133,
143, 144, 159n33; Israeli fears of Arabization and, 150–51; Israeli spatial fictions about, 142–43; militarized checkpoints and, 9, 23, 96, 143, 146, 150; after
1967 War, 36; as porous, 30–31, 150–51;
separation barrier and, 9; tourism
without, 25–28, 133, 143, 144. *See also*
Mobility restrictions on Palestinians in
Occupied Territories

Boycott of Israeli goods, 4, 22, 154n6

British Mandate, 8, 10–12, 11f1, 33, 34f7,
34f8, 35f9, 35f10, 92, 101, 155–56n30

Buses, 56, 132, 139

Butler, Judith, 153n2, 3

Café Moment, 130, 133, 134, 141

Cafés: bombings of, 129–30, 133, 134,
141, 175nn3–4; cartoons and, 135f18,
135f19, 136f20; European culture of,
139–40f22, 144; as figuring political
borders, 142–44; identified with Israeli
nation-state, 147; Israeli nationalization of, 130, 133–34; Israeli political
sensibilities and, 130; politicization of,

133–36, 135ff18–19; in pre-state Palestine, 139–41; as sites of Palestinian absence in Jewish cities, 146–47; as sites of patriotism, 136–37, 176n25; in Tel Aviv, 139–40f22, 177n46; tropes of emptiness of, 144–45, 146; U.S. identification with Israel and, 136. *See also* Patriotism

Camp David Accord, 17, 36, 131, 133

Cartoons in café narrative, 135f18, 135f19, 136f20

Center of the village (*gar'in ha-kefar*). *See* Core of the village

Checkpoints, militarized, 9, 23, 96, 143, 146, 150

Christians, 8–9, 23, 27m2, 116, 159n24. *See also* Russian emigration

Circassian population, 8

Citizenship, Israeli: Ashkenazim, 6, 19, 37–38, 157n40; Christians and, 8–9; Circassian population and, 8; civic equity, 119, 120–22; ethnic identity and, 119; incoming Arab tourism and, 40–42; Law of Return, 159n24; multiculturalism and, 47, 64; Palestinians in Israel and, 23, 38, 48–49; tourist identity and, 150–51; travel narratives and, 19. *See also* Bedouins in Israel; Druze; Mizraḥim

Clandestine travel, 29, 33, 35, 159–60n35, 161n62

Coexistence (*du-kiyum*): "consumer coexistence" or market value of, 7–8, 56–57; discourses about, 105, 155n20; in first-time narratives, 30–32; Israeli state support for, 7–8, 47; multiculturalism and, 47, 64; of Palestinians and neighboring Jewish communities, 102; in tour guide narratives, 55. *See also* Citizenship, Israeli; Consumerism, Israeli; Palestinians in Israel

Collective settlements, 80, 169n40

Colonialism: colonial nature of Israel and, 12, 156n34; imagery of, 91–92; Israeli nation-building and, 12, 156n34; narratives of, 28–29, 60; postcolonialism and, 12, 156n34, 157n3, 160n38; scholarship on, 12, 156n34, 157n3, 160n38; travel narratives and, 12. *See also* Land expropriation

Comparative analogies in tourist narratives, 54, 61–62

Consumer coexistence, 7–8, 56–57

Consumerism, Israeli: attacks on, during second Palestinian Uprising, 129–30, 142–44; "condition of edibility" and, 110–11, 116–18; desire and, 48; elite consumers as national proxies and, 139; as form of political defiance, 136–37, 176n25; impact of, on Israeli merchants, 113; of Israelis shopping in Occupied Territories, 11, 36, 112–14, 159n33; nationalism and, 139; nostalgia for, 111, 115; regional Arab culture as commodity and, 47; shopping activity and, 11, 36, 112–14, 159n33. *See also* Cafés

Core of the village (*gar'in ha-kefar*), 82–83f13, 83–87, 116, 170n42

Culinary tourism. *See* Abu Ghosh; Edibility; Food

Culture of the everyday, 17–18, 59–62, 86–87, 134

Curfews, 9, 96, 106, 132

Dalyat al-Karmil, 49, 61

Dayr Hannah: architectural plan for, 82, 83f13, 84–85, 84f14; development of tourist ventures in, 50, 77, 78, 80–82; Jewish Israeli tourists in, 82; Land Day activism and, 52; Music and Nature Festival in, 53. *See also* Palestinians in Israel

Dead Sea, 24, 33, 34f7, 34f8

de Certeau, Michel, 17–18

Derrida, Jacques, 153n3

De-urbanization of Palestinians, 52, 74–76, 94, 167–68n8, 171n65

Development of tourist market: architectural plans for, 82, 83f13, 84–85, 84f14; construction of tradition and, 94, 171n65; ethnic favoritism in, 79; European market in rural hospitality and, 83–84; geographies of interiority and, 86; by Israeli state planners in, 80–82; by Palestinian entrepreneurs, 88, 89; in rural sector (*migzar ha-kafri*), 78–79; rural tourism, 83–84; state aid for, 78–79, 168–69n27, 169n34. *See also* Israel, State of; Ministry of Tourism, Israeli; Palestinian Galilee

Discovery narrative: as colonial narrative, 29, 157n3, 160n38; as desire, 29–30f6, 159–60n35, 160n36; documentation of, 29–30, 160n38; first-time narratives and, 19, 28–33, 37–38, 41–42; national mythology and, 29–30f6, 159–60n35, 160n36; of Petra, 19, 29–30f6; postcolonialism and, 12, 156n34, 157n3, 160n38; trope of emptiness in, 54, 144–47

Discrepant mobility: definition of, 14; forced migrations of Palestinians, 51, 54, 59, 61, 63, 74, 101, 125–26; population transfer, 146; postarmy itineraries, 13, 156n35; transportation, 24, 32, 56, 132–33, 139; visa restrictions, 9, 23, 40–41, 143, 146, 150–51, 163n96. *See also* Itineraries; Labor force, Israeli

Druze: cuisine of, 118; government aid for tourist development in, 78; Jewish Israeli culinary desire and, 119; Rabin assassination and, 64; state discourse on, 8, 155n21; state regulation of home-based attractions in, 88; village core of, 83, 84, 85, 87; villages of, in Israel, 49, 55, 61, 85, 87. *See also* Palestinians in Israel

East Jerusalem, 28, 38–39, 105, 114, 119

Ecotourism, 89, 170n53

Edibility: Abu Ghosh restaurants and, 111, 119, 124; as analogue of "national intelligibility," 99; definition of, 99; *hummus* and, 97, 100, 103, 127, 173n29; Israeli nationalization of Palestinian food and, 97, 100, 103, 110–11, 127, 173n29; Jewish Israeli consumptive practices and, 110–11; national meaning of, 110; public narratives and, 126–27. *See also* Consumerism, Israeli; Food; Intelligibility, national

Egypt: Camp David Accords, 17, 36, 131, 133; Hilton Hotel bombing in, 149–50; Israeli private sector initiatives and, 22; Israeli tourists in, 24, 36, 149–50; Israel's imagined proximity to, 32; Sinai Peninsula returned to, 36

Eilat, 24, 36

Elections, Israeli, 5, 107, 165n28, 173n21

Emptiness, trope of, 54, 144–47

Entrepreneurship, Palestinian, 17, 50, 56–60, 72, 88–89, 124

Environmentalism, 89, 162n74, 170n53

Erasure: of Arabic identity, 54, 107, 111, 144–46, 173n29; of ethnic identity, 93–94; in first-contact narratives, 32, 38; of Mizrahi identity, 111; of Palestinian exile, 38–39; of Palestinian identity, 56, 60–62, 81–82; of Palestinian modernity, 93, 171n65; rural as locus of, 80

Eretz Yisrael (Land of Israel), 10, 33, 161nn62, 65

Expulsion of Palestinians, 51, 54, 63, 101, 146

Eyal, Gil, 170n43, 171n65

Falafel, 111, 112f15, 173n29

Festivals in Palestinian Galilee, 49–50, 53, 116–17

Film, Israeli, 10, 155n29

First Palestinian Uprising (1987–93), 11, 37, 100, 114, 126

First-time narratives, 19, 28–33, 37–38, 41–42

Food: Americanization of, 116; changing Israeli habits of, 115–16, 118–19; culinary geographies of, 116, 118–19, 127; *falafel*, 111, 112fi5, 173n29; guides, 174n58; *hummus*, 97, 100, 103, 127, 173n29; Israeli-Arab cookbook, 118, 127; Israeli nationalization of Palestinian, 97, 100, 103, 110–11, 127, 173n29; oranges, 173n29; Palestinian Arab sweets, 104; pork industry, 116; Roden on, 173n25. *See also* Abu Ghosh; Consumerism, Israeli; Edibility; Palestinian food

Forced migrations of Palestinians, 51, 54, 59, 61, 63, 74, 101, 125–26

Foreign workers in Israeli, 23, 40–41, 163n96

Foucault, Michel, 153n2

Galilee. *See* Jewish settlements in the Galilee; Palestinian Galilee; Villages in the Palestinian Galilee

Galilee Tours, 24, 26f5

Gaza Strip, 20, 23, 36, 158n5

Geography: of Bedouin tents, 92–93; of café culture, 140–41; core of the village (*gar'in ha-kefar*), 82–83f13, 83–87, 116, 170n42; culinary geographies, 116–19, 127; de-urbanization of Palestinians, 52, 74–76, 94, 167–68n8, 171n65; ethnic portraiture and, 93–94; imaginary, 8, 24–26f5, 27m2, 28m3, 57–58, 61–62, 83f14; imagined proximities and, 6, 8–10, 24–25, 32, 68, 73, 143, 161n56; of interiority, 86–88, 91–93; maps, x, 25–26f5, 27m2, 28m3, 83f14; spatial fictions in political geography, 142–43.

See also Interiority; Intimacy; Proximity; Scale; Space; Villages in the Palestinian Galilee

Golan Heights, 36

Good Food Guide, 174n58

Guide books, 155n30, 174n58

Gulf States. *See* Oman; Qatar

Gulf War, 158n5

Haifa, 24, 74, 116

Hamas, 158n5

ha-Tiyul (the hike). *See* Hike, the

Hebrew language: museum signage in, 65; Palestinian strategic use of, 53–54, 66, 77, 106, 120, 125; spoken by Jewish Israeli tourists in Jordan, 31, 38; state terminologies, 8; status of term "Palestinian" in, 8

Ḥebron, 112, 114

Hike, the (*ha-Tiyul*): in Eretz Yisrael (Land of Israel), 10–11f1, 33, 161n62, 65; in film, 155n29; as nationalist practice, 10; after 1967 War, 36; to Petra, 33–34, 161n62; in Sinai, 162n74. *See also* Itineraries

Hilton Hotel bombing (Egypt), 149–50

Horfeish (Druze Village), 85

Hospitality, value of, 36, 45, 71, 77, 88

Ḥummus, 97, 100, 103, 127, 173n29

IDF (Israel Defense Forces): Bedouins in, 90; curfews and, 9, 96, 106, 132; forced migrations of Palestinians and, 51, 54, 59, 61, 63, 74, 101, 125–26; Golani Brigade, 63; Land Day demonstrations and, 67; militarized checkpoints and, 9, 23, 96, 143, 146, 150; military actions in 'Ilabun by, 54; military travel and, 13, 14, 39, 45–46, 156n35; Palestinian clashes with, 52; Palestinian restaurants patronized by, 111; Palestinians with Israeli citizenship in, 56, 102, 105;

IDF (*continued*)

Sherut Leumi (National Guard), 102, 105; suppression of Palestinian political organizing by, 126. *See also* Mobility restrictions on Palestinians in Occupied Territories; Occupied Territories; *and under* Palestinian Uprising headings

'Ilabun, 53–55, 62–63, 64

Illegal workforce, 40–42, 163n96

Imaginary geography, 8, 24–26f5, 27m2, 28m3, 57–58, 61–62, 83f14

Informal eateries, 117

Intelligibility, national: of Arab culture and places, 6, 7, 56, 61, 111; Butler and, 153nn2, 3; challenges to, 16, 17, 18, 40–42, 69, 150–52; control or reassertion of, 21, 43, 98, 150–51; definition of, 2–3, 153n2; geography and, 13, 46, 58, 61, 73; Oslo process and, 3–4, 6–7, 15, 42–43, 49; of Palestinian Galilee as tourist site, 16, 58; of Palestinian villages, 4, 6–7, 46, 48–49, 61; public mourning and, 63–64, 122; recognition of Palestinian citizens and, 48–49. *See also* Edibility

Interiority: alternative medicine, 89–90; of cafés, 142; consecutive interiority, 86–88; ethnic portraiture, 93–94; photography as, 93; safety of, 132; as a spatial modality, 72; state surveillance, 66, 71, 75–76, 84, 90, 107, 108, 133; tents, 91–93. *See also* Bed-and-breakfast facilities; Geography; Intimacy; Privacy and private spaces; Scale; Space

Intifada. *See under* Palestinian Uprising headings

Intimacy: of Abu Ghosh residents with Israeli state, 120, 122–23; core of the village (*gar'in ha-kefar*) and, 82–83f13, 83–87, 116, 170n42; ethnic portraiture as, 93–94; geographies of interiority and, 86; between hosts and guests, 88–

89, 90; performance of national allegiance and, 106–7. *See also* Interiority; Privacy and private spaces

'Isfiya, 49, 61

Israel, State of: as "accidental state," 77–78; aid for tourism development, 78–79, 168n27, 169n34; changing food habits in, 115–16, 118–19; economic benefits of Oslo process for, 22–23; as European nation-state, 144; heterogeneity of, 47, 58, 151–52; incoming Arab tourism to, 19–20, 39–42, 79, 159n33, 163n88, 169n34; Israeli Independence Day and, 107; as Jewish space, 96; Labor government in, 4, 9, 23, 52, 150; Land of Israel (Eretz Yisrael) and, 10, 33, 161n62, 161n65; Rabin and, 4, 23, 63, 64, 122–23, 123f17, 161n56. *See also* Bedouins; Citizenship, Israeli; Druze; IDF (Israel Defense Forces); Land expropriation; Migration; Ministry of Tourism, Israeli; Mobility restrictions on Palestinians in Occupied Territories; Palestinians in Israel; Wars; Zionist movement

Israel Defense Forces. *See* IDF

Israeli-Arab cookbook, 118, 127

Israeli Independence Day, 107

Israeli Ministry of Tourism. *See* Ministry of Tourism, Israeli

Israeli national artifacts, 64, 97–98, 107

Israeli Parliament (Knesset), 4, 107, 165n28, 173n21

Israeli Society for the Preservation of Nature (SPNI), 162n74

Itineraries: in Abu Ghosh, 101; clandestine travel and, 29, 33, 35, 159–60n35, 161n62; de Certeau's definition of, 17; of exile, 38–39, 42; of illegal labor, 40–41; of Jewish travel in pre-state Palestine, 10–12, 11f1, 33–35, 34f7, 34f8, 35f9, 35f10, 155–56n30; after 1967 War, 36; of

War, 51, 54, 63, 74, 94, 101; in 'Ilabun, 54; Jewish settlements as lookouts (*mitzpim*), 75, 90; militarized checkpoints and, 9, 23, 96, 143, 146, 150; police services and, 108, 138; surveillance of Palestinians within Israel, 66, 71, 75-76, 84, 90, 107, 108, 133. *See also* IDF; Mobility restrictions on Palestinians in Occupied Territories; Occupied Territories; *and under* Palestinian Uprising headings

Military travel, 13, 14, 39, 45-46, 156n35

Ministry of Tourism, Israeli: on Abu Ghosh, 100; aid for Palestinian tourism development and, 78-79, 168n27; core of the village (*gar'in ha-kefar*), 82-83f13, 83-87, 116, 170n42; development in rural sector (*migzar ha-kafri*), 78-79; development of Jerusalem's Old City as Israeli site and, 114; European market in rural hospitality, 83-84; fantasy of borderless tourism and, 25-28m3, 159n33; festivals in Palestinian Galilee, 49-50, 53, 116-17; on incoming Arab tourism, 19-20, 39-42, 79, 159n33, 163n88, 169n34; Misgav Regional Council and, 51-52, 53, 57, 76, 164n7, 165n21. *See also* Development of tourist market; Jewish Israeli tourists; Palestinian Galilee; Villages in the Palestinian Galilee

Misgav Regional Council, 51-52, 53, 57, 76, 164n7, 165n21

Mitzpim, 75, 90

Mizrahim: cuisine of, 111; discrimination against, 14; erasure of Mizrahi identity, 111; migration of, to Israel, 14, 111, 157n40; political influence of, 23, 159n23; tourism to Mizrahi places within Israel, 9; visits of, to Morocco, 38. *See also* Citizenship, Israeli

Mobility restrictions on Palestinians in Occupied Territories: closures, 9, 23, 96, 143; curfews, 9, 96, 106, 132; between East Jerusalem and Ramallah, 28; identity papers, 108; illegal incoming tourism, 40-42; incoming Arab tourism and, 19-20, 39-42, 159n33, 163n88; militarized checkpoints, 9, 23, 96, 143, 146, 150; on movements of Israelis, 10; Palestinian travel after 1967 War, 36; separation barrier, 9; tourism and, 25-27m2, 159n33; transportation and, 24, 32, 56, 132, 139; visa restrictions, 9, 23, 40-41, 143, 146, 150-51, 163n96. *See also* Palestinian Uprising, second (2000-present); West Bank

Moroccan-Israeli relations, 6, 22, 24, 38, 156n35, 159n31

Mourning, public: after assassination of Yitzhak Rabin and, 63, 64, 122-23; geographies of, 63-64, 122, 130, 132; grieving for cafés, 129; for Israeli travelers to Petra, 33, 36; multiculturalism and, 47, 64. *See also* Citizenship, Israeli; Coexistence

Multiculturalism, 47, 64

Museum of Palestinian Folk Heritage (Sakhnin), 53, 65-69

Muslim Arabs, 8-9, 40, 109, 163n88

Nablus, 114, 127

National intelligibility. *See* Intelligibility, national

Nature, 79-80, 89-90, 162n74, 169-70n40, 170n53

Nazareth, 68, 79

Negev, 61, 68

Neoliberalism, economic, 9, 23, 25-26. *See also* Transnationalism

New Jew, New Hebrew, imagery of, 111, 173n25

NGOs, Palestinian, 132

Performance (*continued*)

132; of patriotism, 98–99, 110, 120–23,
126–27

Performativity: Butler on, 153nn2–3; de
Certeau on, 17–18; Derrida on, 153n3;
itinerary and, 17–18. *See also* Intelligibility, national

Petra: clandestine travel to, 29, 33, 35, 36,
159–60n35, 161n62; discovery narrative and, 19, 29–30f6; hike (*ha-Tiyul*)
to, 33–34, 161n62; Israeli and pre-state
photographs of, 29–30f6, 35f10; Israeli
and pre-state travel to, 28–29, 29–30f6,
35f10, 159n30, 33, 35; Israeli-Jordanian
relations and, 29–31; press accounts
of, 29–31; proximity of, to Tel Aviv,
68; Red Rock of, 19, 159–60n35; songs
about, 159–60n35

Photography: of act of discovery, 29–30;
of Arab-Palestinians and Jews in pre-
state Palestine, 97–98; iconography
of traditional and, 93; images of pre-
modernity in, 93–94; of Jewish Israeli
statesmen, 97–98, 107; of Jewish travelers from pre-state Palestine, 11f1,
34f7, 34f8, 35f9, 35f10; Petra and, 19,
29–30f6, 35f10; of victims of Hilton
Hotel bombing, 150

Pik'in, 49

PLO (Palestinian Liberation Organization), 158n5

Police services, 108, 138

Population transfer, 146

Pork industry, 116

Postarmy itineraries, 13, 156n35

Postcolonialism, 12, 156n34, 157n3, 160n38

Posttraumatic stress syndrome, 133

Pratt, Mary, 160n38

Privacy and private spaces: Arabic conversation in, 133; Arab medical practitioners and, 90; authenticity and, 86–87;
bed-and-breakfast facilities, 50; restaurants, 117; social crisis and, 132–33;

value of, 86–87. *See also* Geography;
Interiority; Intimacy; Scale; Space

Proximity: of Arab neighborhoods to
Rehavia, 143; changing Jewish Israeli
perceptions of, 8, 32; coexistence
discourse and, 57–58; Jewish Israeli
perceptions of intra-national and
regional, 6, 8–10, 24–25; Jewish Israeli
travel in Arab Middle East and perceptions of regional, 8, 73; national
intelligibility and, 32; perception of, in
nation-state and region, 32, 68, 73, 143,
161n56; political aspects of, 57–58. *See
also* Geography; Interiority; Intimacy;
Scale; Space

Qatar, 4, 22, 32

Rabin, Yitzhak, 4, 23, 63, 64, 122–23f17,
161n56

Ramallah, 28, 36, 68

Red Rock of Petra (ha-Sela ha-Adom), 19,
159–60n35

Regev, Motti, 176n40

Rehavia, 130, 133, 134, 141, 142–43

Restaurants, 118; informal eateries and,
117; Israeli Jewish consumer confidence and, 124; pictures of Israeli
politicians in, 2. *See also* Abu Ghosh;
Food

Revisionist historiography, 14–15

Right, Israeli, 32, 51, 132, 134–35, 176n24

Rinot, Betsalel, 80–82, 84

Roden, Claudia, 173n25

Rural areas, 46; aesthetics of, 80, 103; de-
urbanization of Palestinians and, 52,
74–76, 94, 168n8, 171n65; development
in, 79–80; discourse of "the rural"
(*ha-kafri*) as symbolic deterritorialization, 80; Israeli state investments in,
79–80, 169–70n40; tourism in, 83–84,
90; underdevelopment as sign of rural
aesthetics, 103. *See also* Interiority

Tourism (*continued*)

cultural value of, 91; ecotourism, 89, 170n53; erasure of modernity and, 93, 171n65; Israeli national identity and, 151; joint (Israeli-Jordan) national projects for, 24; nature, 79–80, 89–90, 162n74, 169n40, 170n53; after 1967 War, 36; promotional material and, 13f3; restaurant sector, 98; shopping, Israeli, 11, 36, 112–14, 159n33. *See also* Cafés; Hike, the; Itineraries; Jewish Israeli tourists; Ministry of Tourism, Israeli; Petra; Restaurants

Tourism, illegal, 40–42

Transnationalism, 22, 73, 118–19, 127, 150–51, 158n13

Transportation, 24, 32, 56, 132–33, 139

Travel guidebooks, 155n30, 174n58

Travel narratives: citizenship and, 19; colonialism and, 12; first contact accounts in, 19, 32, 38; first-time narratives, 19, 28–33, 37–38, 41–42; historical revision in, 38–39; images of exile in, 38–39, 42; pre-state itineraries, 36, 92, 162n78; on travels to Egypt, 36; of Yishuv, 92. *See also* Discovery narrative; Petra

Troen, Ilan, 177n46

Tunisia, 22, 32

Turkey, 22, 24, 32

Unemployment, Palestinian, 23, 75

United States, identification of, with Israel, 136f20

Urban areas: de-urbanization of Palestinians and, 52, 74–76, 94, 168n8, 171n65; Judaization of, 74–76, 168n8; Palestinian Arabs excluded from, 75; respatialization of, 142. *See also* Haifa; Jerusalem; Tel Aviv

Villages in the Palestinian Galilee: alternative medicine and, 89–90; 'Arrabeh,

1–4, 50, 78; core or center of (*gar'in ha-kefar*), 82–83f13, 83–87, 116, 170n42; culinary tourism to, 116–18; erasure of modernity in, 93, 171n65; festivals in, 49–50, 53, 116–17; government aid for tourist development in, 78–79, 168n27; 'Ilabun, 53–55, 62–63; informal eateries in, 117; Jewish settlements in the Galilee, 51–52, 57, 66, 75–76, 90, 136, 164n7, 165n16, 168n15; military rule in, 111; Misgav Regional Council and, 51–52, 53, 165n21; municipal services in, 52, 56, 76, 165n21; performances of civic identity in, 52–53, 165n28; photographs of, 93; restrictions on development in, 52, 75, 94, 168n15, 171n65; as rural (*ha-kafri*), 79–80; surveillance of, 66, 75–76, 84, 90. *See also* Bedouin; Dayr Hannah; Druze; Judaization of the Galilee; Palestinian Galilee; Sakhnin

Visa restrictions, 9, 23, 40–41, 143, 146, 150–51, 163n96

"War for the Peace of the Settlements," 134, 175n15

Wars: Gulf War, 158n5; 1973 War, 162n74. *See also* IDF; 1948–49 War; 1967 War

Washington Declaration, 22, 25f4

West Bank: deteriorating conditions in, 158n5; Israel's imagined proximity to, 32–33; Jewish Israeli consumption and leisure in, 100, 114–15; Jewish Israeli tourism in, 2, 9, 11–12, 32–33, 35f9, 36, 113; military closure of, 23; nostalgia for, 115; Oslo Accords (1993) and, 20; Sharon on military offensive in, 176n24

West Jerusalem, spatial fictions about, 142–43

Yediot Aḥaronot, 30f6

Yemen, 32

Yerka (Druze village), 87

Yiftachel, Oren, 165n21

Yihud ha-Galil. See Judaization of the Galilee

Yodfat, 57, 76, 164n7

Zeh ha-kafeh shelanu, 129

Zionist movement: Abu Ghosh support of, 101, 102; discourse about Bedouin tents and, 92; emigration to Palestine and, 14; ha-Tiyul in Eretz Yisrael and, 10–11, 33, 161n62, 65; idealization of Arabs by youth groups in, 141; Law of Return and, 159n24; Orientalism and, 92; Palmach generation of, 92; tourism promoted by, 11–12, 155–56n30; trope of emptiness produced by, 146; Yishuv, 92. See also 1948–49 War

Zohrot, 156n35

Zoning restrictions, 52, 94, 171n65

Rebecca L. Stein is assistant professor of cultural anthropology and women's studies at Duke University. She is the coeditor of *Palestine, Israel, and the Politics of Popular Culture* and *The Struggle for Sovereignty: Palestine and Israel, 1993–2005*.

Library of Congress Cataloging-in-Publication Data
Stein, Rebecca L.
Itineraries in conflict : Israelis, Palestinians, and the political lives of tourism /
Rebecca L. Stein.
p. cm.
Includes bibliographical references and index.
ISBN 978-0-8223-4251-9 (cloth : alk. paper) — ISBN 978-0-8223-4273-1 (pbk. : alk. paper)
1. Tourism—Political aspects—Israel. 2. Heritage tourism—Israel. 3. Jews—Travel—
Israel. 4. Palestinian Arabs—Travel—Israel. 5. Israelis—Travel—Middle East.
6. Arab-Israeli conflict—1993—Peace. I. Title. II. Title: Israelis, Palestinians, and
the political lives of tourism.
G155.I78S74 2008
338.4'7915694—dc22   2008013526